DIRECT TEACHING TACTICS FOR EXCEPTIONAL CHILDREN

A Practice and Supervision Guide

Joseph J. Stowitschek
Outreach and Development Division
Exceptional Child Center
Utah State University
Logan, Utah

Carole E. Stowitschek
Intermountain Plains Regional Resource Center
Utah State University
Logan, Utah

Jo Mary Hendrickson
Continental Learning Systems, Inc.
Nashville, Tennessee

Robert M. Day
Special Purpose School
Parsons State Hospital and Training Center
Parsons, Kansas

AN ASPEN PUBLICATION®
Aspen Systems Corporation
Rockville, Maryland
Royal Tunbridge Wells
1984

Library of Congress Cataloging in Publication Data
Main entry under title:

Direct teaching tactics for exceptional children.

Bibliography: p. 153
Includes index.
1. Handicapped children—Education. 2. Formal
discipline. I. Stowitschek, Joseph J.
LC4015.D54   1984   371.9   84-11025
ISBN: 0-89443-595-7

Publisher: John R. Marozsan
Associate Publisher: Jack W. Knowles, Jr.
Editorial Director: Margaret Quinlin
Executive Managing Editor: Margot G. Raphael
Managing Editor: M. Eileen Higgins
Editorial Services: Ruth M. McKendry
Printing and Manufacturing: Denise Hass

Library of Congress Catalog Card Number: 84-11025
ISBN: 0-89443-595-7

Printed in the United States of America

1 2 3 4 5

To Fred and Millie Stowitschek,
who had to contend with the results
of both good and poor teaching in our schools.

Table of Contents

Preface

In the last 15 years, the public schools have been called upon to implement educational programs designed to help break the cycle of poverty, to aid in the elimination of racism, and to provide creative educational opportunities in addition to teaching the 3 R's.

With each of these educational policy changes the teacher has been called upon to carry the burden. Generally, this task has been borne with little assistance or special resources. In human terms it is the teacher who has had to make integration harmonious and early education valuable. Now, another social policy is reversing the long history of educational exclusion and segregation of handicapped children. This policy and its supporting laws, particularly Public Law 94-142, mandate a free and appropriate education for all handicapped children.

Several courts have ruled that previously excluded children must be mainstreamed into the public school system. Residential schools and self-contained classrooms were frequently criticized for restricting contact between handicapped and nonhandicapped children within academic settings. Although the courts have provided the impetus to include all handicapped children in the educational process, the responsibility for execution of the law has fallen to the faculty and administrators on the local level. It is there at the local level that mainstreaming succeeds or fails. Each school system now must provide an individualized education program (IEP) for each child who falls under the category of "handicapped child." IEPs are the focal point for assigning the responsibility of free and appropriate education.

When legislation mandates such a global academic shuffle, several difficult problems become evident. For example, "regular" classrooms are already large, and additional students must be assimilated into the present classroom structure. Regular education teachers with little or no training in special education do not feel comfortable in accepting children who have different educational needs. School administrators are not always in a position to be sensitive to teachers who need support facilities and personnel.

Exceptional children as addressed in this book may be found in regular or special classes. Exceptionality is defined here simply as a significant discrepancy between what should have been learned and what has been learned by these children. Exceptionality is largely a matter of degree rather than of condition. We can classify children into numerous distinct types of exceptionality: learning disabled, behavior disordered, language delayed, slow learner, educable mentally retarded, severely mentally retarded, multiply handicapped, hearing impaired, visually impaired, etc. We can employ a variety of experts to tell us what to do with these children: neurologists, psychologists, social workers, diagnosticians. When the diagnostic dust has settled, what ultimately remains, and endures, is the person who is responsible for bringing about educational change . . . the teacher!

This book is designed to assist teachers to develop, improve upon, and utilize teacher-child interaction tactics which are referred to as direct teaching tactics.

Two premises of this book are that: (1) direct teaching approaches show the greatest promise for solving instruction problems; and (2) an increased emphasis in teacher education must be placed on guaranteeing the acquisition and demonstration of direct teaching competence by teachers.

HOW THIS BOOK IS ORGANIZED

The approach taken in this book is to be as helpful to teachers as possible. So, each chapter includes a rationale for its contents, the specific teaching procedures detailed in an ordered fashion, and illustrative teaching examples. Also, supportive materials and forms are included in the appendix to make it easier for teachers to immediately begin using the procedures.

Part I is devoted to planning, measurement and consequation skills that are prerequisite to successful employment of direct teaching tactics, and presents direct teaching tactics for individual and group classroom use. Part II pertains to the supervision of teachers who are learning direct teaching tactics and is to be used by a practicum course instructor or special education district supervisor.

A basic format for systematically applying direct teaching tactics is laid out in Chapter 1. First, a set of procedures for trying out a given teaching tactic is described. Second, a decision sequence for selecting appropriate teaching tactics is presented and discussed. Chapter 2 presents a framework for practice.

Because this book is limited to a detailed explanation of selected teaching tactics, the discussion of general requisites for beginning a program of direct teaching is restricted to these topics. Before a teacher can expect to effectively employ direct teaching tactics, it is essential that he or she, and just as importantly, the student know exactly what is to be taught and learned at each step of instruction. Chapter 3 concentrates on planning strategies that are useful for working with exceptional children: pinpointing and specifying performance behaviors; analyzing instructional tasks; and analyzing concepts. Chapter 4 provides summary descriptions of measurement procedures which permit a teacher to conduct initial assessments to determine children's performance levels and to assess progress that is made while teaching. Thus, the basis for evaluating the effectiveness of a selected direct teaching tactic is provided. Chapter 5 is devoted to a summary discussion of the contingent use of teacher attention. Since this is an essential element of the teaching tactics discussed in this book, it is treated as a critical requisite for direct teaching. The use of other reinforcement techniques as they relate to contingent teacher attention are also mentioned.

The next five chapters present specific direct teaching tactics and applications of these tactics. The focus of Chapter 6 is on tactics for teaching children who do not respond to models, questions, or other instructional stimuli. Tactics for gaining instructional control are also discussed. The next chapter addresses modeling tactics in combination with other teaching procedures. Particular attention is paid to tactics

that were identified in a major teacher competency research project as being critical teacher behaviors. Teacher questioning tactics are described in Chapter 8. Rather than describe the questioning procedures (such as "higher order questions") used in large-group instruction in regular education classrooms, the focus of this chapter is to present questioning tactics that have been found to be effective with handicapped children. The last two chapters of this section present specialized applications of direct teaching. Small-group applications of direct teaching tactics are discussed in Chapter 9, while group-individualized (e.g., desk-work) applications are discussed in Chapter 10.

The second part of the book pertains to the supervision of the acquisition of competence in direct teaching. Since this book is oriented toward the person who intends to do more than just read about direct teaching tactics, it provides the framework for ensuring that the reader who is in a position to try out the tactics under supervised practice conditions will obtain relevant feedback and redirection from the supervisor. Preservice teacher-trainees enrolled in practica or student teaching, or teachers participating in supervised inservice training are in a position to benefit from the supervision section of this book. The last two chapters are closely coordinated with Chapter 2 because the same forms presented for practicing direct teaching are the basis for supervision procedures presented later. These procedures were derived from the Field-Based Special Teacher Education Project and are the key element in the success of that project. Chapter 11 is devoted to procedures for organizing direct teaching practice, inspecting teacher planning records, and observing teacher-child interaction. Chapter 12 explains procedures for giving feedback and redirecting trainees' practice and concludes with a discussion of teaching competency verification.

It is hoped that the approach taken in this book will help teachers to find immediate classroom applications of direct teaching tactics. The problems of exceptional children pose immediate problems for teachers and require immediate attention. Many texts dealing with procedures for exceptional children provide background information and describe several teaching strategies for general classroom application. Because these texts are intended to be comprehensive, they are seldom able to deal extensively with any one teaching tactic or set of tactics. While this book does not deal extensively with background information and comprehensive teaching strategies, it does provide thorough guidelines for implementing a precise set of selected direct teaching tactics. These tactics are based on research that has empirically verified teaching behaviors that have demonstrable and predictable effects on the performance of handicapped children (Shores & Stowitschek, 1977; Shores, Roberts, & Nelson, 1977).

Acknowledgments

The authors would like to extend their appreciation to the following:

Richard E. Shores, who knows what it means to dig at a mountain with a teaspoon.

Staff of the Field-based Special Teacher Education Program at George Peabody College for Teachers of Vanderbilt University, whose efforts helped evolve many of the procedures described in this book.

Bev Lewis   Cynthia Langford
Mary Margaret Kerr   Jerry Blackman
Robert Gable   Vaughn Stagg
Judy Armstrong-Iacino   Kathy Riggs
Thomas Hennessey Powell   Jane Goodwin
Clifford Young   Marion George
Peter Gordon   Bill Brown
Tony Hecimovic

The graduates of the Field-based Special Teacher Education Program, who demonstrated that teaching competence and child change are interdependent.

Connee Polak, for her assistance in the preparation of this book.

Part I
Direct Teaching Tactics for the Practitioner

A reanalysis of our schools is underway as a result of the presidential report *A Nation at Risk*. A major emphasis is on teaching, and especially, achieving excellence in teaching. It presents a rare opportunity to make extensive and far-reaching improvements in education in general and teaching in particular. However, educators arc in danger of stopping short of substantive improvements in favor of administrative responses such as across-the-board salary increases and career advancement based on seniority. Salaries and career advancement are needed but will not guarantee the improvement of instruction without giving teachers the wherewithal to systematically improve teaching skills.

Far from being excluded from this process, special educators are joined with mainstream educators to provide least restrictive educational alternatives for handicapped children. Special educators are in a position to contribute by encouraging the general adoption of an orientation toward immediate child change. The contribution of this orientation to teaching is the ability to discern ineffective from effective teaching behaviors, on an ongoing basis instead of after the fact. There is a growing interdependence between mainstream, resource, and self-contained special classroom educators as a result of the mainstream education movement. This interdependency must also include the achievement of excellence among teachers.

The achievement of excellence is less related to talent than to hard work and continual striving for improvement. The acquisition and improvement of teaching skills must be carefully guided. There is a technology developing that is applicable to this guidance process. It consists of

- a framework that places the practice of a teaching tactic in perspective with all requisite elements of systematic teaching
- concentrated practice on clearly defined and validated teaching competencies
- a direct reference of that practice to child performance
- supervisory feedback and redirection on teaching.

Part I directly addresses the practice framework, the teaching tactics and the child reference, and lays the foundation for supervision of practice.

Chapter 1

A Decision Sequence

Mainstreaming, more than any other social policy change, has had a direct and profound impact on both regular and special education teachers. Teachers are faced with children who have been excluded from regular classes and, in many cases, from the entire educational process. Not only must teachers accept children who have "problems," but also, under the law, they are accountable for the remediation of those problems.

BROADLY VARYING HANDICAPPING CONDITIONS

Who are these handicapped children? How different are they? The handicapped children who have previously been enrolled in special classes or have been excluded from school altogether have acquired significantly fewer skills than have their nonhandicapped peers. The discrepancy in performance can be slight, moderate, or severe. These children have not learned as rapidly as others under normal instructional circumstances and require more directive attention from the teacher. For example,

- Tommy T. is in the third grade and still unable to name all the letters of the alphabet. He has almost no word attack skills, although he sight-reads 25 words.
- Janice L. is being readied to leave the special learning disabilities class that she has attended for the past 2 years and enter a fifth-grade math class. She has mastered numeration skills and basic math combinations, but her progress in solving higher level computations is extremely labored and slow.

- Sophia B. is 12 years old and has yet to follow directions correctly (e.g., "Stand up." "Come here."). She occasionally imitates a movement, such as putting an object in a can. Sophia is scheduled to leave the state institution for the mentally retarded and enroll in a public school classroom for severely mentally retarded persons.
- Artell D. is a constant disruption to his class of fourth graders. His favorite ploy is to shove or pull classmates from their desks when they are off guard. Bruises, abrasions, and contusions have resulted. Artell will remain in the same class for at least the coming year because he has not progressed academically and because children with behavior disruptions of this sort are not being placed in special classes.

These children are exceptional in that they have significant learning difficulties. Some may be certified as exceptional, some may not. Regardless of their official status, these children pose serious problems to their teachers.

Although the provision of a free and appropriate education for all handicapped children is a worthy policy, it presents classroom teachers with a myriad of problems. Teachers have expressed the following specific concerns:

1. teaching time

   "I'm really concerned about adding special education students to my class. I'm already unable to help all my regular students who are having trouble. What's going to happen when I have kids with behavior problems or learning handicaps?"

"I've just had a course in special education and all the professor talked about was measuring student progress and changing behavior. It seemed like a good idea, but who has that kind of time? I have to teach. I don't have time to sit around and record everything a kid does."

2. materials

"With my normal children, I have to hustle to get enough materials together. These mainstreamed kids are all at different skill levels. They each need something different. Who's going to prepare or buy materials for these kids? My supplies budget hasn't been increased in the last 3 years."

3. prerequisite skills

"I spent a lot of time making special worksheets for a learning-disabled child in my class last year who couldn't read short vowel words. I tried to make them interesting, you know meaningful, but she still had problems completing them. Then one day I realized that she was having trouble with the worksheets because she couldn't figure out what I wanted her to do. She really had the skills, it was the worksheets themselves that completely confused her. I can't be responsible for teaching my fourth-grade curriculum as well as what the first-, second-, and third-grade teachers were supposed to teach!"

4. behavior problems

"It's hard enough to get normal kids to work. Some of these new kids are going to be discipline problems. I'm worried about their effect on other kids. Will my kids copy them when they are bad?"

"I've got a severely handicapped child in my class. Sometimes he self-stimulates, hurts himself or even attacks another child. He throws anything he touches down on the floor. One day he threw a puzzle at me. With this kind of stuff going on, it's almost impossible to teach anything to the other children."

5. teaching and learning

"I've spent hours with several of my SMR students just trying to get them to follow simple directions like 'stand up' and 'come here.' I just feel like I'm getting nowhere. It's all very frustrating."

"I tried to include a special education kid in my social studies class. I'd ask a question and try to get the children to think about the different countries. But this little kid just didn't get anything out of it. He wouldn't even raise his hand. I just don't know what to do. He's so far behind the other children."

Discouraging as these problems are, many teachers have experienced some success in dealing with them:

1. teaching time

"I've found that I can use some of my students to help the kids who are having problems. Both the handicapped children and the normal children seem to really enjoy the experience, and I've found that I have more time to work with my small groups."

"One of the things that helped me a lot is to realize that I can make my teaching strategies more efficient, like getting a set pattern started for using demonstrations or questions."

2. materials

"It's a lot easier to find effective teaching materials now that I have an accurate measurement system that tells me where my kids are working on specific skills. In a lot of ways the key to this whole problem of time and materials has been made easier by my being more aware of children's individualized needs and organizing materials around these needs."

3. prerequisite skills

"In the last 2 years that I have had handicapped children in my class I found that, in many instances, I can get around problems they have in reading directions and in understanding what work is to be done. One way is to have some of my good readers tape-record instructions for the math assignments so that my nonreaders can complete the assignments. Another way is to have readers and nonreaders work in pairs."

"Well, when it comes to students who lack the necessary prerequisites to work in my class, I could have washed my hands of the problem by saying that I'm hired to teach science, not reading. But, something just doesn't ring true. If I don't do something, it is the child who loses out regardless of who should have taught the child to read."

4. behavior problems

"At first, I had some terrific disruption problems in my classroom. But, by learning to use my attention more judiciously as a reward to children who worked hard and by making materials appropriate to the individual child's needs I've cut these disruptions way down."

5. teaching and learning

"The most exciting thing about working with my handicapped kids is to watch them learn a new skill. They've had so much failure that the successes they do begin to have are a real thrill to them and to me. With my normal kids, who are so used to learning, I'm not nearly as rewarded as I am when my slower students start to progress."

Whether the primary problem is believed to be insufficient teaching time, inaccurate materials, disruptive behavior, or a combination of other problems, a key factor in providing an appropriate education for handicapped children lies in the way teachers interact with these children.

NONDIRECT INSTRUCTION APPROACHES

With nondirect instruction, the teacher is not necessarily involved in the act of teaching. Instead, the child and the setting are considered the most crucial instructional elements. The teacher is a guide or facilitator of learning who works from the sidelines. Three examples of nondirect approaches are: the experiential learning strategies, discovery learning, and self-directed learning, which overlap considerably.

- Experiential learning strategies are designed to provide learners with as many varied experiences relating to an educational goal as possible. Children participate in relevant real life experiences, rather than merely read about or discuss them. The teacher's role is to organize

and structure these experiences, as well as to bring learners into contact with them; this function is somewhat similar to that of the tour guide.
- The goal of discovery learning is to develop cognitive problem-solving strategies. With this approach, an educational task is viewed as a problem to be solved. Learners often work with each other in special projects that are organized by the teacher. Again, the teacher refrains as much as possible from direct teacher-child interactions that are task-oriented.
- Self-directed learners work mostly at learning how to learn. Instead of teaching educational tasks per se, the teacher strives to provide learners with the tools and methods of learning. The teacher makes the learners aware of possible avenues toward learning an educational task, but again, does not get involved in teaching the task.

Although these nondirect approaches produce exciting improvements in educational performance for some children (as do most approaches), they may hold some distinct disadvantages for exceptional children. First, because nondirect approaches often rely heavily on the learners' cognitive problem-solving ability and on their powers of observation and deduction, they are often too sophisticated to be useful in educating handicapped persons. Second, because the teacher acts primarily as a facilitator, responsibility for learning under these indirect approaches rests squarely on the shoulders of the learner. This responsibility can be overwhelming to handicapped children. Furthermore, there is no evidence to indicate that direct teacher involvement in instruction precludes experiential, discovery, or self-directed learning when they are coordinated to gain the same outcomes.

DIRECT TEACHING TACTICS

Instructional activities that involve teacher-child interactions are considered direct. In totally independent instruction, the student interacts with textual materials or with mediated materials, or the teacher waits for the student to initiate a learning activity; in direct instruction, the teacher is in full command of instruction, directing and prompting students to respond correctly to tasks. Teaching refers to those direct actions performed by a teacher that produce measurable improvement in educational performance of learners. This definition is not prescriptive as to specific types of teacher actions, but to the outcomes that those actions produce in terms of behavioral changes in students. Tactics are those particular patterns of direct teaching and student responses that are likely to produce desired effects on the educational performance of students. Teaching, by this definition, is taking responsibility for learning outcomes.

SELECTION OF APPROPRIATE TACTICS

Proficiency in the use of each teaching tactic is important, but the ultimate goal, improving the educational performance of children, may not be attained if the teaching tactic selected for the instructional situation is inappropriate. No single teaching procedure can be successful for all instructional objectives or for all children. Nowhere in education does this reality become so quickly apparent as in teaching handicapped persons. The use of inappropriate teaching procedures may (1) waste the teacher's time, (2) waste the child's time, (3) frustrate the teacher, (4) frustrate the child, or (5) do all of the above. Furthermore, when the teaching procedures, including the ways in which teaching and learning are measured, are completely inappropriate, many teachers do not suspect that their teaching is at fault. Then the consequences are even more severe (for the children), because these teachers may place the responsibility for failure on the children, their parents, or even on societal conditions as a whole, rather than consider a change in their teaching methods.

Some special educators have been convinced that a single teaching tactic or strategy is *the* tactic to use. The materials-purchasing behavior of teachers (Bleil, 1975; Stowitschek, Gable, & Hendrickson, 1980) indicates that many seek a panacea and thus become discouraged with and discard materials that could be effectively used if the teaching tactics were varied. The only sure way to determine whether a selected teaching tactic is the right one is to use it and measure its effects on child learning.

A DIRECT TEACHING DECISION MODEL

There are many elaborate models and processes for guiding teachers' instructional decisions. Unfortunately, the models are often difficult to use. A simple series of decisions leading to the selection of an appropriate direct teaching tactic is displayed in Exhibit 1–1. Prioritizing curriculum targets, specifying instructional objectives, and analyzing instructional tactics are the primary decisions pertaining to what to teach. Identifying the exact measurement purpose and selecting appropriate assessments are important determinants of how the measurement of child performance should be carried out. The identification, selection, and use of reinforcers are also key instructional decisions. Finally, decisions regarding which teaching tactic is to be selected and in which format it is to be used help the teacher to determine how instruction is presented to the learner.

A sequence of decisions based on this model is shown in Tables 1–1 and 1–2. This sequence can be quite valuable as a checklist for the teacher beginning this decision process, as it helps to ensure that important factors in the selection of

Exhibit 1–1 Decision Model

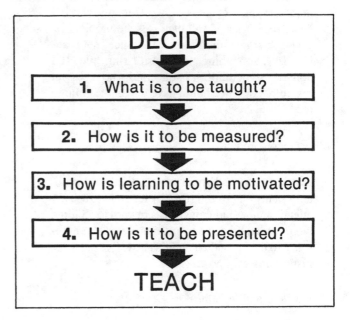

teaching tactics are not overlooked; however, it would obviously be cumbersome to use it every time an instructional decision is to be made. Fortunately, these decisions can become automatic in a teacher's planning repertoire, and a guide such as this is no longer required.

The table consists of four columns:

1. Steps, the determining factors for what to teach, how to measure, and how to motivate
2. Questions, aids to the teacher in relating initial program decisions to the day-to-day teaching considerations that will result from their decisions
3. Response, a checklist for each step
4. Action, the action to be taken as determined by the response to each question

The steps for the first major decision area, determining what to teach, were selected to (1) ensure teachers that they have selected a skill that is important for the learner to acquire; (2) provide a means of checking whether objectives, once written, are precisely stated and are still relevant to the skill to be taught; and (3) determine which analysis tactic should be employed for a given objective. In some cases, the conditions under which the behavior is to occur are the subject of analysis; in other cases, the behavior itself is broken down into parts and sequenced. In still other instances, the criteria to which the behavior is to be performed may be systematically adjusted.

In the second major decision area, determining how to measure, the first step is to consider whether the assessment instrument or procedure matches the purpose for which it is

Table 1-1 Direct Teaching Decision Sequence

Determining What to Teach

Steps	Questions	Response	Action
Step I: Prioritize.	(1) Is the skill being considered related to ultimate functioning (given a skill under consideration)?	Yes _____ No _____	Go to (2).
	(2) Does this skill help to learn another skill?	Yes _____ No _____	Go to (3).
	(3) Is the skill important to parents or other persons responsible for the learner?	Yes _____ No _____	Go to (4).
	(4) Are items (1), (2), or (3) checked yes?	Yes _____	Decide to teach that skill and go to step II.
		No _____	Select a higher priority skill and repeat step I.
Step II: Specify target objective.	(1) Does the objective specify an action (given an objective in mind)?	Yes _____ No _____	Go to (2).
	(2) Can the same behavior be demonstrated by different people when they read the objective description?	Yes _____ No _____	Go to (3).
	(3) Do conditions for performance specify the stimulus precisely?	Yes _____ No _____	Go to (4).
	(4) Do the conditions specified reflect *how* that skill will be realistically used later on?	Yes _____ No _____	Go to (5).
	(5) Do the criteria specified reflect countable units?	Yes _____ No _____	Go to (6).
	(6) Do the criteria match levels of "age competent" use?	Yes _____ No _____	Go to (7).
	(7) Are items (1) through (7) checked yes?	Yes _____	Use the objective as written and go to step III.
		No _____	Rewrite objective where it is deficient and recheck using items (1) through (7).
Step III: Analyze the objective.	(1) Is it a concept? (Will the learner be expected to generalize to instances not taught directly?)	Yes _____	Do concept analysis and go to (3).
		No _____	Do task analysis and go to (2).
	(2) Is it a single or series of motor responses that the learner must perform?	Yes _____	Analyze behavior first and go to (5).
		No _____	Go to (3).
	(3) Is it a series of discriminations requiring a response that the learner can already do?	Yes _____	Analyze conditions first, then analyze criteria.
		No _____	Go to (4).
	(4) Are responses and discriminations already in the learner's repertoire, but at low levels of accuracy or rate?	Yes _____	Analyze criteria, then go to (5).
		No _____	Go to (5).
	(5) Do the behavior conditions and/or criteria in the subobjectives add up to the performance specified in the target objectives?	Yes _____	Go to "determining how to measure."
		No _____	Repeat analysis, rework analysis, and repeat (1) through (5).

Table 1–1 continued

Determining How to Measure

Steps	Questions	Response	Action
Step I: Identify the purpose of measurement.	(1) To help determine what to teach?	Yes _____ No _____	Go to (2).
	(2) To determine whether the learner needs to be taught a selected objective?	Yes _____ No _____	Go to (3).
	(3) To determine where in a skill sequence to begin teaching?	Yes _____ No _____	Go to (4).
	(4) Items (1), (2), or (3) checked yes?	Yes _____	Purpose is initial assessment, go to step II.
		No _____	Go to (5).
	(5) To pinpoint initial performance trends?	Yes _____ No _____	Go to (6).
	(6) To determine whether progress is occurring following instruction?	Yes _____ No _____	Go to (7).
	(7) To determine whether mastery has occurred?	Yes _____ No _____	Go to (8).
	(8) To analyze errors?	Yes _____ No _____	Go to (9).
	(9) Items (5), (6), (7), and/or (8) checked yes?	Yes _____	Purpose is progress checking, go to step III.
		No _____	Think again.
Step II: Select an initial assessment approach.	(1) Is the behavior of interest sampled sufficiently for purposes listed in steps I (1) through (5)?	Yes _____ No _____	Go to (2).
	(2) Do assessment conditions match those of ultimate use?	Yes _____ No _____	Go to (3).
	(3) Does the selected assessment yield separate scores for subskills besides one composite score?	Yes _____ No _____	Go to (4).
	(4) Does the assessment yield information on error patterns?	Yes _____ No _____	Go to (5).
	(5) Is the administration time practical for initial assessment purposes?	Yes _____ No _____	Go to (6).
	(6) Items (1) through (5) checked yes?	Yes _____	Consider using this assessment; go to step III.
		No _____	Use step II to examine other instruments and select the one that checks out the best, then go to step III.
Step III: Select a progress check.	(1) Do the learner's responses match the behavior specified in the target objective?	Yes _____ No _____	Go to (2).
	(2) Is the progress check designed to sample daily or weekly performance?	Yes _____ No _____	Go to (3).
	(3) Can the progress check display data relative to the criteria specified in the target objective?	Yes _____ No _____	Go to (4).
	(4) Do the conditions of assessment match the conditions specified in the target objective?	Yes _____ No _____	Go to (5).
	(5) Is the progress check consistent over time?	Yes _____ No _____	Go to (6).
	(6) Are the data displayed clearly enough to facilitate reporting to colleagues or parents?	Yes _____ No _____	Go to (7).
	(7) Items (1) through (6) checked yes?	Yes _____	Consider using this progress check, go to "determining how to motivate."

Table 1–1 continued

Determining How to Motivate

Steps	Questions	Response	Action
Step I: Identify potential reinforcers.	(1) Are the learners verbal?	Yes _____ No _____	Go to (2).
	(2) Do they respond reliably and accurately to questions?	Yes _____ No _____	Go to (3).
	(3) Items (1) and (2) checked yes?	Yes _____	Ask them what they would like, go to step II.
		No _____	Go to (4).
	(4) Is time available, and do you have an assortment of reinforcers?	Yes _____	Consider using reinforcement sampling, go to step II.
		No _____	Go to (5).
	(5) Do you have written records describing the learner's past educational experiences?	Yes _____ No _____	Go to (6).
	(6) Can you ask someone who knows the learner from previous educational experience?	Yes _____ No _____	Go to (7).
	(7) Items (5) and (6) checked yes?	Yes _____	Consider using reinforcement history to select reinforcers, go to step II.
		No _____	Check and try out various potential reinforcers.
Step II: Select practical reinforcers.	(1) Can you easily deliver the reinforcer?	Yes _____ No _____	Go to (2).
	(2) Can you control (limit) the dispensing of the reinforcer?	Yes _____ No _____	Go to (3).
	(3) Does it approximate naturally reinforcing conditions, and/or can it be paired with social reinforcers?	Yes _____ No _____	Go to (4).
	(4) Items (1) through (3) checked yes?	Yes _____	Consider using that reinforcer, go to step III.
		No _____	Use items (1) through (4) to examine other potential reinforcers.
Step III: Use the reinforcer.	(1) Can you specify how the reinforcer can be used contingently?	Yes _____ No _____	Go to (2).
	(2) Do you have alternative reinforcers and methods (project check) of determining when the selection is no longer reinforcing?	Yes _____ No _____	Go to (3).
	(3) Items (1) and (2) checked yes?	Yes _____	Go to "determining how to present."
		No _____	Reexamine how reinforcers will be used and repeat step III, then go to "determining how to present."
		No _____	Select another progress check and reexamine it using items (1) through (6), or adapt this progress check, then go to "determining how to present."

Table 1–2 Teaching Tactics Decision Matrix: Determining How to Present

Tactics/Formats	Utility for Teaching	Preliminary Considerations	Teaching Demands	Primary Instruction Purpose
Modeling	Rote, one-step responses Response chains	Child must be able to imitate.	May have to arrange for individual tutor sessions Simple teaching tactic when used consistently as part of a sequence Used in one-to-one tutoring or roving tutorial formats	Response building Remediation
Questioning	Conditional discriminations (problem solving) Post hoc skills (e.g., reading, comprehension) On-the-spot diagnosis	Child must be able to respond differentially to questions (yes/no).	May have to arrange for individual tutoring sessions Follow-up with another teaching tactic (e.g., modeling) Somewhat complex when used as the sole teaching tactic May be used in one-to-one or roving tutorial formats Best used for on-the-spot problem diagnosis	Response building Error analysis
Training, learning prerequisites (sitting and attending, imitation, direction following, match-to-sample discriminations)	Rote, one-step responses Response chains	Child has motor skills, as well as sensory skills, for making a response.	Typically a one-to-one teaching arrangement May require a second adult teaching assistant Variety of tactics included May involve considerable experimentation to arrive at successful use	Instructional control[a] Response building
Consequation only	All types of responses	Child has the desired response in his or her repertoire but at low rates or levels of appropriate use.	Must be able to observe the behavior readily Adherence to schedule of reinforcement Practice commitment required for proficiency	Instructional control[a] Proficiency practice
Small-group direct instruction	Rote, one-step or short chain responses Oral responses	Child must be able to imitate and to respond differentially to questions. Group instructional control[a] is a must.	3–5 learners (up to 12 older learners) Must accommodate rest of class for 10–20 minutes while teaching pretraining (e.g., DISTAR workshops) Commitment to practice required before teaching proficiency is attained	Response building Generalized responding

[a]The intent in establishing instructional control is not necessarily to teach a functional skill, but to bring some behavior of the child under the control of the teacher as a prerequisite for teaching other skills that may be more functional.

Table 1-2 continued

Tactics/Formats	Utility for Teaching	Preliminary Considerations	Teaching Demands	Primary Instruction Purpose
Group-individualized instruction	Instruction without direct teaching presentation of each stimulus	Responding (whether correct or incorrect) must be under the control of a stimulus other than the teacher (e.g., printed work page, set of objects to be manipulated, computer screen). Response must produce a permanent product. Child must be able to work independently, proceeding from one stimulus to the next (e.g., problem on a worksheet).	Materials appropriate for the intended instruction Control of the entire class Work with children, one at a time to help them overcome problem areas Learning tasks introduced prior to group-individualized instruction	Proficiency practice

to be used. If the measurement purpose is to determine a child's entry level, the considerations critical to the selection of the appropriate assessment approach differ from those required when the measurement purpose is to determine the extent of a child's progress through an instruction sequence.

The set of decisions in the third major decision area, determining how to motivate, permits the teacher to select appropriate motivational events. Once potential reinforcers have been identified, another decision process helps the teacher to arrive at the most suitable reinforcer for a particular child. There are some important considerations in order for an *intended* reinforcing event to become an *actual* reinforcing event.

The Questions in Table 1-1 contain the "meat" of the decision process. The Response column may be used literally as a record of decisions made; however, it is expected that teachers who use the process will automatically incorpo-

rate it into their program planning. The Action column contributes system to the decision process. It provides an objective means of deciding when a program element, whether a skill to be taught, a written objective, an assessment instrument, or a potential reinforcer, should be discarded or included in the program. In some cases, it also suggests a best tactic for further planning.

Decisions for selecting a presentation tactic usually involve a comparison of different tactics and the factors that determine their successful use. So, this portion of the decision process is presented as a matrix (Table 1-2) to facilitate comparison of presentation modes in (1) their usefulness for teaching a particular skill; (2) the prerequisite behaviors or levels of pupil performance desired; (3) allowances that the teacher must make, and (4) the purpose of instruction in terms of pupil outcomes (e.g., to begin to acquire a behavior or to become proficient in a skill).

Chapter 2

A Practice Framework

Practice alone probably won't make perfect (Lovitt, 1977). It must be carefully guided and shaped. So must practice at teaching be guided. A framework for practice designed around child programs provides a logical guide. Hence, the planning forms presented here permit the specification of both child objectives to be achieved and teacher behaviors to be practiced.

Four planning forms are consistently used to guide the day-to-day practice of direct teaching: (1) Direct Teaching Program Checklist, (2) Preprogram Planner, (3) Teacher Presentation Guide, and (4) Daily Planner (Exhibit 2–1). It is crucial that it be recognized that these forms are not a program in and by themselves. They are summaries of other documents such as IEPs, tests, observations, instructional materials, and/or graphs. Because they are generic to any systematic instruction program, the planning forms are unique. They permit practice in the use of direct teaching tactics with ongoing instruction programs. When proficiency is attained in the use of direct teaching tactics, the planning forms may be either dropped out or assimilated into ongoing instruction.

The Direct Teaching Program Checklist (Exhibit 2–2) is designed to serve as a direct translation between Individualized Education Programs (IEPs) and daily teaching activities. On this checklist, the teacher describes the program from start to finish, including what is said and done in the daily teaching session. The teacher can use the checklist to plan basic elements of teaching for each child or group of children to be taught. The elements of teaching to be planned on the checklist are

1. Target: the task to be taught. This may be an abbreviated reference to an IEP short-term objective, but it *must* be behaviorally specified elsewhere, including conditions for performance and criteria for mastery. The targeted objective should also be justified as high priority for the child(ren) to be taught.
2. Analyze: the analysis tactic selected to determine the component subtasks or subobjectives.
3. Assess: the instruments or methods used to determine which objective is to be taught and the child(ren)'s entry level.
4. Intervene: the name for the particular intervention tactic selected.
5. Arranged Event: the social and/or other deliverable event(s) intended to reinforce appropriate child responses and the contingent relationship.
6. Arrangement: the scheduled delivery of consequent events, whether continuous or intermittent.
7. Check Progress/Mastery: the means by which the daily progress of the child(ren) is to be measured (i.e., a test). This may be the same procedure as that used for initial assessment and is typically used to determine whether the objective has been met.
8. Redirect: a planned option if the intervention fails. It describes corrective procedures or a change in the planned intervention procedures.

The remaining three planning forms are subsidiary to the checklist and serve to provide more detailed planning information on the components of the checklist.

Exhibit 2–1 The Planning Forms

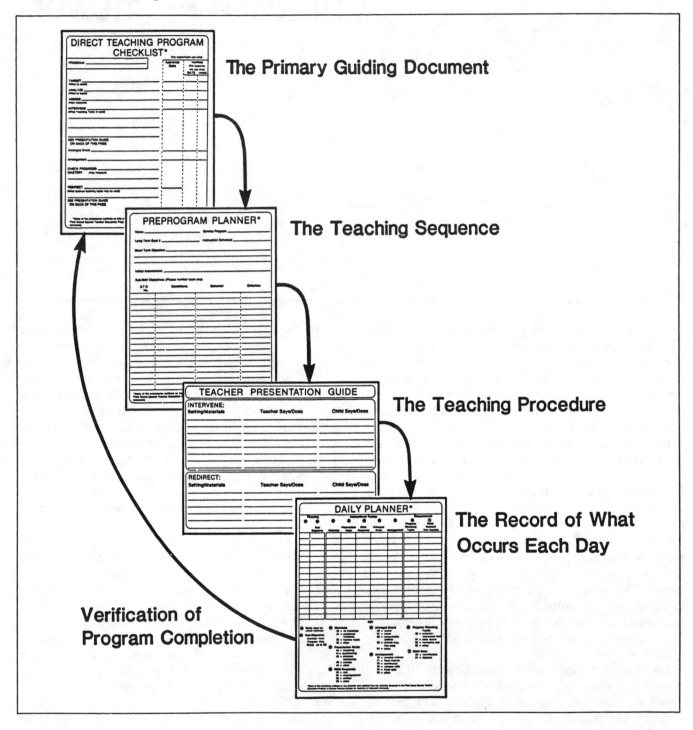

The Preprogram Planner aids the teacher in analyzing and sequencing the IEP short-term objectives to be taught (Exhibit 2–3). If the IEPs are to be effective, there must be a means for the teacher to relate short-term objectives directly to teaching behavior. The Preprogram Planner is a linear sequential list of results of task, concept, or other forms of analysis used. The subtasks are assigned a short-term objective number (STO number) and written in three separate parts (conditions, behavior, criterion). The STO number is useful for quick identification of the skill that the objective represents. Table 2–1 shows a simple numbering system that may be used.

Exhibit 2–2 Checklist

DIRECT TEACHING PROGRAM CHECKLIST*

(For supervisors use only)

PROGRAM *Handwriting : Group-Individualized*

	Approved Date	Verified (For supervisors use only) DATE Initial

TARGET *Copy lowercase cursive letters*
(What to teach)

ANALYZE *Task analysis*
(What to teach)

ASSESS *Placement test – DLM Program*
(How measure)

INTERVENE *Worksheet practice – Teacher*
(What Teaching Tactic is used)

Feedback

(SEE PRESENTATION GUIDE ON BACK OF THIS PAGE)

Arranged Event *Redrawn letters, praise*

Arrangement *fixed ratio, then variable ratio*

CHECK PROGRESS/ *daily probe - copy first*
MASTERY   (How measure)
row of worksheets letters unassisted

REDIRECT *copy single letters instead*
(What back-up teaching tactic may be used)
of entire row.

(SEE PRESENTATION GUIDE ON BACK OF THIS PAGE)

*Many of the procedures outlined on this checklist were adapted from the materials developed in the Field Based Special Teacher Education Program at George Peabody College for Teachers of Vanderbilt University.

Exhibit 2–3 Preprogram Planner

PREPROGRAM PLANNER*

Name _John P._   Service Program _Trask Elementary_

Long Term Goal # _17.0 Cursive letters_   Instruction Schedule _9:00–9:20 a.m., daily_

Short Term Objective _Given a row of models, copy lower case cursive letters so that they match the DLM placement test standards on three consecutive worksheets_

Initial Assessment: _DLM placement test_

Sub-Skill Objectives: (Please number each one)

S.T.O. No.	Conditions:	Behavior:	Criterion:
17.1	Given a–f models	copy letters	3 consec. wksts
17.2	Given g–l models	" "	" "
17.3	Given m–r models	" "	" "
17.4	Given s–z models	" "	" "
17.5	Given any combination	" "	" "

*Many of the procedures outlined on this checklist were adapted from the materials developed in the Field Based Special Teacher Education Program at George Peabody College for Teachers of Vanderbilt University.

Table 2–1 Numbering System for Short-Term Objectives

Category for Annual Goal	Category for Short-Term Objective
Motor skills	1.0 Gross motor skills 2.0 Fine motor skills
Self-care skills	3.0 Feeding 4.0 Dressing 5.0 Cleanliness 6.0 Home cleaning and care
Language skills	7.0 Receptive language 8.0 Expressive language
Reading skills	9.0 Word attack (phonic/linguistic) 10.0 Oral reading 11.0 Comprehension
Math skills	12.0 Numeration 13.0 Basic computation 14.0 Advanced computation
Spelling skills	15.0 Spelling
Handwriting skills	16.0 Manuscript letters, numerals, words 17.0 Cursive letters, numerals, words
Social skills	18.0 Social language (greeting, handshaking, etc.) 19.0 Social requisites (grooming, table manners, etc.) 20.0 Social interaction
Community living skills	21.0 Transportation 22.0 Consumer skills 23.0 Leisure skills 24.0 Work skills

Subtasks for a given short-term objective can also be numbered; for example, copying cursive letters *a* through *f* may be numbered 17.1. Once the sequence of tasks to be taught has been established, other planning decisions fall into place in the proper perspective. This list should be considered as representative and not necessarily exhaustive.

A Teacher Presentation Guide (Exhibit 2–4) is printed on the back of the Daily Planner for two reasons. First, it permits the teacher to plan in writing the *exact* intervention and redirection procedures that are needed. Second, it pro-

vides, in scriptlike fashion, a guide for the teacher to follow in carrying out daily lessons. The guide is divided into two sections: Intervene and Redirect. The three parts of the intervention section are

1. Setting/Materials. Setting features are described only when they pertain directly to the teaching stimuli (e.g., the setting must be a building if language commands such as "Open the door." or "Walk down the hall." are to be taught). Materials include those to be presented as teaching stimuli (e.g., flashcards, worksheets, or objects).
2. Teacher Says/Does. The statements or actions a teacher uses to prompt a child's response (antecedent events) and the statements or actions a teacher uses to react to the child's response (consequent events) are listed.
3. Child Says/Does. Usually the child response remains unchanged. However, in some cases, it may be necessary to reanalyze the task and specify a less complex response for the child to perform. Expect to make changes in the presentation procedure once instruction gets underway.

Redirection is a planned change in the intervention procedure, whether in setting, event, or materials; in what the teacher says or does; or in what is entered under the appropriate column. Typically, this entry is made after the program is underway and the child is not progressing.

The Daily Planner (Exhibit 2–5) is a visual record of both teaching and learning activity over time. It incorporates features of is-does planning, criterion-referenced decision making and teacher supervision models. It functions as a "check-and-balance" sheet. Objectives, teaching procedures, and child learning are balanced against each other to ensure that (1) one subobjective is not dwelled upon for too long or left too soon, (2) the planned teaching procedure is consistently followed, (3) teaching procedures are changed when a child is not making progress, (4) teaching procedures are *not* changed when a child is making progress. Once the teacher adopts the Daily Planner, the need for time-consuming descriptions is reduced. Teacher-trainees who have used the Planner often required less than 30 seconds per program per child, because the trainee's daily response was to enter a code numeral or ditto mark under each column. Because the planner corresponds to both the Direct Teaching Program Checklist and the Preprogram Planner, most of the "thinking" part of the planning has been done and it is a matter of transferring this information to the Daily Planner. Definitions for each teaching competency code and format definitions are in Appendix A.

Exhibit 2-4 Teacher Presentation Guide

TEACHER PRESENTATION GUIDE

INTERVENE:

Setting/Materials	Teacher Says/Does	Child Says/Does
Group-individualized, Cursive letter work-sheets containing Model letter row at the top of the work-sheet.	Praises child for 3 or more correct letters. Overmarks incorrect letters with highlighter pen erases child's error portions	Writes one row of letters redraws letter to match highlighted letter—moves to next row

REDIRECT:

Setting/Materials	Teacher Says/Does	Child Says/Does
Individual blank overlay page to reveal one letter Column → [A]	same as above but for single letter	Write one letter at a time redraws letter—moves to next letter in column

Exhibit 2–5 Daily Planner*

DAILY PLANNER*

Planning		Instructional Tactics					Measurement	
Ⓐ	Ⓑ	Ⓒ	Ⓓ	Ⓔ	Ⓕ	Ⓖ	Ⓗ	Ⓘ
	Sub-Objective	Materials	Presentation Mode	Child Response	Arranged Event	Arrangement	Progress Checking Tactic	Child Mastery/ Non Mastery
10/28	17.1	31	40, 44	51	60	74	81	90
10/29	17.1	''	'' ''	''	''	''	''	90
10/30	17.1	''	'' ''	''	''	''	''	91
11/1	17.2	''	'' ''	''	''	''	''	90
11/4	17.2	''	'' ''	''	''	73	''	90

KEY

Ⓐ **Date:** date for which planned

Ⓑ **Sub-Objective:** (number from Program Plan Sheet - up to 30)

Ⓒ **Materials:**
30 = no materials
31 = published materials
32 = teacher made
33 = other

Ⓓ **Presentation Mode:**
40 = modeling
41 = questioning
42 = physical assistance
43 = prompt
44 = other

Ⓔ **Child Response:**
50 = oral
51 = motor/gestural
52 = written
53 = other

Ⓕ **Arranged Event:**
60 = social
61 = token
62 = consumable (edible)
63 = activity (e.g., free play)
64 = other

Ⓖ **Arrangement:**
70 = variable interval
71 = fixed interval
72 = continuous
73 = variable ratio
74 = fixed ratio
75 = other

Ⓗ **Progress Checking Tactic**
80 = criterion-referenced test
81 = daily record
82 = normative test
83 = other

Ⓘ **Child Data:**
90 = non-Mastery
91 = Mastery

*Many of the procedures outlined on this checklist were adapted from the materials developed in the Field Based Special Teacher Education Program at George Peabody College for Teachers of Vanderbilt University.

Chapter 3

Specification and Implementation of Behavioral Objectives

SUCCESSFUL AND UNSUCCESSFUL PROGRAMMING

Washington Elementary School serves grades 1 through 6 in a midwestern town. The two resource teachers in the school, Mr. MacMahon and Ms. Martin, were hired to teach remedial math and reading classes. Mr. MacMahon serves the older children (grades 4 through 6), while Ms. Martin usually serves the younger children. Both teachers have 5 or more years of teaching experience and have been at Washington for several years.

The other teachers at Washington Elementary feel that the remedial opportunities offered in math and reading are important for children with academic performance problems. The teachers from the regular classes appreciate the support they receive from both resource teachers. Further investigation revealed, however, that the other teachers feel that children from Ms. Martin's classes return to their regular classes with greatly improved skills in the referral area, but that children from Mr. MacMahon's classes were "hit and miss." Some children who returned from his classes had improved skills, but more children were unchanged and even further behind than when they left their regular classes. The teachers attributed this to the extra difficulty of helping older children once they have developed academic problems.

The differences between the two teachers can be examined by simulating the methods they use to deal with the same referral problem.

Richie and Bobby are third graders who read well but have had frequent problems with math. They have difficulty keeping up with their classmates and usually require more repetition on each learned skill than do other children. Their teachers must provide considerable support and careful monitoring to avoid gaps in knowledge. This is not their first referral to a resource teacher.

Richie and Bobby have been referred to the resource room this time because they cannot add figures with multiple columns, even though they have mastered basic addition and subtraction facts. They have been taught to carry and can manage when there are only two columns of figures, but they have not generalized to multiple column problems. Carrying across zeroes is particularly problematic. They guess at answers when they are stumped.

After receiving Richie on a referral basis, Mr. MacMahon places Richie in a remedial math class with other students. He gives Richie a Wide Range Achievement Test to determine his functional grade level. Richie's raw score is 29, which places him at a grade level of 3.6. Mr. MacMahon determines from the test that Richie is having problems with carrying in addition problems, borrowing in subtraction problems, and basic multiplication facts. Therefore, his planning for Richie's remedial program includes mixed problems of these types. He plans for Richie to work with him on the misunderstood concepts at the beginning of each period and then to complete worksheets at his desk. Mr. MacMahon and Richie's regular teacher decide that Richie should catch up on basic concepts before continuing on in his regular math class, and the remedial class replaces Richie's current math program. Mr. MacMahon allows all the children in the class to raise their hands for help whenever they feel that they need assistance. Richie asks questions frequently.

Bobby is referred to Ms. Martin's class, where he is also placed in a remedial math class. However, Ms. Martin requests that Bobby remain in his regular math class while taking the remedial class. Ms. Martin also acts as a support teacher for Bobby in his regular class whenever he needs additional help.

Ms. Martin's remedial class is split into two sections with three children in each section. After conferring with Bobby's teacher about his problems, Ms. Martin administers a teacher-made test with 50 mixed addition problems. By means of this test, Ms. Martin determines that Bobby has mastered two-column addition problems with carrying, but cannot generalize to more difficult addition problems. Ms. Martin assigns Bobby worksheets that concentrate on these specific math facts. Each worksheet includes a permanent model on the upper left corner of each page. After an initial training session on the carrying operation with this type of problem, Ms. Martin begins each session by working individually with Bobby for a few minutes. She demonstrates a correct model and next requests that Bobby correctly work a problem for her before practicing on the worksheet by himself.

There are several reasons why Ms. Martin has more success with children than does Mr. MacMahon. First of all, she bases her assessment on the referral information provided by the teacher. Once the problem has been pinpointed, she plans remediation to focus specifically on that problem through intensive teaching and practice sessions. She also tries to keep the child in regular placement whenever possible. In contrast, Mr. MacMahon fails to consider the information gleaned from the referring teacher, makes an inadequate assessment, and bases programming on the nonspecific problem.

WHAT TO TEACH

The first task a teacher must tackle when planning a program for a particular child is to determine what to teach the child. Although this may sound self-evident, it cannot be overemphasized that the program must be based on an accurate analysis of the child's deficit. In other words, in order to provide programming that will remediate a specific problem, the teacher must first identify the exact problem(s).

Most handicapped children exhibit more than one behavior that requires remediation. Problems may arise in the social, academic, and behavioral areas. Therefore, the teacher must consider all deficit areas, assess the functional level of the deficits, and, finally, prioritize the instructional plan according to the child's greatest need. It is the teacher's responsibility to decide which skills will benefit the child most. These skills are given the highest priority and are taught first. In the case of Richie and Bobby, basic addition skills are a high priority, because they must become proficient in basic skills before moving on to higher math skills. Once a child's problem has been pinpointed, the design of an individualized education program (IEP) is underway.

TEACHER USE OF BEHAVIORAL OBJECTIVES

When initially planning an instructional program for a child, teachers should be concerned with four major questions:

1. What is the child's current educational performance level (making the initial assessment)?
2. What are the child's long- and short-term goals (determining behavioral objectives)?
3. What methods and/or materials should I use to teach the child (designing the instructional plan)?
4. How will I know when the child has mastered these objectives (Howell, Kaplan, & O'Connell, 1979)?

All these questions are relevant to the specification and implementation of behavioral objectives.

Making the Initial Assessment

As mentioned earlier, it is the teacher's responsibility to select the most critical tasks to teach—tasks that, when mastered, will help the child the most in the future. The procedure usually begins with a diagnostic evaluation to determine the child's placement and instructional needs. This initial assessment procedure yields a variety of quite specific data concerning the child's current skill levels. From this information, the teacher can derive reasonable long- and short-term goals for the school year. The task of prioritizing what is to be taught remains.

Frequently, an IEP team determines the most outstanding needs and establishes these as the primary concerns to which the objectives are directed. This is a particularly important part of IEP preparation, because not only school personnel, but parents are involved. Once the goals have been determined, the highest-priority goals become annual goals. Next, the IEP team attempts to bridge the gap between the child's current performance level and the annual goal by breaking the short-term objectives into teachable subobjectives. The short-term goals then become the blueprint to be used by the teacher in planning instruction for the child. The behavioral objective is the beginning of this plan.

Determining Behavioral Objectives

It is important for teachers to write objectives in such a way that another teacher can read and implement them. They should be precise and accurate because they become an integral part of the instruction plan. Clear behavioral objectives are also a part of the IEPs required by law for handicapped children. Parents, teachers, and administrative personnel must agree on behavioral objects for each handicapped child. Therefore, these objectives must be written so that anyone (parents, teachers, and administrators) can easily interpret them.

To date, numerous volumes have been written on the basic "how to" of behavioral objective writing (e.g., Mager, 1962, 1969; McNeil, 1967; Wheeler & Fox, 1972). These noted authors agree that behavioral objects should always be written to include three components: (1) observable behaviors, (2) conditions, and (3) criteria of acceptable performance.

Observable Behaviors

The first step in writing an objective is to specify the desired behavior change. It is important to state the desired change in terms of publicly observable behavior. Teachers often defend nonbehavioral objectives by saying, "Well, I *know* what I want the children to do." Nonbehavioral objectives serve little useful purpose, however, because others (e.g., parents, the principal, next year's teachers) may not *know* what the child was to do, may not read and interpret the written objectives in the same way, and, thus, may not be able to measure the child's ability to perform the task. The behavior specified in the objective must be observable so that student mastery can be assessed accurately.

Examples of observable behaviors include

- The child will *write* the answers to 50 single-column addition problems.
- The child will *place and keep his hands at his sides* during line-up for lunch.
- The child will *say* each word aloud.
- The child will *catch* the ball.
- The child will *draw* and label the parts of the amoeba.
- The child will mark commas and periods in appropriate places in a written paragraph.

Examples of behaviors that are not directly observable are

- The child will solve mathematics problems.
- The child will feel that her behavior has improved.
- The child will become a competent speller.
- The child will be able to analyze written math problems.

- The child will learn to read.
- The teacher will present the concepts big, bigger, biggest.

These behaviors are ambiguous. It is difficult to count the number of times the child feels "that her behavior has improved." It is impossible to specify when the behavior begins and when it ends. Similarly, it is impossible to count instances in which the child becomes a competent speller. When writing a behavioral objective the teacher should state the behavior so that its readers can ask the child to "Show me how you _____."

Conditions

A behavioral objective should include the conditions under which the behavior is to be observed. The conditions answer the questions, "when," "where," or "given. . . ." This part of the objective further describes the behavior to be exhibited. It frequently begins "When given . . ." or "Given . . ." or states a specific place "When on the playground. . . ." For example,

- When given 50 single-digit subtraction problems in the form (A − B = C)
- After reading "The Emperor's New Clothes"
- Given a baseball and glove while on the playground
- When given a diagram of an amoeba
- Given a 50-word paragraph without commas or periods

This part of the behavioral objective is critical, because it states what is required before the behavior can be completed. When the provisions of the objective are known, the entire outcome objective is clarified.

Criteria of Acceptable Performance

The third component of a behavioral objective is the statement of criteria that must be met before the teacher can consider the objective attained. In other words, the objective should contain a standard by which judgment can be made concerning achievement of the objective. Without criteria, a teacher may either stop teaching before the behavior is sufficiently established in the child's repertoire or may continue teaching after it is no longer necessary. Examples of criterion statements are

- For 5 minutes continuously, making no more than five errors in 30 problems
- Eight out of ten attempts completed correctly
- Six consecutive trials
- With no more than two misread words per minute of oral reading

Teachers should also keep in mind the appropriateness of criteria for task completion. Criteria must be high enough to demonstrate that the learner has mastered the tasks, but not so high that, to the learner, the criteria seem unreachable goals. If criteria must be set at high levels to ensure task mastery, the teacher should consider using several successively introduced objectives that bring the learner to the goal in smaller steps. In either case, the teacher must carefully consider the task, determine what constitutes mastery, and set objectives so that the learner can make steady progress toward the goal.

Designing the Instructional Plan

Many teachers select materials and teaching methods for use with a particular child according to a "best guess" technique based on experience and education. There are quantities of literature on effective instructional techniques (Brophy & Good, 1974; Stevens & Rosenshine, 1981). Similarly, a great many commercial materials are available to assist the teacher in carrying out instruction, and systematic procedures for selecting materials have been described in other works (e.g., Stowitschek et al., 1980). Even so, the predominant mode of choice may still be an educated guess. In any case, the teacher must implement the instructional plan with the child and determine by the child's performance whether the choice was appropriate.

The teacher must always consider what, exactly, the child should practice. Teachers frequently ask children to perform tasks that are related, but are not the same as the task stated in the objective. Assignments should pertain only to the specific task stated in the objective, however. For example, if the objective calls for the child to mark commas and periods correctly within written paragraphs, the teacher should not ask the child to capitalize words in the paragraph; capitalization is a separate task. Likewise, if the objective requires the child to compute single-digit subtraction problems in the

form $\begin{array}{c} A \\ -B \\ \hline C \end{array}$, the teacher should not include problems in the

form $A - B = C$ in the assignment (although the student may soon be asked, in a new objective, to apply subtraction skills to the linear format).

Teachers must be judicious not only in the selection of teaching methods and the construction of teacher-made materials, but also in the selection of appropriate commercial materials. Teachers must become evaluators of their own teaching and materials so that they present the child with tasks specifically related to the desired objective and exclude other tasks. In other words, teachers should use the objectives that they have written. They should consider objectives tools for making correct decisions.

PLANNING TACTICS

Task Analysis

Implicit in the programming for behavior change is the teacher's choice of an instructional planning tactic. In order to make this choice, the teacher must first examine the terminal behavior (task) that is expected of the child. If the child cannot perform the terminal task, it can be assumed that the child has not adequately learned all or some part (i.e., subtask) of the terminal task. This approach is called task analysis and refers to the preliminary step in instructional planning, which involves isolating, sequencing, and describing the essential components of a task (Howell et al., 1979).

The teacher must decide if a task analysis approach is appropriate for a given objective. The best way to determine this is to try to analyze the task that the child is expected to perform and divide it into subtasks that are to be performed in sequence. If the task can be divided into discrete conditions, behaviors, or levels of criteria (subtasks) that can be assessed and subsequently taught, if necessary, task analysis is an appropriate instructional planning technique. It is not necessary for teachers to conduct a task analysis of every skill taught to children in their classes, however. Task analysis is best used to help a child who is not progressing with more global instructional approaches or to fill in instructional gaps, such as the teaching of skills required to begin an instructional program.

In using task analysis as a planning tactic, two questions may be asked: (1) is the task a motor task with easily observed movements (e.g., manipulating objects)? and (2) are rote discriminations (e.g., pointing to an object) the intended outcome of the objective? If so, the task analysis approach is a good choice for instructional planning. The terminal goal can be analyzed into substeps that, when individually mastered, lead to task mastery. For example, if the terminal goal is washing hands, the teacher may list the following substeps:

1. Turn on tap.
2. Wet hands.
3. Grasp soap between hands.
4. Rub hands over soap to lather.
5. Lay soap down.
6. Wash tops of hands.
7. Wash palms.
8. Wash between fingers.
9. Rinse soap off hands.
10. Turn off tap.
11. Get towel.
12. Dry hands.
13. Replace towel.

This linear task list contains the specifics that constitute (1) the terminal behavior, (2) the subtasks to be taught in the instructional program, and (3) the subtasks the teacher should monitor to determine progress toward task mastery.

Task Analysis: A Hierarchical Model

Thiagarajan, Semmel, and Semmel (1974) described the steps needed to perform a task analysis as follows:

1. Specify the main task.
2. Identify subtasks at the preceding level of complexity (e.g., "What skills should the trainee possess in order to perform the task?").
3. Treat each subtask as a main task and repeat the analytic procedure.
4. Terminate analysis when subtask reaches the entry level of the teacher trainees.

Figure 3–1 shows how the model proposed by Thiagarajan and co-workers can be applied to the analysis of social skill development in preschoolers. Task descriptions must become behavioral statements that describe what the learner is expected to do.

After the task analysis has been constructed, Thiagarajan and associates suggested the use of a checklist to review the task analysis for the following conditions:

1. relevance. Is the main task relevant to the effective performance of a teacher in a real-world classroom with handicapped children?
2. completeness. Are enough subtasks listed to cover the performance of the main task? Has any essential subtask been omitted?
3. triviality. Is any subtask included which is simpler than the entry level of the target trainees?
4. necessity. Is each subtask necessary for the performance of the main task? Are any of the subtasks unnecessary?
5. redundancy. Is any subtask repeated more than once with or without minor changes in wording? Is any set of

Figure 3–1 Portion of a Hierarchical Task Analysis

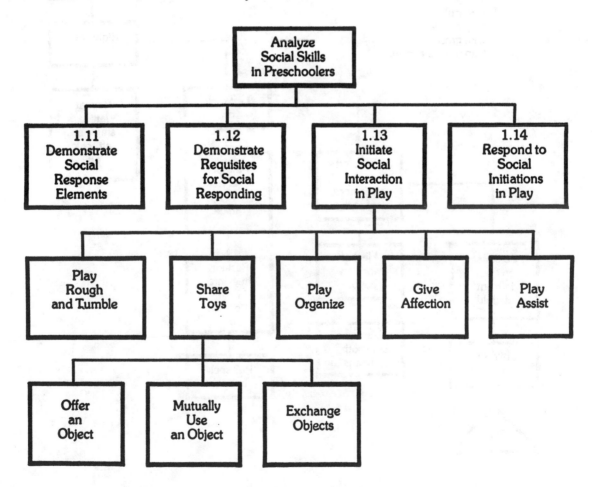

subtasks an alternate for the performances contained in another set of subtasks? (p. 41)

The advantage of a carefully planned instructional sequence is obviously a program that runs smoothly. Teachers frequently complain that the completion of a carefully prepared task analysis is a time-consuming task, however. Although the initial outlay of time is substantial, teachers who plan and evaluate their instructional programs carefully actually save time because future program alterations are minimized.

Task Analysis: Modified Lattice System

Another task analysis approach that teachers can use to plan the best way to help children achieve instructional goals is the modified lattice system (Smith, 1981; Smith & Snell, 1978). The system is similar to the hierarchical model devel-

oped by Thiagarajan and associates (1974), but it provides a visual blueprint or format from which a teacher can develop an instructional program. The steps used to develop this model are as follows:

1. Define the terminal goal.
2. Identify main tasks and place on ridge line.
3. Identify subtasks and place in sequence below main tasks.
4. Develop other miniprograms within a more complex program (optional).
5. Determine prerequisites.

The terminal goal represents the desired outcome of the program and should be stated in observable and measurable terms. It is always placed in the uppermost box on the right side of the lattice. In Figure 3–2, for example, the terminal goal is "socks on."

Figure 3–2 Portion of a Lattice System of Task Analysis

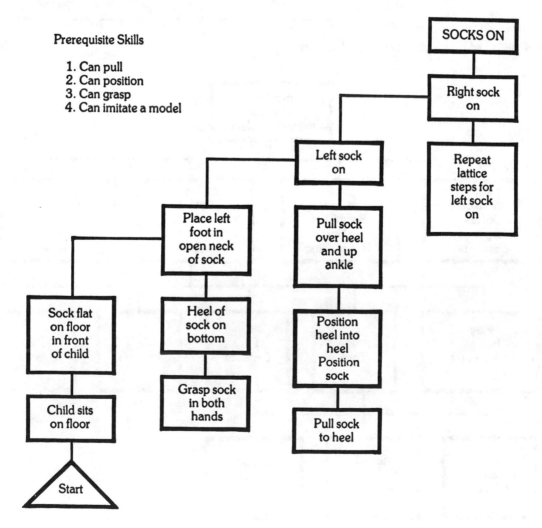

Next, the teacher must determine the main tasks required to complete the terminal goal. In this example, the first main task is to position the child on the floor with the sock flat on the floor in front of the child. Other main tasks are "left sock on" and "right sock on." Main tasks are positioned at the top of each column of subtasks, reading from left to right. The ridge line is an outline of the total picture.

Each main task is divided into the subtasks needed to arrive at the desired outcome. The teacher must determine the appropriate size of the steps. If the child does not meet with program success, more discrete subtasks or miniprograms may have to be developed. The subtasks are positioned below each main task, reading from bottom to top, left to right.

In some cases, a lattice may include a cluster of related programs under one more general terminal goal. For example, putting on clothes, taking off clothes, and putting clothes away may be three separate miniprograms under the more general terminal goal of dressing skills. Each miniprogram is developed and taught independently, but they are nested as minilattices under the more general lattice for dressing skills. Each miniprogram is positioned as a separate minilattice within the larger lattice, and the miniprograms can be taught in any order.

Finally, the teacher must carefully determine the skills that the child needs to begin the program. The teacher must also determine the point of division between the prerequisites needed and the subtasks taught within the program. Student entry level skills should match the subtasks being taught in the program. If the child has difficulty mastering the program, alterations may be required to teach unlearned prerequisite skills.

Transfer of Task Analysis to Direct Teaching

Once completed, the task analysis can be used to prepare the instructional program. Exhibit 3–1 illustrates how the "Socks On" program can be transferred to the Teacher Presentation Guide. The program branches in that teacher prompts cease if the child can complete one or more steps unaided or if the child completes the task without further prompting. In addition, the Socks On task analysis can be transferred to the Preprogram Planner (Exhibit 3–2), which allows for specification of the main objective and each short-term objective (STO) needed to produce the final objective.

Exhibit 3–3 shows another task analysis transferred to the Preprogram Planner. In this example, the child is learning to share toys. The behavior and criterion remain unchanged throughout the training, but the conditions vary. At first, the teacher interacts with the child in a classroom; then the emphasis is shifted to child-child interaction—still in the classroom—with successive changes occurring until the child is interacting with various children during free play.

Exhibit 3–1 Results of Task Analysis Translated into Teacher Presentation Instructions

TEACHER PRESENTATION GUIDE

INTERVENE:

Setting/Materials	Teacher Says/Does	Child Says/Does
socks (with heels)	(nothing, if child sits down)	child sits
	"Sit down, Nicky!"	child sits
child seat with sock	"Put your socks on"	socks on unaided
	"Pick up the sock"	picks up sock
	"Put one hand on e/ side"	holds sock w/ two hands
	"Put your toe in sock toe"	puts toe in sock
	"Place sock heel on bottom"	sock heel on bottom
	"Pull sock to heel"	sock heel in place
	"Pull sock to ankle"	sock on

Exhibit 3–2 Task Sequence Transferred to Preprogram Planner

Sub-Skill Objectives: (Please number each one)

S.T.O. No.	Conditions:	Behavior:	Criterion:
4.11	"sit down"	child sits	10/10 trials
4.12	"pick up sock"	picks up sock	10/10 trials
4.13	"hold with two hands"	holds sock correctly	10/10 trials
4.14	"put heel on bottom"	positions sock	10/10 trials
4.15	"put foot in hole"	foot in opening	10/10 trials
4.16	"pull to heel"	pulls sock to heel	10/10 trials
4.17	"position heel"	positions heel	10/10 trials
4.18	"pull sock to ankle"	pulls sock to ankle	10/10 trials
4.1	"put on your socks"	puts on socks	10/10 trials

Exhibit 3–3 Task Sequence in Which Response Conditions Vary

S.T.O. No.	Conditions:	Behavior:	Criterion:
20.11	T. & child (in class rm.)	shares toys	25/25 trials
20.12	child & 1 other w/ T. present (in class rm.)	shares toys	25/25 trials
20.13	child & 1 other w/o Teacher	shares toys	25/25 trials
20.14	child & 1 other (in free play)	shares toys	25/25 trials
20.15	child w/ others (in free play)	shares toys	25/25 trials

In a task analysis of two-digit addition with carrying, the conditions and behavior remain the same throughout the program, but changes in criteria occur as the child reaches different levels of proficiency (Exhibit 3–4). The first criterion specifies 80% mastery, a reasonable expectation during initial acquisition of the skill. A criterion of 100% mastery might be established after the child has mastered the skill. The next two criteria are based on rate per minute; the mastered skill is built to a high level of proficiency. Finally, a maintenance level in terms of rate per minute is specified.

Exhibit 3–4 Task Sequence in Which Performance Criteria Vary

S.T.O. No.	Conditions:	Behavior:	Criterion:
13.11	30 math facts	2 digit add. w/ carrying	24/30 correct
13.12	30 math facts	2 digit add. w/carrying	30/30 correct
13.13	30 math facts	2 digit add. w/ carrying	20 correct/Min.
13.14	30 math facts	2 digit add. w/ carrying	30 correct/Min.
13.15	30 math facts	2 digit add. w/ carrying	[maintain] 25 correct/Min.

Sub-Skill Objectives: (Please number each one)

Concept Analysis

Another instructional planning technique that may be employed by teachers is concept analysis. This technique is particularly applicable to objectives designed to generalize learning. Concepts are analyzed by arranging their characteristics into dichotomized groupings of critical and irrelevant attributes. By repeated presentation, children learn to discriminate between examples and nonexamples so that, ultimately, they can recognize an instance of the concept when presented with a unique example (one form of stimulus generalization).

Markle and Tiemann (1970) suggested a format for developing a concept analysis that begins with the identification of the constant attributes of the concept. In other words, it is necessary to determine the specific attributes that produce a consistent response when they are present and no response when they are absent. These attributes are called critical attributes. Irrelevant attributes, or attributes that can be varied because they are not indigenous to the concept, must also be determined (Exhibit 3–5).

Following the identification of critical and irrelevant characteristics, the teacher must determine examples and nonexamples to be used to teach the concept. At first, the examples and nonexamples are exaggerated so that differences are clearly discernible; as learning progresses, however, finer discriminations are expected. Examples become more varied, and nonexamples become closer in character to examples so that fine distinctions must be made. Examples and nonexamples that were not used in teaching are used similarly to test concept acquisition.

Since the Direct Teaching Program Checklist is designed to serve as an intermediary stage between the IEP and daily teaching, it can be used to display a concept analysis procedure (Exhibit 3–6). The concept analysis can also be transferred to the Preprogram Planner (Exhibit 3–7), where each short-term objective (STO) is assigned a number and the conditions, behavior, and criteria are specified.

Programming for Generalization

Even when a concept is not involved, teachers can often manipulate the conditions of an objective to include a plan for generalized responding with the behavior being taught. In other words, teachers can structure the conditions of their teaching so that the child will be able to generalize learning to new applications, discriminating not only among the stimuli presented during teaching, but also among stimuli not previously presented. Becker, Engelmann, and Thomas (1975) stated that teachers can plan for generalization by stressing commonalities of stimulus characteristics during teaching and providing subsequent discrimination training.

Whitney and Striefel (1981) described how generalization must be programmed across persons, settings, or other relevant dimensions. They used a matrix of nine cells to illustrate generalization under these conditions (Figure 3–3). Generalization is said to occur if a behavior is demonstrated in a cell without training either by that person, in that setting, or both. The arrows show the steps to be followed through the matrix when planning for generalization. Each new step requires the child to respond correctly, either with a new

Exhibit 3–5 Concept Analysis: Square

Attributes	Critical	Irrelevant
1. Closed geometric figure	X	
2. 4 sides of equal lengths	X	
3. Sides are perpendicular to each other	X	
4. Size		X
(a) large (b) medium (c) small		
5. Orientation of position		X
(a) horizontal (b) vertical (c) slanted		
6. Color		X
(a) single (b) multi (c) varied		
7. Texture		X
(a) smooth (b) rough		

Teaching Examples	Rationale	Teaching Non-Examples	Rationale
1. 12″ by 12″ square of red construction paper	4a, 5b, 6c, 7a	1. Equilateral triangle of red paper	lacks 2, 3
2. 2″ by 2″ square of blue wood	4c, 5a, 6b, 7b	2. 6″ by 12″ rectangle of green wool	lacks 2, 3
3. 6″ by 6″ square of clear glass	4b, 5c, 6a, 7b	3. A square with 1 open side	lacks 1
4. 1″ by 1″ square of sandpaper	4c, 5c, 6b, 7a	4. A trapezoid drawn on white paper	lacks 2, 3
5. 4″ by 4″ square drawn on white paper	4b, 5a, 6c, 7a	5. Star of blue construction paper	lacks 2, 3

Testing Examples	Rationale	Testing Non-Examples	Rationale
1. 12″ by 12″ square of puce construction paper	4a, 5b, 6c, 7a	1. A circle of blue silk	lacks 2, 3
2. 2″ by 2″ square of black wool	4c, 5c, 6a, 7b	2. A rectangle (1″ by 2″) drawn on paper	lacks 2, 3
3. 5″ by 5″ square of wood	4b, 5a, 6b, 7a	3. An open sided trapezoid	lacks 1, 2, 3
4. 1″ by 1″ square drawn on paper	4c, 5a, 6c, 7b	4. The letter S cut from green wool	lacks 2, 3

Exhibit 3–6 Results of Concept Analysis Represented on Direct Teaching Checklist

DIRECT TEACHING PROGRAM CHECKLIST*

(For supervisors use only)

PROGRAM _Shape recognition --oral_	Approved Date	Verified (For supervisors use only) DATE Initial
Freddy S.		

TARGET _identification of square_ (What to teach)			
ANALYZE _concept analysis_ (What to teach)			
ASSESS _present examples & nonexamples_ (How measure)			

Exhibit 3–7 Results of Concept Analysis Represented on Preprogram Planner

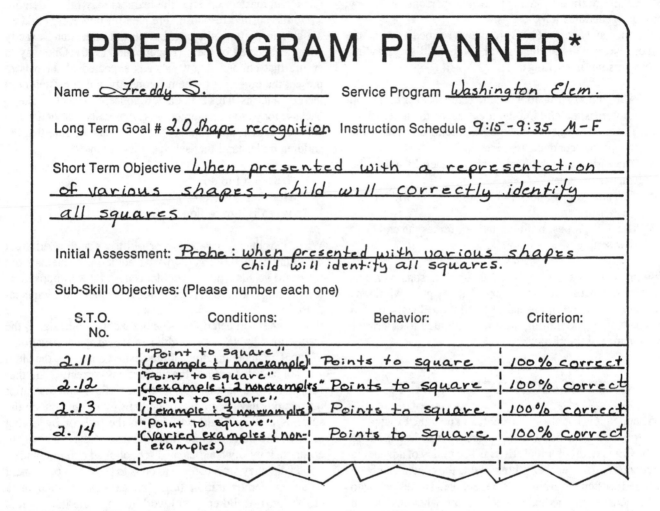

PREPROGRAM PLANNER*

Name _Freddy S._   Service Program _Washington Elem._

Long Term Goal # _2.0 Shape recognition_ Instruction Schedule _9:15 - 9:35 M - F_

Short Term Objective _When presented with a representation of various shapes, child will correctly identify all squares._

Initial Assessment: _Probe: when presented with various shapes child will identify all squares._

Sub-Skill Objectives: (Please number each one)

S.T.O. No.	Conditions:	Behavior:	Criterion:
2.11	"Point to square" (1 example & 1 nonexample)	Points to square	100% correct
2.12	"Point to square" (1 example & 2 nonexamples)	Points to square	100% correct
2.13	"Point to square" (1 example & 3 nonexamples)	Points to square	100% correct
2.14	"Point to square" (varied examples & non-examples)	Points to square	100% correct

Figure 3–3 Steps in Training for Generalization

	Teacher	Aide	Parent
Classroom 1	Teacher in Classroom 1	Aide in Classroom 1	Parent in Classroom 1
Classroom 2	Teacher in Classroom 2	Aide in Classroom 2	Parent in Classroom 2
Home	Teacher in Home	Aide in Home	Parent in Home

Source: Reprinted from "Functionality and Generalization in Training the Severely and Profoundly Handicapped" by R. Whitney and S. Striefel, *Journal of Special Education Technology*, 1981, *4*(3), with permission of the authors.

person or in a new setting. Teaching continues until the child exhibits the desired behavior with new persons or in new settings (generalization).

Whitney and Striefel (1981) further described a procedure that can be used to transfer control of the child's responding across persons and settings:

1. After initial acquisition training, the teacher trains and reinforces the child in the presence of the aide.
2. The aide assumes the task of reinforcing the child while the teacher conducts training.
3. The aide trains and reinforces the child while the teacher observes.
4. The aide trains and reinforces the child without the teacher present.
5. The aide probes, or trains and reinforces the child in a new setting.

This procedure can be extended to new persons and new settings. If generalization is observed at any point within the procedure, further training can be discontinued while probes are conducted. Monitoring must be continued to determine maintenance of the behavior.

DETERMINATION OF MASTERY

Although it is not always possible to know the exact point of instruction at which mastery occurs, it is important to establish some sort of initial criteria. The policy of advancing a student when the teacher "thinks" that the content has been mastered is often too arbitrary to be reliable. The teacher who uses a nonspecific method of determining when instruction should change or cease may move children into content for which they are not ready or allow them to sit for days (or even weeks) on a task that has been mastered.

The teacher should quantify mastery criteria for the behavior specified in the objective:

- When given a 50-word paragraph without commas or periods, the child will place commas and periods at appropriate places in the narrative with 92% accuracy (22 of 25 possible).
- When requested to "eat your breakfast" and given a spoon and bowl of cereal, the learner will voluntarily place spoonfuls of cereal in his mouth without spilling on a minimum of eight consecutive spoonfuls for 3 consecutive days.

Even if criteria are arbitrarily established at first, they can be adjusted later when the child and teacher have had experience with the specified behavior and can better determine mastery criteria.

In spite of carefully written statements of behavior, conditions, and mastery criteria, the learners may fail to demonstrate the desired response. Frequently, however, children are able to perform the task but do not understand exactly what is expected of them (Engelmann, 1970). One way to ensure that children know what is expected of them is to present the objective to them frequently and consistently in their own terms. This is not a new concept to most teachers, because they are accustomed to giving daily instructions to children in their classrooms. Teachers must be sure that the children understand the task specifics, such as

1. What am I to do?
2. How is it to be done?
3. When is it to be done?

When introducing new tasks or old tasks with a different presentation mode (e.g., working addition problems from the board versus working problems out of a workbook), the teacher must be sure that the child understands the expectations.

A teacher can determine whether a child understands the instructions by asking the child to repeat the instructions. Without an understanding of the desired outcome, the child will not be able to repeat the instructions correctly. Another simple method is to observe the child's work just after instructions have been given, perhaps by roving among the students as they begin working on the task or by asking selected children to demonstrate the task. A sure-fire way to ensure that mildly handicapped school-aged children understand what they are expected to do is to provide a permanent model or demonstration (e.g., an example written on a chalkboard). Children could work through the item as it is presented. The result is a trial performance of the task and permanent model of how to complete the task. Use of these simple techniques should provide children with a sufficient opportunity to grasp the task requirements and to ask questions if they do not understand what to do.

CONCLUSION

The value of behavioral objectives in teachers' instructional planning has long been recognized in education circles. Mager and McCann (1961) found that child learning increased when precisely stated objectives were shared with the child at the outset of instruction. A number of subsequent studies also showed child gains when specific objectives were used (McNeil, 1967; Peniston, 1975). Although research does not universally support the effectiveness of the use of behavioral objectives, most research supports the importance of instructional planning by means of behavioral objectives (Burney, 1976). In general, educators agree that behavioral objectives are useful in stating to parents, teachers, and to the child exactly what terminal behavior is expected.

Passage of Public Law 94-142 (P.L. 94-142), the Education for All Handicapped Children Act, and state mandates have made it necessary for schools to use behavioral objectives in their planning procedures in order to comply with the law. Section 4(a)(19) of the act contains the following description of IEP components:

a written statement for each handicapped child developed in any meeting by a representative of the local education agency or an intermediate educational unit who shall be qualified to provide, or supervise the provision of, specially designed instruction to meet the unique needs of handicapped children, the teacher, the parents or guardian of such child, and whenever appropriate, such child, which statement shall include (A) a statement of the present levels of educational performance of such child, (B) a statement of annual goals, including short-term instructional objectives, (C) a statement of the specific educational performance anticipated duration of such services, and appropriate objective criteria and evaluation procedures and schedules for determining, on at least an annual basis, whether instructional objectives are being achieved.

Although P.L. 94-142 provides detailed requirements on what should be included in an IEP and the conditions under which the plan should be developed, it does not specify the planning process to be followed. Many teachers who write IEP objectives to comply with the law neglect to use them for educational planning (Stowitschek & Shores, 1977). This can invalidate the effectiveness of the behavioral objectives. Therefore, it seems that teachers would best meet their responsibility of remediating deficits of handicapped children by writing annual goals and short-term objectives that not only fulfill legal requirements, but also provide a blueprint for the development of an accountable instruction program.

Chapter 4
Measurement

A relatively inexperienced seamstress may use a company-made, no frills shirt pattern, while a master tailor may design an original pattern or cut the fabric without a pattern. In either case, seamstress and tailor go through a similar series of activities before arriving at the final product. Each works in the most efficient manner possible, given the skills each brings to the task at hand. Each has one goal in mind—to finish the shirt according to specifications in the least amount of time possible. In that effort, each makes many decisions based on measures, mainly objective measures, made before and during the course of making the shirt.

Like shirt makers, teachers use both subjective and objective data in their initial assessments of tasks, in varied goal-directed activities, and in follow-up evaluations. Just as the tailor selects color, style, and fabric to meet the needs and preferences of the consumer, so the teacher sets instructional priorities to meet the educational needs of the student, preferences of the parents, and demands of society. Early in the decision-making process, both tailor and teacher often rely heavily on experience, past success, and local or regional priorities and standards. Once larger and more general goals have been determined, the tailor and the teacher use more objective measures in assessing their objectives. For the tailor, the main variable is size. After noting the general size of the consumer, the tailor more precisely assesses arm length, wrist size, neck size, girth of the waist, and so on. Thereafter, all cutting and sewing progress in relation to these objective measurements. At times, the future wearer may be asked to try on the shirt before final cutting or stitching is done. If at last the shirt is a perfect fit—all dimensions correspond correctly to the consumer's size and personal preferences—the tailor's work has been successful.

Unfortunately, children are not easily categorized into educational "sizes," nor do their instructional needs readily "fit" many commercial learning products. Consequently, teachers are often required to modify prepackaged programs or to "cut" their own instructional patterns to meet the unique needs of the exceptional learner. For the inexperienced or inadequately trained teacher, cutting instructional patterns to coincide with the exact learning problems of each student may be particularly difficult and time-consuming. Fortunately, there are many shortcuts and standard assessment procedures for measuring student needs and progress. For the teacher who learns to use them, accurate and efficient teaching is possible. Furthermore, students who respond favorably to certain instructional procedures and materials in one area of learning are likely to respond favorably when the same approaches are used to teach other skills and concepts. When teachers more quickly identify effective approaches for their students, less planning and reprogramming are needed in the future.

Like the tailor, most teachers, particularly if they are inexperienced or have not worked extensively with a given student, find that a frequent "fitting" is the best way to ascertain whether a program is effective with that student. Measuring a student's progress toward an objective on a continuous or intermittent basis appears to be as critical to successful teaching as identifying that objective and specifying its dimensions. The sooner the tailor or the teacher discovers the need to change plans, e.g., to increase the length of the sleeve or to include a verbal prompt to lower error rate, the faster the objective is likely to be met and the less time and money wasted in ineffective, inadequate, or even deleterious action.

MEASUREMENT IN INSTRUCTIONAL DECISION MAKING

In the not too distant past, the mention of educational and psychological measurement and testing to some teachers and laypersons conjured up esoteric tests and test reports or protocols that could be interpreted only by the "experts." More recently, others have associated measurement in the classroom with a cool, detached teacher-technician who punches stopwatches, sets timers, carries clipboards, charts every student response imaginable, and generally dissects learning while busily tallying the occurrence of its components. In the first case, the teacher was believed to be receiving information from "authorities," information that helped the teacher sympathize with the child and parents but did little to assist the teacher in the instructional process. In the second case, the teacher was believed to be a data collector and manager, with little time for teacher-child interaction.

Today, fortunately, teachers and parents expect measurement activities to be much more educationally pragmatic than the bestowing of generic labels or the collecting of data on every minute behavior. Indeed, measurement is now seen as a critical tool that the teacher can use to assess specific student strengths and deficits and to monitor student learning. When assessment experts are employed, they are expected to provide information that is directly relevant to the needs of the classroom.

Measurement is the key to targeting an appropriate skill/task/concept for teaching. By using measurement tactics and tools (e.g., criterion-referenced tests or daily behavior counts), in a straightforward manner, the teacher can identify skills mastered, skills in the process of being mastered, and skills that have not yet been acquired. The initial assessment of student skills allows the teacher to determine where to direct instructional time and resources so as to avoid expenditure of valuable instructional time on skills or subskills that have already been mastered. The teacher not only can set priorities in a systematic and confident manner, but also can explain to others why those skills have been targeted.

In the course of monitoring student progress and mastery, teachers are concomitantly assessing the effectiveness of different teaching tactics and instructional materials. No single strategy or material is 100% effective with all children or even with the same child from skill to skill. Gathering data on the effectiveness of specific strategies and materials greatly facilitates the daily task of selecting and managing materials. Teachers can spend progressively less time searching for materials and effective teaching strategies as they gain information on the approaches that have produced the best results with their students. By using appropriate measurement tools and the resulting data, teachers can confidently set instructional priorities, make and modify instruc-

tional plans, and select curricular materials and teaching strategies that are most likely to be successful.

Measurement procedures that are overly time-consuming, complicated, or unrelated to the instructional decision-making process are meaningless. Measures of student performance are nonfunctional if they cannot be used to guide decision making. Data need not be extensive to be useful, however. For example, sampling of individual or group performance for short periods of time, e.g., 1 to 5 minutes, can give an accurate picture of student progress. Nor is it necessary to collect data on every skill every day. Depending on the precision needed, the teacher may choose to sample a child's performance only intermittently. The child who has mastered a skill needs occasional checks to see that the skill is being maintained. A child who is learning a new skill needs more frequent checks to be sure that learning is progressing satisfactorily. Measurement activities can be distributed across the day and related to instruction so that there is little, if any, disruption in the daily teaching routine.

The responsibility of collecting and analyzing data need not fall entirely on the shoulders of teachers. With training and supervision, even first-grade students can collect some of their own data, score their work, and chart their progress. By teaching children these skills, teachers not only reduce their own workload, but also promote self-management and goal-directed behavior of students, an educational outcome that Hansen and Eaton (1978) pointed out is the real goal of schooling.

Regardless of their experience, teachers cannot be expected to perform their tasks without some specific measures to guide their decisions and help prevent them from making costly errors. Even the most organized, experienced teachers cannot be asked to make initial assessments, check progress as needed, make daily instructional decisions, and accurately determine the best present and future course of instruction for their students without some objective guides. Measurement provides those guides. At best, the teacher who does not make instructional decisions on the basis of objective measures is not being educationally accountable to the student, parents, school system, or community. At worst, that teacher may be making inappropriate and inaccurate decisions, thereby depriving children of their right to an education.

A MEASUREMENT SCHEMA

It is not always easy for educators to decide which form of measurement to use for which purpose. With the wide array of educational measurements available for an equally wide array of purposes, some means of classifying them systematically according to their instruction and materials application is needed (Stowitschek, Gable, & Hendrickson, 1980).

In the schema developed by Stowitschek and associates (1980), types of tests and measures were classified according to their levels of sensitivity and their purposes (Figure 4–1). The term *sensitivity* refers to the number or duration of responses sampled (often the number of test items) per skill or subskill assessed. Generally, the more subskills assessed by a test, the less sensitive the test for sampling student performance on each subskill. Although the measurement purposes presented in the pyramid are somewhat arbitrary or overlapping, the question to be answered by measurement preceding instruction (What should be taught?) differs from those to be answered by measurement during instruction (Is teaching/learning occurring?) or following initial instruction (Has the skill been acquired and retained?). Furthermore, the information obtained is used in different ways.

Teachers must balance the time they devote to measurement with the time they spend planning and teaching. Initial assessments should allow a teacher to determine progressively more discretely which subskills to assess later in depth. Conversely, after instruction, assessments of the relationship of subskills to skills and, in turn, the relationship of skills to overall achievement should be progressively more global.

The schema presented in Figure 4–1 is intended to ensure not only that subskills are identified before instruction as a result of measurement, but also that the synthesis of the subskills into the terminal skill is assessed following instruction. The levels of assessment and their relationship to instructional materials are depicted as follows:

1. global achievement screening. Standardized achievement tests, often group-administered, help identify which skills in a given subject area are above, at, or below the norm, thus pointing in the direction for further skill assessment.
2. skill deficit identification. Diagnostic tests that focus specifically on identifying deficits or teacher-prepared assessment tools can be used for this purpose. Tests with this level of sensitivity may help teachers select skill kits, e.g., time telling or money concepts.
3. pinpoint diagnosis. Precise specification is needed to begin instruction with many handicapped students. This level of assessment identifies the student's performance on specific subskills and the pattern of errors associated with that performance. For example, the Diagnostic Arithmetic Combinations Test—Addition (Hofmeister, 1970) is such an assessment tool.
4. daily-weekly progress assessment. One of the most essential levels of assessment, daily measures of pupils' performance, as well as pretests and post-tests, can be used to help govern decisions related to work in a given material.
5. mastery assessment of specific tasks and skills. Before instruction is discontinued on a subskill or task, mastery must be assessed. The same type of assessment used for pinpoint diagnosis can be used for this purpose, but the criterion decision is critical at this stage.

Figure 4–1 Purposes of Assessment Related to Levels of Sensitivity

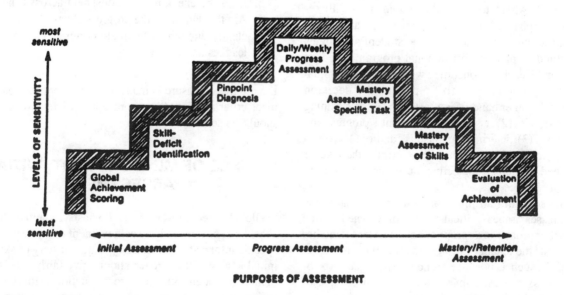

Source: Reprinted from *Instructional Materials for Exceptional Children: Selection, Evaluation, and Adaptation,* p. 157, by J. Stowitschek, R. Gable, and J. Hendrickson, with permission of Aspen Systems Corporation, © 1980.

6. evaluation of achievement. Most school systems require end-of-year evaluation of student achievement. The purposes of this level of assessment are increasingly shifting toward overall competency testing; often, the measures used for global achievement screening are again used here.

HOW TO MEASURE

More specific than the measurement schema just described, the direct teaching decision sequence (see Exhibit 1–1) allows teachers to plan for and measure direct instruction systematically. At first glance, determining how to measure appears to be an isolated issue, the second major decision point in the decision sequence. In truth, measurement influences what is taught, helps determine if the conditions of motivation are appropriate, and ultimately reveals the instructional worth of the teaching strategy(ies) and material(s). The selection of a measurement method should be carefully and thoroughly addressed if the entire direct teaching decision-making process is to retain its integrity.

There are three essential steps in the measurement decision-making process:

1. Step I: Identify the purpose of measurement.
2. Step II: Select an initial assessment approach.
3. Step III: Select a progress check.

Step I helps the teacher decide whether the purpose of measurement is initial assessment or progress checking. If the purpose of the measurement is to determine (1) what to teach, (2) whether the student needs instruction on a specific objective, or (3) where to place the student in a skill sequence, the purpose is initial assessment. In any initial assessment, the purpose is to assess the student's strengths and deficits and to plan an instructional program based on that assessment. Teachers concerned with selecting an initial assessment approach move to Step II in the decision sequence. On the other hand, if interested in (1) determining performance trends, (2) assessing the student's progress and rate of progress, (3) determining mastery, and/or (4) assessing the kind, frequency, and pattern of errors, the teacher should proceed to Step III (selecting a progress measure) in the decision sequence.

In Step II, selecting an initial assessment approach, the teacher addresses issues critical to deciding whether one measurement approach is appropriate or superior to another approach. First, the teacher must decide if a given measurement approach, such as norm-referenced tests, checklists, or observational assessments, involves a sufficient sample of the behavior to be measured. Second, the teacher must decide whether the conditions under which the skills are to be

evaluated should be similar to or the same as those in which the student will ultimately use the skills. Third, the teacher must select an assessment approach that yields separate scores for subskills in addition to a composite score, since individual subscores provide the more precise information necessary for program placement and instructional management. Fourth, the teacher must consider whether the assessment procedure provides information on the pattern, kind, and frequency of student errors. Fifth, it is very important for the teacher to consider the practicality of administering the test. The time required to administer and score the test should be balanced against the kind of results the test provides. If the assessment tool is inadequate in any of these areas, it may be advisable for the teacher to select another instrument to evaluate the targeted skill(s).

The considerations in Step III, selecting a progress check or measure, differ from those in Step II. When preparing to make progress checks, the teacher should consider the following six questions in the decision sequence:

1. Do the learner's responses match the behavior that is specified in the instructional objective? (The teacher should have an objective written by this point.)
2. Is the progress check giving an adequate sample of the student's responses, e.g., is the behavior sampled daily or weekly, are there enough test items or trials to ensure reliable results?
3. Can the progress check be used to display the data in relation to the criteria that have been specified in the instructional objective?
4. Do the conditions of assessment (observing or testing) match the conditions specified in the target objective?
5. Does the check remain consistent across time?
6. Are the data from the progress checks being displayed clearly enough to facilitate communication with colleagues and parents?

If a progress measure is inadequate, it may be redesigned to meet criteria or another more appropriate progress check should be selected.

USES OF MEASUREMENT: INITIAL ASSESSMENT

Global screening, such as IQ tests, adaptive behavior checklists, or standardized achievement tests, do not provide specific information on mastery or nonmastery of skills. The initial assessment approach should give fairly precise information on student skills prior to instruction so that the teacher can decide what to teach and can set up meaningful, well-sequenced instructional programs. Initial assessments should enable the teacher to differentiate between critical unlearned skills and skills that have already been mastered by the student. Generally speaking, teachers gain such information through informal measurement procedures, norm-referenced tests, and/or criterion-referenced tests, although the teacher may have a more specific purpose in administering a test than was originally intended by the test developer.

Norm-Referenced Tests and Criterion-Referenced Tests

Although norm-referenced tests and criterion-referenced tests both have value in the instructional decision-making process, these tests were developed for different purposes. Norm-referenced tests are usually intended to show how the performance of a student or group of students compares with that of other students of the same age. The result indicates that a given student is functioning at a level below, equal to, or above age mates. Norm-referenced tests are static measurement approaches, however; they tell what has happened, not what is happening. Their items generally vary in difficulty and complexity so that errors are not easy to interpret in terms of educational planning. Items at any level are seldom repeated more than once, making identification of error patterns difficult.

In contrast, criterion-referenced tests are designed specifically to identify what the student does or does not know in relation to a given skill or concept. They are both diagnostic and prescriptive. Because scores on criterion-referenced tests are interpreted in relation to a fixed standard, interpretation of their results is more consistent across time than that of norm-referenced tests. Generally, items on a criterion-referenced test are repeated at the same level of difficulty often enough for the teacher to discover error patterns and relationships between errors. Once a student's skill level has been identified by means of a criterion-referenced test, it is fairly simple to determine what to teach—teach those skills/concepts that have not been mastered.

Since norm-referenced tests compare a student's performance to the performance of others and criterion-referenced tests compare a student's performance to a specific skill or task level, criterion-referenced tests theoretically should be of much greater instructional value than are norm-referenced tests. Indeed, this is often the case. Criterion-referenced tests state the objective, criteria, and materials, enabling the teacher to replicate testing/teaching conditions or, conversely, to construct a criterion-referenced test to assess the skills/knowledge taught in the classroom. The best criterion-referenced tests examine only the behaviors or discriminations that are relevant to the skill or concept of interest. Not all such tests are well designed and sequenced, however, and some lose their validity by virtue of errors in format, admin-

istration, or item sampling. The teacher using a commercial criterion-referenced test embedded within the body of the material must be sure that the objectives are precisely stated and that the behavior required to demonstrate mastery matches the behavior stated in the performance objective. For instance, a spelling objective may state that the student is independently and correctly to spell (write) 9 of 10 words that follow the "*i* before *e*" rule, but the test may require the student to find misspelled words. Proofreading and writing the same words correctly are not equivalent terminal behaviors. Data derived from tests that measure behavior other than that stated in the objective are of questionable validity. Another problem is that the results of criterion-referenced tests may not be summarized in a way that is readily usable by teachers.

Adaptation of Tests for Initial Assessment

If teachers were required to develop all of the tests they ever used, including the selection of test items, development of forms, administration procedures, as well as interpretation and scoring procedures, a great deal of planning time would be consumed in test preparation alone (Stowitschek et al., 1980). Therefore, it is fortunate that many standardized norm-referenced diagnostic tests and criterion-referenced tests can be useful in the initial assessment process, even though this was not the purpose for which they were designed. By modifying the manner in which the results of already developed tests and subtests are used, e.g., not using stanines or grade equivalencies, and implementing a practical procedure for assessing mastery, teachers can make use of a wealth of potential initial assessment tools. Norm-referenced and criterion-referenced tests with fairly lengthy subtests may be ideal for the initial assessment of specific skills. For example, the Basic Educational Skills Inventory (BESI; Adamson, Shrago, & Van Etten, 1972), may be used in this manner. Subtests of the BESI can be administered easily to determine mastery of certain skills. While administering the entire test may be cumbersome and unnecessary, using a specific subtest may prove worthwhile and time-saving.

Often teachers find that standardized tests such as the California Achievement Test (CAT; Tiegs & Clark, 1970) are also useful in initial assessment. This test provides lists of objectives that are assessed by the CAT. Items missed by the student may be related to the objective. If necessary, more specific criterion-referenced tests can be designed by the teacher to measure the targeted skill(s), once they have been generally identified. Tests such as the CAT may be used not only to assess a child's overall performance and identify skill deficit areas, but also to evaluate students' proficiency or maintenance of skills (Stowitschek, et al., 1980).

Criteria for Selecting Initial Assessments

As when evaluating any initial assessment test, the teacher should always consider the direct teaching decision sequence (see Table 1–1). Most importantly, the teacher adapting a test should determine whether the test or subtest samples the desired range of skills and whether enough items are tested in each skill to ensure that the sample is representative of a child's performance. While there is no set rule on the number of items an initial assessment test should devote to a given skill or subskill, fewer than three or four items should greatly reduce a teacher's confidence in the test. In any case, when selecting a test, the teacher must weigh the number of test items against the amount of time required to administer and score the test. Stowitschek and associates (1980) discussed a set of procedures for adapting tests for initial assessment purposes.

Several assessment tools that may be used by teachers to pinpoint skill deficits are commercially available. Some are norm-referenced instruments that sample skills and subskills sufficiently to allow the teacher to make some instructional decisions based on items passed and missed. Some are criterion-referenced tests intended to be used independently of any curricular material; other criterion-referenced tests are designed to accompany a specific set of instructional material, but could be readily employed by teachers for their own assessment purposes. Tests that teachers may wish to investigate further include

- Brigance Diagnostic Inventory of Basic Skills (Brigance, 1977), criterion-referenced tests to assess readiness and academic skills in key subject areas, kindergarten to sixth-grade level. Subtests may be used independently. Administration instructions are brief, but the entire test requires considerable time to administer.

- Diagnostic Mathematics Inventory (Gessel, 1975), criterion-referenced inventory, two levels with traditional and nontraditional mathematics objectives, grades 1.5 to 8.5. Learning activity guide and valuable interim evaluation tests are available.

- Basic Educational Skills Inventories: Reading, Math (Adamson, Shrago, & Van Etten, 1973), criterion-referenced test, two levels, kindergarten through sixth grade. Single skills are assessed by subtests, and a sufficient item sample is used to permit pinpointing and diagnosis. It is time-consuming to administer the entire test, however, and instructions for administering the test are brief.

- Criterion Reading: Individualized Learning Management System (Hackett, 1971), criterion-referenced test,

two series, kindergarten through seventh grade (basic adult), process skill-oriented. Although called a reading test, it includes skill areas such as gross motor skills and balancing; thus, it may have use outside the reading area. Reading objectives and test items must be carefully evaluated by user.

- Analysis of Skills: Reading (Anderhalter & Shands, 1976), criterion-referenced test, four area scores, three items per skill, group-administered. The content of this test is well defined, skills clearly stated, and items representative of skills tested.

- Individualized Criterion Referenced Testing: Reading (Educational Development Corporation, 1976), criterion-referenced management system, kindergarten through eighth grade, nine levels, 46 tests. The test is attractively packaged, but it is questionable whether the instructional continuum is well sampled.

- Wisconsin Tests of Reading Skill Development: Word Attack (Wisconsin Design for Reading Skill Development, Kamm et al., 1972), criterion-referenced tests with 6 to 12 single skill scores at five levels. The tests are exceptionally comprehensive, lead to objective evaluation of strengths and weaknesses, and provide activities and materials to accompany skill training.

- Woodcock Reading Mastery Tests (Woodcock, 1973), norm-referenced tests with two parallel forms, kindergarten to 12th grade, five subtests. Some items are diagnostic; some are predictive. The test is easy to administer, but it is difficult to score. It is a good general skill screening instrument.

- Stanford Diagnostic Mathematics Test (Beatty, Madden, Gardner, & Karlsen, 1976), norm-referenced test that has a number of subtest areas. This test may be used to identify gross areas of difficulty that should be assessed more precisely.

- Key Math Diagnostic Arithmetic Test (Connolly, Nachtman, & Pritchett, 1976), basic subtest areas, preschool through sixth-grade skills. The test is simple to administer, requires no reading, and is very prescriptive.

In summary, a teacher evaluating any initial assessment approach should be sure that the target behavior is sampled adequately, that the assessment conditions are related to ultimate functioning of the skills and knowledge tested, that subtest and composite scores are available, and that the time and complexity of administration are not unwieldy. Those interested in descriptions and evaluations of other potential tests are referred to *The Eighth Mental Measurements Yearbook* (Buros, 1978).

USES OF MEASUREMENT: PROGRESS CHECKING

Once specific skills/concepts have been targeted for teaching, materials and teaching strategies selected, and criterion levels established, progress checks should be made on a frequent basis. Since test scores derived at widely spaced intervals may lead to erroneous conclusions regarding the process of instruction or the materials used, frequent measurement is essential (Lovitt, 1977). It provides information on the effect of teaching before an undue amount of time has been spent employing an unsuccessful strategy. By carefully and consistently monitoring student progress, the teacher can recognize immediately when changes in programming need to be made to facilitate an individual's learning rate. The more intense the measurement procedure, the more sensitive it is to the needs of the individual learner. Lovitt (1978) also pointed out that the frequency of measurement may vary with the stage of instruction, i.e., skill acquisition, proficiency, and skill maintenance. In the initial stages he suggested frequent measurements. Maintenance checks may be taken less frequently, yet still routinely.

In addition to checking progress on new skills and concepts as they are being acquired, the teacher should conduct progress checks on subskills and terminal objectives to determine if mastery of the subskills indeed adds up to progress and mastery of the main objective. Furthermore, mastery checks on all previously learned skills permit the teacher to "recycle" or provide additional instruction that may be needed to maintain skills.

Progress checks may be implemented in a variety of manners. Regardless of the measurement approach, each check should be conducted with consistency across time. Permanent product measures, which provide a permanent record of the student's performance, or teacher observational assessments, may include simple tallies of student behavior, records of time on task or at a particular activity, or oral probes of student knowledge, which may be used effectively as progress and mastery checks.

Permanent Products to Measure Progress

The term *permanent product* refers to any tangible byproduct of learner behavior, such as the outcome of a written assignment, whether it be a math worksheet, a written spelling test, a handwriting exercise, or written response in another subject area (Hall, 1971). Unlike teacher observations of student behavior or oral responses, a permanent product of a child's school performance can be reviewed as often as the teacher, child, or parent wishes. These products can be saved for comparison of performance across time.

They can also be rechecked to verify that an accurate and reliable assessment was made.

Criterion-referenced tests allow the teacher to set up instructional procedures that follow in one-to-one correspondence with the assessment approach. By using a criterion-referenced approach to progress measurement, the teacher can see the student's current performance level and the relationship of mastered subskills to terminal objectives. Generally, criterion-referenced tests (or other end-of-unit tests) are given on a regular, if not daily basis. Guidelines have been developed for constructing teacher-made criterion-referenced tests pertaining to the mastery of any skill (Howell, Kaplan, & O'Connell, 1979).

Many teachers prepare their own tests because they need precise information during instruction. Worksheets and other prepared material may be used for testing purposes and as permanent products of student performance. Many of the practice exercises and materials designed for instruction can also be used to measure progress, since there is only a fine line between the responses students make during instruction and those students make during testing. The essential differences are in the conditions under which the responses are made and the way in which the results are used. Worksheets and drill pages are most useful for probing and assessing mastery of single skills. In short, pages from workbooks, texts, ditto sheets, and even magazines may be employed not only for teaching, but also for measurement purposes.

Lovitt (1978) presented a sample arithmetic sheet that could be teacher-constructed or adapted from a set of commercially available math materials (Exhibit 4–1). At the top of the sheet, there are spaces for the student's name, date, and the time the test session begins. When told to stop, the student enters the time ended and calculates the total time spent on the task. At this point, the teacher or the student may tally and enter the number of correct and incorrect responses, finding the rate of each. A series of similar worksheets dated and placed sequentially in the student's file may give both teacher and student a clear idea of the progress being made. To accompany these sheets, teachers should design a raw data tally sheet, containing the information that was entered at the top of the test sheet, on which the results of each test can be entered. These summary sheets provide a good picture of progress and can be used in the transfer of data to a visual display, such as a line graph.

Although daily measurement of student progress may be the most desirable means of assessing the effect of a particular teaching procedure or instructional material, time spent evaluating performance must be kept within reasonable limits. In place of the traditional test, which may last from 20 minutes to 1 hour, a probe may be used. Probes are based on specific objectives, usually last from 1 to 5 minutes, and are administered daily preceding or following instruction. They

Exhibit 4–1 Sample Arithmetic Sheet

ARITHMETIC				
Name _____	# Correct _____		Correct Rate _____	
Date _____	# Incorrect _____		Incorrect Rate _____	
Time begun _____	Time ended _____		Total time _____	
25	71	51	31	91
−8	−6	−8	−5	−3
54	71	22	31	63
−9	−4	−5	−5	−4
52	41	31	67	23
−3	−8	−3	−8	−4
41	32	52	41	31
−5	−5	−8	−9	−8
81	25	92	81	42
−5	−9	−8	−6	−3
23	62	95	21	54
−5	−5	−9	−9	−9

Source: Adapted from "Arithmetic," p. 135, by T. Lovitt, in *The Fourth R: Research in the Classroom*, edited by N. Haring, T. Lovitt, M. Eaton, and C. Hansen, with permission of Charles E. Merrill Publishing Co., © 1978.

should be a quick sample of what is being taught (Haring & Gentry, 1976). As a measurement tactic, probes are useful only when instruction is held constant and materials do not vary from day to day. Haring and Gentry (1976) reported that the features of probes may vary according to the nature of the material being tested. Features a teacher should consider when constructing probes include

- the length in terms of the number of probe items, e.g., from 5 to 50 items
- the way the learner responds to each item, e.g., oral, written, motor-gestural
- the location of the probe administration, e.g., child's desk, hall, cubicle
- the time allotted for completing probe items, e.g., 15 seconds to 5 minutes
- the materials used in the probe, e.g., flashcards, skill sheets, readers
- the establishment of uniform administration and scoring procedures

Permanent products provide excellent, clear records of student performance. It is not necessary to keep every product completed by the student, however; teachers should maintain summary records of student performance and intermittently file representative samples as permanent long-term record samples.

Observational Assessments to Measure Progress

During the course of the day, teachers have many opportunities to observe their students' work. Some observations are informal and barely noted; others are formal assessments to monitor learning and redirect instruction. When a permanent product is not potentially available or desirable, teachers may simply observe and record student responses under specified testing conditions during predetermined time periods. Teachers may use flash cards or oral probes to present test items; they may observe students reading passages from texts, completing motor tasks or self-help skills, or demonstrating their linguistic skills in a naturalistic environment. Consistency in these observations across time is a primary goal for accountable, effective teachers. To achieve that goal, they may ask an aide, student, or volunteer to make occasional reliability checks, or they may use a tape recorder or a videotape to create a permanent record to be reviewed later. In any event, by collecting, checking, and summarizing their own observational data, teachers gain immediate knowledge of student response levels. With carefully designed data collection and summary sheets, student responding can be interpreted rapidly and easily.

The use of observational assessment requires teachers to direct their attention toward collecting data, following the test administration procedures reliably, and maintaining accuracy in scoring responses. The more complex the behavior being observed, the more elaborate the data collection systems usually become. Only the most pertinent data should be collected, however. When a teacher has complex behaviors as terminal objectives, more than one assessment approach may be needed to evaluate the terminal skill. Generally speaking, most behaviors should be amenable to observation. Proficient observation and data collection are teaching competencies that require practice, but the effort is well worth the time expended.

METRICS AND SUMMARIZING DATA

Different evaluation systems stress measurement of different kinds of responses. For measurement to be direct, however, it must measure observable behavior. In selecting any metric the teacher needs to consider the complexity of the skill, the stage of learning, e.g., acquisition, proficiency or skill maintenance, and the degrees of measurement sensitivity needed to address the purpose of measurement.

Selecting metrics that are appropriate for the type of behavior and information the teacher wishes to gather is fundamental to meaningful measurement. Depending on the skill or concept measured, the teacher may use frequency counts, percentage, rate, or latency and duration. In addition, the teacher should choose ways to summarize or display the data visually for easy interpretation and communication to others. Charts, line and bar graphs, cumulative graphs, and trend lines may be employed for this purpose.

Frequency/Tally Summaries

A tally of student behavior is one way to measure the frequency with which a response occurs. A simple count of correct and error responses, for example, is one of the most often used procedures for collecting data on students in traditional classrooms. Unless the number of responses tested is held constant, however, the usefulness of tallies in comparing performance across time is limited. Frequency counts can be used to assess progress across time only if the time period and the number of responses available to the student during testing are equal each time an assessment is made. Furthermore, since time is not usually considered an important variable in a tally procedure, it is not possible to obtain information on the proficiency of a student's performance based on frequency alone.

Nonetheless, tallies can be useful. They are easy to keep and are usually one of the first types of data collection students learn to use. When lessons vary in length, tallies can be converted to percentage by dividing the number of correct responses by the total number of responses and multiplying by 100. Exhibit 4–2 shows a daily/weekly tally sheet that was used to record a student's oral reading responses. The teacher merely placed a check mark to show whether the student read the word correctly or incorrectly. This tally sheet can be used to keep simple frequency counts or to calculate percentage and rate (if time is recorded).

Percentage Summary

The advantage of percentage scores is that they can be compared from one day to the next even when there are differences in the material used and the number of responses available. Comparisons of correct responses across teaching sessions may be misleading, however, if only a small number of responses are tested. For instance, a child's performance of 75% correct on 4 test questions is not equal to a performance of 75% correct on 40 test questions. Because percentage data provide a good measure of a student's accuracy, they are often most appropriate for assessing skills that are being acquired or skills that include speed as an important variable, such as reading comprehension tasks.

Rate Summary

Generally, rate yields more information than do other educational measures. It indicates not only accuracy (as percentage does), but also fluency of performance, i.e., the amount of work and the time period in which it was done. For educational purposes, rate is usually reported on a per minute basis. Rate per minute is calculated by dividing the total number of behaviors by the number of minutes needed to complete the task. Error and correct rates are useful for monitoring progress with great precision. Howell, Kaplan, and O'Connell (1979) reported procedures for displaying rate data on six-cycle semilogarithmic paper, which allows trends to be plotted as straight lines. Using precision teaching techniques, the teacher can record where the child is, in relation to an objective, where the child is going, and when the child should arrive at mastery of the objective. Other authors have also described procedures for displaying and interpreting rate data in detail (e.g., Eaton & Hansen, 1978; White & Liberty, 1976; Young, 1972).

Latency and Duration

Both measures of time, latency and duration are most often used for collecting social or linguistic behavioral data. Latency measures the time lapsed between presentation of a stimulus and the occurrence of the behavior, for example, the amount of time that transpires between a teacher's instruction and a student's response to the instruction. Sometimes it is important to know the actual amount of time a behavior continues. Teachers typically measure the duration of behaviors such as temper tantrums, out-of-seat time, and off-task time.

Visual Data Display

The standard data displays used by teachers and educational researchers vary greatly. Three of the most commonly used visual displays are line graphs, cumulative graphs, and bar graphs.

A standard line graph is the simplest and most common method of plotting performance data (Hall, 1971). It permits teachers to inspect pupil performance data visually and to determine the extent to which an intervention is succeeding. A line graph is completed according to a standard procedure (Exhibit 4–3). Along the vertical line, the amount of behavior is recorded, usually in percentage, rate, or frequency of occurrence. Information on the horizontal axis consists of the number of sessions, minutes, days, or weeks, according to the frequency with which assessments are conducted. Line graphs can be used to chart individual or group data; they can be personal records kept by the student or class records posted on a highly visible wall or bulletin board. A line graph is noncumulative in that each score represents a single unit of measurement and stands independent of scores recorded before and after it.

The information recorded on a cumulative graph after each session is added to that recorded previously. In this way, all

Exhibit 4–2 Daily/Weekly Tally Sheet

Response

DAILY / WEEKLY TALLY SHEET

Student _Gini T._

Task _calling out reading words_

Item	Date	3/4		3/5		3/8						Item mastered	error type
	Time (min.)	cor.	inc.	cor.	inc.	cor.	inc.	cor.	inc.	cor.	inc.		
1 come		✓		✓		✓							
2			("cane")		("came")		("come")						
3 dome		✓		✓		✓							
4			("down")		("down")		("dome")						
5 here		✓		✓		✓							
6			("her")		("here")		("here")						
7 like		✓		✓			✓						
8			("look")		("lack")		("love")						
9 play		✓		✓		✓							
10			("plug")		("plug")		("plug")						
11 not		✓		✓		✓							
12			("Tom")		("not")		("Tom")						
13 had		✓		✓		✓							
14			("Dad")		("had")		("had")						
15 let		✓		✓			✓						
16			("yell")		("let")		("tall")						
17													
18													
19													
20													
21													
22													
23													
24													
25													
26													
27													
28													
29													
30													
Total		cor.	inc.	cor.	inc.	cor.	inc.	cor.	inc.	cor.	inc.		
Percent													
Rate													

Percent Finder on reverse side of page.
Rate Finder on reverse side of page.

Compare your response to the sample responses in Appendix A.

Source: Reprinted from *Instructional Materials: Selection, Evaluation, and Adaptation*, p. 175, by J. Stowitschek, R. Gable and J. Hendrickson, with permission of Aspen Systems Corporation, © 1980.

Exhibit 4–3 Examples of Graphs

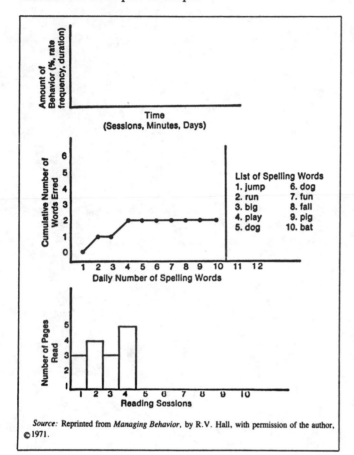

List of Spelling Words
1. jump   6. dog
2. run   7. fun
3. big   8. fall
4. play   9. pig
5. dog   10. bat

Source: Reprinted from *Managing Behavior*, by R.V. Hall, with permission of the author, © 1971.

earlier performances are part of the most recent entry on the cumulative graph. The middle graph in Exhibit 4–3 is a cumulative line graph.

The graph at the bottom of Exhibit 4–3 is a bar graph. Bar graphs are familiar to all teachers and most children, as such graphs are used on many commercially produced instructional materials to depict student progress and class profiles. Several curricular areas can be recorded for one student or several students' behaviors can be recorded on the same graph.

CONCLUSION

In evaluating behavior to be measured in relation to specified terminal objectives, the teacher must decide on the type of measurement approach, as well as the metric and data summary technique, to be used. There is no single answer to establishing functional measurement procedures. Consequently, the teacher has more decisions to make, but more meaningful alternatives from which to choose.

The value of measurement in establishing and conducting direct teaching strategies cannot be overstated. Measurement allows teachers to assess the immediate relevancy and effect of their efforts and to redirect their teaching as dictated by the learning needs and characteristics of the student. Measurement is meaningless, however, if the teacher does not establish a process for tying measurement results to the instructional decision-making process.

Chapter 5
Contingent Attention

Robert M. Day and Sarah Rule

At the heart of any successful teaching program is the student's motivation to learn. The ease with which many children learn new skills suggests that simple accomplishment is often reward enough. These children enter school with eager anticipation, ready to achieve and expand their skills. For them, the educational process is a rewarding and often exciting experience. For children with learning problems, however, this enthusiasm is often muted by repeated frustration and failure; the educational process is often a difficult and painful experience for them. Many such children simply stop trying rather than risk failing. They may create diversions from academic work by disrupting the efforts of other children or daydreaming.

A good teacher must help motivate children by being enthusiastic and positive about students' work. Positive teacher attention in such forms as praise, happy faces, or stars may be all that is needed to maintain a child's interest and motivation. Such attention alone is rarely sufficient for children who have experienced great difficulty in acquiring new skills, however. For these children, motivational tactics must be carefully planned.

The successful use of direct teaching tactics requires contingent teacher attention. The term *teacher attention* refers to events that follow responses by children. These events may include looking at, touching, or talking to children. It is important to remember that talking to children is attention whether it is in the form of praise, assistance, or criticism. Because most students will do things to get attention, teacher attention can be a positive reinforcer. The challenge to the teacher is to encourage children to do constructive things, such as working on academic tasks, by making attention contingent on desirable classroom behaviors, such as staying in one's seat, working on an assignment, or following direc-

tions. The teacher must give little or no attention to undesirable behaviors, such as daydreaming. Simply increasing the amount of attention a teacher gives to children does not necessarily alter their behaviors, nor does giving praise or happy faces. In order to effect changes in student behavior, the teacher's attention must be conditional—it must depend on desirable classroom behavior. Consistent and immediate attention to the students' constructive behaviors and minimal attention to nonconstructive behaviors ensure that the students understand the relationship between those behaviors and their consequences.

A number of studies have demonstrated that disruptive classroom behavior can be altered by teacher attention given in a systematic, i.e., contingent, manner. Becker, Madsen, Arnold, and Thomas (1967) worked in public schools with teachers whose students had high rates of disruptive behavior. Each teacher was taught to use attention in such forms as praise or smiles when children behaved in an appropriate manner. The result was a dramatic decrease in disruptive behavior with concurrent increases in cooperative responses. In a subsequent study, Thomas, Becker, and Armstrong (1968) demonstrated that disruptive classroom behaviors increased with the rate at which disapproval of such behaviors was expressed, while the expression of approval for appropriate responses increased the frequency of appropriate on-task behaviors. They showed that students would engage in whatever behaviors produced relatively more teacher attention. The *form* of the attention was not important. Students engaged in disruptive behavior when it produced attention, even though the attention was in the form of criticism or disapproval. These studies and others show that the conditions under which the attention is given, i.e., whether it follows appropriate or disruptive behavior, determine which behaviors students display. Positive attention must be given consistently for a specific set of behaviors; attention must be withheld for misbehavior. It is this relationship between student behavior and teacher attention that is the key to the successful use of direct teaching tactics.

The definition of the desired student response determines the conditions under which the teacher provides specific reinforcement to the child. This establishes a critical if-then relationship between the response and consequences. If the child is engaged in the desired response, then attention may follow. If the student is not engaged in the desired response, attention is withheld.

Teacher attention involves the planned use of specific and consistent types of teacher behaviors. This attention may take the form of systematic praise; it may be accompanied by other events, such as tokens, happy faces, or food items, depending on students' responses. As an instructional tactic, teacher attention must be consistently present following desirable behaviors and consistently absent following undesirable behaviors. Whether *all* attention is withheld following undesirable behavior depends on whether the behavior is dangerous or severely disruptive.

PLANNED IGNORING

The most difficult aspect of learning to use contingent teacher attention is usually learning which behaviors to ignore and when to ignore them. The following examples illustrate common classroom situations in which teachers ignored desirable behavior and failed to ignore undesirable behavior.

The teacher observes Bill looking out the window instead of doing his seat work. "Bill, I've told you at least five times today to get to work. You're behind in math because you're always daydreaming." Bill looks back at his page, and the teacher moves on down the aisle. She comes back in about 5 minutes, and Bill is looking around on the floor for the pencil he dropped. "Bill, I see you haven't finished the first problem yet. I'd better help you get started."

Teacher (*holding up an addition fact flashcard*): "Five plus three equals _____?"
  Child: "Five plus three equals nine."
  Teacher: "Nice try, but think about what you're doing. Five plus three equals eight."
Teacher (*holding up the next card*): "Three plus six equals _____?"
  Child: "Three plus six equals, let's see, oh, ten."

Teacher: "You were close; it's nine. Now try this one, four plus five equals _____?"
  Child: "Uh, nine."
  Teacher: "Now try this, eight plus two equals _____?"

The teacher is talking to a student about not completing her assignment. "I've told you over and over that you need to complete your work. I'm really tired of this; now get back to your seat." The student returns to her seat and completes the worksheet. The teacher says, "Well, it's about time."

These teachers attended more to the students' incorrect or undesirable responses than to their correct answers or appropriate behavior. It is easy to fall into this trap. Unfortunately, the effect of attending to failures, such as daydreaming or giving wrong answers, while ignoring successes, such as correct answers and obeying the rules, is that students may learn to increase their rate of errors and misbehaviors to get attention.

Some teachers confuse planned ignoring (i.e., ignoring undesirable behavior for the moment, waiting for a more desirable behavior to occur, then paying attention to that desirable behavior) with a failure to instruct. They think that even a momentary ignoring of a misbehavior is tantamount to letting the student get by with undesirable behavior. When Bill was looking out the window, for example, the teacher felt that she ought to correct his behavior, so she instructed him. Other teachers give more attention to undesirable behavior than to desirable behavior out of simple frustration. If their attempts at discipline have repeatedly failed and they have tried over and over to teach a concept to a student who consistently forgets it the next day, the teacher may feel that there is no desirable behavior to be praised.

The following examples illustrate situations in which teachers have learned how to use planned ignoring successfully.

Bill is looking out the window instead of doing his math seat work. The teacher looks at the child next to him, who is working a problem, and says, "Ellen, I like the way you are working. Let's check the problems you've finished so far." Out of the corner of her eye, she sees that Bill is looking at his paper. A few seconds later, he has pencil in hand and is writing. "I like the way you are working, Bill. As soon as I'm through checking Ellen's paper, I'll check yours."

In this example, the teacher gave Bill no attention at all for his inappropriate daydreaming. Instead, she attended to someone who was behaving appropriately. She was careful to acknowledge Bill when he was working, however. She was not oblivious to him; she was simply withholding her praise and assistance until he was behaving appropriately.

A variation of planned ignoring is shown in the following example.

> Teacher (*holding up a word flashcard with the word "cape"*): "What's this word?"
> Child: "Cap."
> Teacher: "No, cape. Try again."
> Child: "Cape."
> Teacher: "Great. You got it right this time. It's cape." (*holding up a new card with the word "tape"*) "What's this word?"
> Child: "Tape."
> Teacher: "That's right, this is tape. You knew that *e* at the end of the word makes the *a* say it's own name. You got tape all by yourself."

In this brief exchange, the incorrect response received a minimal amount of attention, only enough to prompt a correct response. Differentially attending to the child's responses assisted the child in distinguishing those responses that were correct from those that were not.

The first step in using planned ignoring is to define the appropriate classroom behaviors that will receive attention. The next step is to define inappropriate behavior and to decide when and how to ignore it. Some inappropriate behavior can be totally ignored; behavior that disturbs no one can usually be ignored until a more appropriate behavior occurs; some inappropriate behaviors can never be ignored.

Ignoring Errors

Sometimes errors can be ignored altogether. The teacher simply says nothing when the child makes an error and proceeds to a new question. Ignoring errors is *not always* appropriate, however. The word *planned* denotes the fact that the teacher must determine in advance whether ignoring is appropriate. When errors are careless or appear to be random, planned ignoring is appropriate. If the errors seem to follow a pattern, further instruction is in order. In the following math problems, for example,

$$\begin{array}{ccccc} 9 & 7 & 6 & 9 & 5 \\ +12 & +12 & +15 & +14 & +13 \\ \hline 11 & 19 & 11 & 13 & 18 \end{array}$$

all the errors center on the student's inability to rename in the tens place. In this instance, no matter how much praise is given, accuracy is unlikely to increase because the error pattern indicates a lack of skill or knowledge rather than a failure in motivation or discrimination. When errors are

made in predictable patterns, correction and instruction are appropriate.

Praising Good Behavior

When minor misbehaviors occur, the technique of choice is to

1. ignore the child engaging in the misbehavior
2. find someone who is not misbehaving
3. praise the student who is "good" in specific terms
4. wait until the behavior of the misbehaving student improves
5. praise the child who had been misbehaving

There are a few considerations that must be taken into account when using this technique.

First, the teacher must be sure that the child is capable of performing the desired behavior. It is safe to assume a child is capable if he or she has performed the behavior in the past. Confronted with a hyperactive child, the teacher should not expect that child to sit in a seat for 45 minutes or even for 15 minutes. The teacher should praise the student for sitting in a chair for 1 minute, if that is the longest that the student has ever sat.

Timing is important in Steps 4 and 5 of the procedure. If students who have been behaving badly are praised immediately after they cease misbehaving, they may learn an unfortunate chain of behaviors. Discovering that they receive attention when they stop misbehaving, they whisper to other children, stop whispering, and wait for the teacher to tell them how quiet they are. Teachers can prevent the development of this behavior sequence by gradually lengthening the time between the end of the misbehavior and the teacher attention. For example, Mrs. Saavy may praise Zeke a few seconds after he stops whispering once or twice just to teach him that he can get attention when he is quiet. If she waits too long, he may start whispering again. However, she must gradually lengthen those few seconds between whispers and attention to 5, 10, 20, 30, or 50 seconds, eventually praising him only occasionally and only when he has been quiet for a considerable length of time.

The pattern of attention a student has been receiving from the teacher must also be considered. If Mrs. Saavy has consistently told Zeke to be quiet when he whispers, he expects that attention. If she suddenly withholds it, his behavior will get worse before it gets better. Receiving no attention for whispering, he will try harder to get attention; he may whisper louder, speak aloud, or poke a classmate in the ribs. If Zeke's behavior is to change, Mrs. Saavy will have to praise many children around him who are quiet and—without fail—praise him after a few moments of quiet. In technical terms, Mrs. Saavy must place Zeke's behavior on extinction. When she withholds the positive reinforcer, attention, that she used to give, an increase in the rate of the previously reinforced behavior, whispering, will generally occur. Eventually, the behavior will subside, but only if it is never reinforced. If Mrs. Saavy lets frustration get the better of her and tells Zeke even once to be quiet, his whispering, and perhaps his talking and poking, will persist, and Mrs. Saavy will have to resort to other techniques.

Using Planned Ignoring Wisely

Planned ignoring is not the technique of choice for behaviors that are dangerous to persons or property or those that interfere with other students' work. Such behaviors require intervention strategies, such as contingent observation (Porterfield, Herbert-Jackson, & Risley, 1976), overcorrection (Azrin & Besalel, 1980), or some form of punishment sanctioned by the parent, teacher, and school system. The effective use of contingent teacher attention and planned ignoring from the outset will prevent the occurrence of many behaviors that require intervention, however. Teachers who focus their attention on desirable classroom behaviors and withhold attention to minor misbehaviors can generally avoid escalation of minor into major misbehavior.

FORMS OF CONTINGENT ATTENTION

When a student is learning a new task or behavior, teacher attention must be delivered immediately after the behavior occurs and every time it occurs. Once the behavior is learned, the attention should be faded, i.e., delivered only occasionally for performance of the behavior. The timing of attention may influence the form of attention chosen by the teacher.

There are many ways to attend to a student's appropriate classroom behavior, for example, by praising, by touching, or by presenting tokens or tangible items. The form of attention selected for use with a particular student must be based on the responses of that student. There is no universal way to motivate all children or to motivate one child all the time. Apparently, one child's chocolate chip cookie is another child's spinach. The value of any specific type of teacher attention can be judged only by its effect on children's learning. In general, if a teacher has consistently given attention after a desired response but the child does not learn, a change in the form of teacher attention is in order. If the child is learning, the teacher has probably found an effective motivator.

Praise

It is reasonable to use the simplest form of attention that is sufficient to motivate a child. Praise is the easiest, least time-consuming, and most economical form of attention. If the teacher says something nice ("good") when the student does something desirable and states what the student did ("you read that whole sentence correctly"), praise can have heuristic value. Praise should be enthusiastic and should include a description of the correct response:

- "That's good, John, you spelled Democrat."
- "Excellent work on these division problems!"
- "Nice going, Matt, I like it when you say the whole thing."
- "You're working hard, good for you."

Different forms of praise that may accompany a description of desirable behaviors are

- That's right.
- Good!
- I like the way you _____.
  (state behavior)
- Yes, _____ is the right answer.
  (state answer)
- Fantastic!
- Excellent!
- Wonderful!
- Fine.
- You worked hard.
- That's the best _____ on the whole
  (state letter or number)
  page.
- You did that _____.
  (quickly, right, nicely, well)
- You _____ neatly.
  (wrote, drew, ate)
- Thank you for _____.
- Super!
- Okay! Give me five.
- Perfect.
- You worked until you got it right.
- Nice job.
- I'm proud of the way you _____.
  (state behavior)
- Great!

Sometimes praise alone is not sufficient to motivate a child. If the child will not attempt the task and has never performed it correctly, the teacher should question whether the child is capable of the behavior. It may be necessary to break the task into smaller steps or to clarify the directions. However, if the teacher has observed that the child has done a given task in the past, but does the task inconsistently, it is possible that praise alone does not motivate the child.

Consequences to Accompany Praise

If praise does not motivate a child, it must be accompanied by stronger motivators, such as tangible items (e.g., food or trinkets) or activities. The teacher will learn over time which consequences, when they consistently follow a child's behavior, result in the child's doing more of the behavior or doing it better. At first, however, the teacher must use a trial-and-error approach. The chosen consequence must be delivered immediately after the child's response and every time it occurs, at least initially.

Food and trinkets can be given immediately, but tangible items may become expensive and the child may quickly lose interest if these items are given every time the child gives a correct response. Therefore, the teacher may consider using intangible items, such as activities or extra recess time. Activities cannot be delivered immediately and every time the child behaves appropriately, however, so the teacher must decide how to mediate between the child's behavior and the activity. One way is to praise the child, give a point for every correct response, and explain to the child that 10 points will be worth 10 minutes of time to listen to story tapes or draw. The child must have enough receptive language to understand the mediation procedure, or the teacher must teach the child about the procedure before trying to use mediators, such as tokens, to motivate learning.

The teacher usually determines what activities might motivate students by watching what they do in their free time, listening to activities they discuss with friends, or noticing what they ask to do. As Premack (1959) observed, activities that people engage in frequently (high probability behaviors) can be used to motivate them to engage in activities that they engage in rarely (low probability behaviors) by making the high probability behavior contingent on the low probability behavior. If a child likes to draw but hates to do arithmetic, the child is allowed to draw after working on arithmetic. Conversely, the child is not allowed to draw until the arithmetic assignment is finished. If there are many responses to be made, as there are in arithmetic, the teacher may mediate by giving the child a token for every correct answer and allowing the child to draw when a certain number of tokens have been earned.

Activities are usually readily available to classroom teachers. Children generally like a variety of activities, and their choices may vary from day to day. Using activities contingently requires planning and organization, since access to activities must be restricted to those who have earned them. In addition, the teacher must discover a way to mediate between behaviors and the activities.

Some severely handicapped students may not freely engage in activities that are appropriate in the classroom. Left to their own devices, they may sit and stare or engage in self-stimulatory behaviors. Initially, it may be necessary for a teacher to use tangible items, perhaps small bites of food, to help these students develop skills. The skills they learn may eventually be used as preferred activities that are available contingent on their working to learn new skills. Hall and Hall (1980) discussed a variety of items and activities available as motivators when simple attention is insufficient to help students learn.

Additional things or events should always be paired with praise when they are delivered. Children who are not initially motivated by praise may become motivated by it over time when it accompanies something that they value. As they master a response, the additional thing or event can be gradually withdrawn. Then praise alone should be sufficient to maintain the already learned response.

TIMING AND FREQUENCY OF CONTINGENT ATTENTION

In general, the less time that elapses between the child's appropriate behavior and the delivery of the contingent attention, the more powerful the tactic, since the contingent relationship between the reinforcer and the behavior is more firmly established:

> Mr. Burrows has set up a vocational task for his moderately handicapped students. They are to assemble as many 12-piece bicycle brakes as they can in one half-hour. At the end of the half-hour, the students leave for a 20-minute lunch break. Upon returning, Mr. Burrows gives the students a token for every complete brake. These tokens are then exchanged for free time at the end of the day.

Mr. Burrows has committed a disastrous error. He has allowed too much time to elapse between the desired behavior, assembling the bicycle brakes, and the delivery of the reinforcing token. If he wanted to use his tokens effectively, he should have given one each time a student assembled a complete brake, thus reducing the time gap between the desired behavior and the contingent attention.

When a child is learning a new response, attention should be given after every response. When the child has learned the response, the use of intermittent teacher attention, in which some, but not all, correct responses are followed by teacher attention, is more effective than is attention to each correct response:

> Mrs. Jones (*holding up an addition fact card*): "Four plus two equals _____?"
> Student: "Six."

Mrs. Jones: "Good. Five plus three equals _____?"

Student: "Eight."

Mrs. Jones: "Good!" (*gives the child a token and goes on to the next card. This continues throughout the lesson, i.e., the child receives a token for every second correct response and praise for every correct response.*)

Research has shown that, once a behavior has been learned, intermittent schedules can produce more durable behavior than can continuous schedules in which every correct response is reinforced.

Intermittent schedules also affect the rate of student responding, and one behavioral objective may be to increase the rate of responding. When students are working on reading fluency, for example, an intermittent schedule of praise is more likely to increase a student's rate than is praise for every correct response. Figure 5-1 is a graphic depiction of two students' "say word" rates. The first graph shows the effect of praising every correct response to a flashcard word; the second shows the effect of praising every third correct

response. In most cases, proficiency tasks, such as drill work and maintenance tasks, are best suited to intermittent reinforcement schedules.

Two types of intermittent schedules may be used. One, a ratio schedule, varies the reinforcement according to the number of responses, regardless of time. For example, a token may be given for every fourth correct response on a math sheet. The other schedule, an interval schedule, is related to time. The teacher may praise students who are on task every 3 minutes of the period, for example. A ratio schedule is most often used during instruction; an interval schedule, for students' independent tasks.

Either a ratio or an interval schedule may vary. A student may be praised sometimes for doing two problems, sometimes for doing five, and sometimes for doing three. This type of ratio schedule makes it difficult for students to predict when the teacher will attend, so they are unlikely to pause after finishing each problem. Similarly, the teacher may praise a student sometimes after 3 minutes of work, sometimes after 10 minutes, and sometimes after 5 minutes.

In deciding the schedule of attention, the teacher must remember that too much reinforcement is safer than too little. Insufficient attention may reduce the student's motivation to learn or respond correctly. With this in mind, the schedule of intermittent attention should be adjusted slowly. If the number of correct responses declines with increased ratios or intervals, it is likely that the teacher is requiring too many responses before giving reinforcement, and the ratio or intervals should be reduced.

Students who are capable of performing a behavior (staying in their seat or working a certain type of math problem) are likely to exhibit more of the behavior if they cannot predict when the teacher may attend to the behavior. If students are seated in a circle and the teacher calls on each student in turn from right to left, the child on the right may stop listening after answering the question until all the others have answered their questions. The child on the left may not start listening until the teacher calls on the children nearby. If the teacher calls on students at random, however, they are likely to pay attention more of the time.

MATERIALS FOR USE WITH CONTINGENT ATTENTION

The developers of a number of teaching materials have suggested the use of contingent reinforcement, specifying various forms that contingent attention can take. For example, *DISTAR Reading I* (Engelmann & Bruner, 1975) is a sequenced reading program designed to train students to decode words. The DISTAR program precisely defines correct student responses and uses a group instructional format with both group unison and individual responding. These

Figure 5-1 Performance under Conditions of Continuous and Intermittent Reinforcement

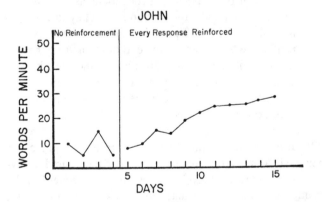

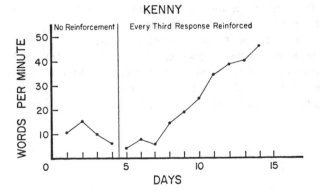

materials are scripted, outlining precisely how the skill is to be presented, as well as how and what kind of teacher attention is to be used. Engelmann and Bruner suggested both pointed and general praise for appropriate responses. The responses to be praised are behavioral (e.g., attending to the task) and academic (e.g., reading correctly). Accuracy and speed are stressed in the lessons. Incorrect responses are to be corrected by using a mild "no" and modeling the correct response. Similar programs in arithmetic and language are available (Engelmann & Carnine, 1970, 1975, 1982; Engelmann & Osborne, 1973, 1976).

The purpose of the materials in *Essential Math and Language Skills* (Steinberg, Sedlar, Cherkes, & Minich, 1978) is to teach students basic cognitive relationships important to mathematics achievement, such as same and different. Such concepts are based on a concrete relationship of objects and are thought by the authors to relate to a basic understanding of mathematics. The materials specify a series of student responses that are targeted objectives. Precise stimulus cues are provided by the teacher. Although the teacher is told to reinforce correct responses, the exact form of the reinforcer and the schedule are not included; they are left to the teacher's discretion.

I Can (Wessel, 1976) is a program designed to provide the learner with a wide range of physical education activities related to a series of objectives that specify desired student behaviors. Wessel recommended the use of reinforcement to help motivate students. Stressing social reinforcement as the most effective method of altering student responding, Wessel recommended that social approval for correct responses be provided "every once in a while" unless the task is extremely difficult or just being learned. The contingent nature of the attention is not as clearly specified in this program as in the DISTAR Reading I, partly because it is more difficult to specify correct responses as precisely in a physical education activity.

As in DISTAR, specific instructions for providing praise are included in *Corrective Reading* (1978). In addition, a system for awarding points that may be exchanged for reinforcing events is included. The teacher's guide of the 1974 version contained suggestions for ways in which teacher attention and other consequent events may be used contingently to overcome specific behavior problems.

RELATED RESEARCH

Few teaching tactics have been as widely documented as the use of reinforcement. Two decades of research have demonstrated that teachers can systematically alter a wide assortment of student behaviors, including academic responses, through contingent management of their own behavior.

Reinforcer Type

A number of studies have demonstrated that edible reinforcers may be effectively used to increase desired responding in a number of teaching situations. Wolf, Risley, and Mees (1964) used small pieces of food to facilitate a severely disturbed boy's acquisition of speech. Reese (1973) used edibles to train a severely retarded child in beginning arithmetic skills and number labeling. Meyerson, Kerr, and Michael (1967) used edible reinforcers to shape walking skills in a 9-year-old retarded child. These early studies and a host of others that followed demonstrated that edible reinforcers can be effective motivators for learning, particularly with more handicapped youngsters. The teacher must keep in mind, however, that the child can become satiated or tired of an edible reinforcer.

Hall, Panyan, Rabon, and Broden (1968) showed that teacher attention, a study game, and loss of break time increased the study behavior of an entire class. Thomas, Becker, and Armstrong (1968) successfully used contingent attention to increase the study behavior of a number of classes; they asked teachers to attend to and praise study behavior but to ignore disruptive or off-task behavior. In another study, Hasazi and Hasazi (1972) found that contingent teacher attention decreased the rate of digit reversals made by an elementary school child, thus demonstrating that corrective feedback that focuses on errors can maintain incorrect responding. When the teacher stopped attending to incorrect responses and began ignoring errors and praising only correct responses, the child's performance showed a dramatic shift in accuracy.

As mentioned earlier, Premack (1959) noted that access to high-frequency behaviors contingent on the emission of the low-frequency response increases the frequency of such responses. Hopkins, Schutte, and Garton (1971) found that first- and second-grade students completed copying assignments more quickly when they could have access to a playroom only after completing and scoring their assignments. Lovitt, Guppy, and Blattner (1968) determined that the spelling accuracy of fourth-grade students improved systematically when access to leisure time was made contingent on accuracy of spelling assignments. Osborne (1969) used access to free time to increase the amount of time a class of deaf students stayed in their seats; students were given a 5-minute free period for every 20 minutes they were in their seats. All the students in the class dramatically reduced their disruptive out-of-seat behavior.

Token Economies in the Classroom

A great many studies have demonstrated the effectiveness of token economies in the classroom (see O'Leary & Drabman, 1971, for a thorough review). An early application of a token economy in a classroom was reported by Birnbrauer, Wolf, Kidder, and Tague (1965); their study demonstrated, among other things, that token reinforcement programs were effective when praise had failed to control students' behavior. O'Leary, Becker, Evans, and Saudargas (1969) reported on the institution of a token economy for seven second-grade students whose behavior was unruly and disruptive. The token program not only systematically reduced their disruptive behavior, but also seemed to have a positive influence on their academic achievement and attendance. A study by Lahey and Drabman (1974) was designed to examine the effects of token reinforcement on the acquisition and retention of reading skills in second-grade students. Two groups of students were taught a list of 30 sight words. One group received praise for correct responses, while the other received tokens that could be exchanged for pennies. The token group met the established criteria faster than did the praise only students, and they retained more words over a longer period of time.

In another study (Rowbury, Baer, & Baer, 1976), tokens were used to encourage a group of preschool children to complete academic tasks. The children could earn plastic chips for completing each of seven possible tasks during a 1.5-hour "work time." The teacher ignored dawdling and inattention, but provided assistance if a child had a problem on a specific task. The tokens were exchanged for 5 minutes of free time in a popular play area. At the end of the 5-minute play time, the child returned to the work area. Results of this study indicated that the free time did indeed motivate the preschool children to complete their work.

Literally hundreds of studies have clearly demonstrated that systematic, i.e., contingent, teacher attention, sometimes paired with other reinforcers, can dramatically increase the skill acquisition of schoolchildren. When deciding to use contingent reinforcement, however, the teacher may need to spend some time determining which events are effective reinforcers for a specific student. Effectiveness is determined by whether the student's behavior changes as a result of the contingent attention.

Chapter 6

Learning Prerequisites for Direct Teaching

K. Richard Young and Robert M. Day

How often do teachers make unwarranted assumptions about what a child can or should do during instruction? The third-grade teacher expects children to have acquired certain skills in the second grade, and the second-grade teacher assumes that certain skills were acquired in the first grade. Even the first-grade teacher expects children to be able to follow some procedures, such as answer questions, stay in their seats, hold a pencil, open a book to the first page, and look at the teacher during a demonstration. Academic programs are based on a hierarchy of prerequisite skills that are essential for students' progress.

Most children acquire basic learning prerequisites, such as paying attention, imitating behaviors demonstrated (modeled) by others, following directions, and matching objects that are the same, as part of their normal sensory and sensorimotor development. Traditionally, these skills are learned in the home. Infants learn to follow moving objects with their eyes and focus on a person's face. Toddlers learn to imitate the speech and movement of others, follow directions, and match or point out objects or pictures of objects on request. Preschoolers learn to sit quietly and attend to one task for progressively longer periods of time. Thus, it is natural for the elementary school teacher to assume that these behaviors have been acquired to some degree.

Some handicapped children do not answer questions, follow directions, repeat what is said to them, stay in their seat, point at an object, or even look at the teacher. In fact, the more severely handicapped a child is, the more likely it is that the child lacks one or more of these essential behaviors. Students who are behaviorally deficient in these learning prerequisites require special pretraining before they can begin more complex learning tasks:

Physically, Billy appeared to be a normally developing 5-year-old boy. His motor development, while at times animated, was within normal ranges. Observation of Billy's behavior, however, revealed an extremely limited behavioral repertoire. Billy would not sit in his seat or work at tasks independently. During one-to-one sessions with the teacher, he did not make eye contact, frequently had tantrums and bit his hand when he was corrected by the teacher, and spent a great deal of time filtering light with his hands before his eyes. Billy did not have any verbal language and did not seem to learn from observing his surroundings.

Suzanne was a severely retarded 10-year-old girl. She had poor motor development and was extremely small for her age. During the instructional sessions, Suzanne remained seated and looked at the teacher when her name was called. When her teacher attempted to show her how to complete a task, Suzanne failed to follow the teacher's demonstration. Suzanne could not match similar objects, such as a toy car with another toy car. In fact, almost all of Suzanne's responses had to be physically prompted (i.e., the teacher had to guide her through each response). Suzanne had made virtually no progress over the last 4 years of school.

Both of these children have extreme deficits in learning. Billy lacks the basic attending skills necessary to learn in a structured setting, while Suzanne requires separate instruction for every response. Both children could benefit from extensive training in basic learning prerequisites, since continued training while they lack such behaviors would more than likely result in minimal behavior change. The initial training in these learning prerequisites can be time-consuming, but the acquisition of these skills is essential to the success of future instruction. Fortunately, there is a burgeoning technology from which strategies and tactics for training handicapped children in these learning prerequisites can be drawn.

A note of caution should be added here. Some children may have these learning prerequisites in their repertoires, but do not exhibit them in a teaching situation. These children are demonstrating noncompliance, a problem that may be addressed through the manipulation of contingencies (see Chapter 5), rather than extreme skill deficits that require pretraining before other instructional activities are undertaken.

SENSORY AND SENSORIMOTOR DEVELOPMENT

From the moment of birth, children begin to see, hear, feel, smell, and taste. Since visual, auditory, and tactile sensory development are essential for learning, teachers must assess handicapped students to ensure that prerequisite skills such as visual fixation, visual tracking, sound localization, auditory discrimination, and tactile exploration of the environment are part of their behavioral repertoire. Only a small number of handicapped children are deficient in these areas, but it has been noted that these skills are critical for learning (see Robinson & Robinson, 1978; Van Etten, Arkell, & Van Etten, 1980).

PAYING ATTENTION

In working with a handicapped child, especially one who is severely impaired, the teacher must have control over the student's attending and readiness behavior. When the teacher signals that it is time for instruction to begin, the student should sit (or stand) quietly, hold feet and hands still, and look at the teacher or the appropriate materials. The student should also stop any verbal or motor behavior that may interfere with the learning process. The tactics involved in helping the student acquire these behaviors are verbal instructions, shaping, prompting, fading, reinforcement, and extinction.

These tactics are frequently used in discrete trial formats. One format that has been successful has five steps:

1. The teacher presents the instruction to the child (e g., "*Johnny*, look at me."). This is called a discriminative

stimulus because it signals Johnny that, if he looks at the teacher, he will be reinforced. If he does not look, he will not be reinforced.
2. If the student does not respond correctly (e.g., looks at the table), the teacher prompts the response.
3. The child responds (e.g., looks at teacher's face).
4. The teacher reinforces correct responses or ignores incorrect responses (e.g., teacher praises eye contact or turns away from the child).
5. Then there is a short intertrial interval, which helps to provide clear beginning and ending points for each trial. It also affords the teacher time to record the child's performance (e.g., teacher pauses for approximately 3 to 5 seconds and marks the data collection form).

After a number of successful trials with this format, the stimulus (look at me) becomes a controlling stimulus and provides the teacher with the control needed to proceed with other tasks.

Shaping

Often, the desired behavioral response is very different from the child's current behavior; sometimes, the correct behavior is complex, involving a series of chained responses. If either or both of these conditions exist, it is unlikely that the child will be able to make the new response immediately when instructed to do so. Thus, the new behavior must be shaped.

Shaping is the process of reinforcing successive approximations to the desired response. Panyan (1980) described the shaping process as a series of 10 steps:

1. Define both initial and goal behavior in specific terms including the condition under which the behavior is to occur. This first step in the shaping process requires an exact statement of the initial behavior of an individual as well as the long range goal.
2. Identify a behavior that the individual currently performs relatively often and that roughly approximates the desired target behavior.
3. Reinforce this current behavior, even though it may only remotely resemble the target behavior. Reinforce improvement, not perfection. Individualize your reinforcer to the needs and preferences of those you are teaching.
4. Withhold reinforcers for behaviors that are not clear steps toward the target behavior. Be judicious in your delivery of reinforcement. If

the behavior is not equal to or better than previous attempts, do not reinforce it.

5. Reinforce closer approximations to the target behavior and discontinue reinforcement for previously reinforced behaviors that are less similar to the goal behavior.
6. Increase the requirement for reinforcement when closer approximations begin to occur with some regularity.
7. Consistently reinforce any relatively new approximation.
8. Continue to withhold reinforcers for behaviors that are not in the direction of the goal behavior.
9. Increase the requirement until the goal behavior is fully developed.
10. Reinforce every instance of the goal behavior until it occurs consistently. (pp. 3–4)

The processes of reinforcement (e.g., contingent praise) and extinction (e.g., planned ignoring) are key aspects of shaping a behavior. As described in Steps 3 through 10, acceptable approximations of the desired behavior are reinforced, and unacceptable responses are extinguished.

If, for example, the objective is to have the student look at the teacher and maintain eye contact for 3 seconds, the teacher first sits facing the child and says, "*Sue*, look at me." The child does not respond on several consecutive trials, so the teacher prompts the behavior. The teacher holds an edible reinforcer (e.g., a raisin) in front of Sue's eye, then slowly moves the reinforcer next to her (the teacher's) eye. A student with visual tracking skills will generally follow the movement of the reinforcer and end up looking the teacher directly in the eye. The teacher maintains the eye contact for 1 second and then reinforces the child by quickly placing the edible in her mouth, saying "Good looking at me!" and patting or hugging the student.

After the child has met the criterion for that step (e.g., 10 consecutive correct responses), the response requirement increases. The student must now maintain eye contact for 2 seconds. The teacher no longer reinforces the lower level of performance, extinguishing it or ignoring it, and the student learns that reinforcement is contingent on a higher level of performance. After the 2-second requirement has been mastered, the teacher reinforces only 3 seconds of eye contact. When the student has achieved the final goal, the prompt (visually tracking the edible reinforcer) is gradually withdrawn.

Prompting and Fading

During the initial training of a new behavior, severely handicapped children frequently need to be prompted. Some commonly used prompts are verbal instructions, gestures, partial physical assistance, and complete physical assistance.

An attending program developed by Jensen, Carlson, Saunders, and Hinerman (1980) demonstrates how prompting and fading are combined with shaping to teach a child to pay attention. The objective of the attending program is to have the child respond to the instruction "Get ready" by (1) sitting in a chair with the feet on the floor, (2) placing hands on knees, (3) being quiet for 3 seconds, and (4) looking at the teacher. The four steps of the behavior are taught consecutively. The child and the teacher sit facing each other, and the teacher says, "*John*, get ready." The teacher then adds the verbal prompt, "Put your feet on the floor." If the student does not respond, the teacher may gesture, e.g., point to John's feet and then to the floor. Verbal prompts and gestures are frequently used in combination. If more assistance is needed, the teacher may grasp the child's feet and gently guide them to the correct position (physical prompt). The teacher should always use the least involved prompt that will produce the desired behavior, i.e., a verbal prompt with a gesture rather than a physical prompt, if possible.

Any prompts used during the acquisition of a new response must be eliminated before teaching is considered complete. This process is called fading. After Sue has learned to maintain eye contact, for example, the teacher fades the edible reinforcer used in the visual tracking by gradually (over several trials) moving the hand away from the eyes, first to the cheek, then beside the mouth, and so on until the hand is back to the table. Then Sue must make eye contact in response to the instruction "Look at me" without prompts. Fading is difficult with some students; it may have to be done slowly, with only small increments of change in the position of the hands.

In teaching John to get ready, any use of verbal, gestural, or physical prompts must be faded after he has mastered the responses. The teacher first fades from more involved prompts (physical) to lesser involved prompts (gestural or verbal). If John initially needs a full physical prompt to place his feet in the proper position, the teacher changes to partial physical prompts as soon as possible. For example, after several trials using the full physical prompt, the teacher gives the instruction "*John*, get ready," followed by the verbal prompt "Put your feet on the floor," and waits 2 seconds. If there is no response, the teacher takes hold of John's feet and starts to move them into position, but releases them to see if John will complete the task with only a partial physical prompt. This is further faded to the point where it is necessary only to touch John's feet and, eventually, only gesture. For some severely handicapped children, the fading process may involve several small steps and hundreds of trials. Physical prompts may be reinforcing for some children; they may not respond until the teacher touches them. In other words, the child is reinforced by the physical prompt for waiting patiently. Shadowing or time delay procedures may help eliminate this problem.

When prompts have been reduced to verbal instruction, the final fading begins. If the verbal prompt was "Put your feet on the floor," the instruction may be modified to "Feet on floor." or even "Feet." Verbal prompts may also be faded by gradually reducing the volume at which they are spoken until they are said so softly that they can be completely dropped.

After the first component in the sequence (feet on floor) has been mastered, the same procedures are applied in teaching the second component (hands on knees). The new behavior is taught one component at a time until the entire behavior is under the control of the discriminative stimulus ("Get ready."). By using shaping, prompting, fading, reinforcement, and extinction, the teacher has acquired control. When a teacher says, "Get ready," the student will sit facing the teacher, feet and hands down, sit quietly, and look at the teacher, in other words, pay attention and be ready to learn.

IMITATING A MODEL

Generalized imitation is an important learning prerequisite. Striefel (1981) defined generalized imitation as learning the rule "Do what I do right after I do it" (p. 17). If the child learns to perform the behavior correctly the first time that it is demonstrated, all the instructional time that would be spent shaping each individual behavior is saved. Once they have learned to watch the teacher, parent, sibling, or other individuals and do what they do (imitate their behavior), students can learn many new skills quickly through direct instruction.

Most children learn to imitate the behavior of their parents or other caregivers early in life. As part of caring for an infant, parents smile at the child, play pat-a-cake with the child, and talk to the child. Parents may even physically assist the child in some motor responses. As the infant begins to imitate, the caregiver reinforces the child with hugs, kisses, tickling, more smiles, talk, and games. Because these events are reciprocally reinforcing, the behaviors of both the caregiver and the infant are strengthened and continue to increase in frequency of occurrence. At first, the infant's responses are not topographically exact, but rough approximations. The excited parent eagerly accepts the behavior, reinforcing it and continuing to coach and prompt gradual improvement.

As the child grows, the variety of behaviors modeled increases, as does the variety of settings, times, and people involved. The child learns the rule "Do what I do." As imitation becomes generalized, the child is likely to imitate both appropriate and inappropriate behavior. Parents typically accept and reinforce those behaviors that they consider appropriate (e.g., good manners, polite talk, sharing) and ignore or punish those that they consider inappropriate (e.g., swearing, fighting, quarreling). By this process, the child learns to imitate some classes of behaviors and not others.

All humans learn a great deal through observing others and imitating their behavior. Early in life, much of the language and many other basic skills are learned through imitation. As children mature, they learn to adapt to new situations. Even adults learn through imitation; if uncomfortable in a social or vocational setting, they observe others and imitate them if their behavior seems appropriate. Many severely handicapped children do not learn to imitate through this natural developmental process, however. This failure to learn by observing the behavior of others limits the severely handicapped person's capacity to acquire new skills. Since generalized imitation facilitates rapid acquisition of many new skills, as well as lifelong learning and adapting, it is a critical learning prerequisite to student progress.

Teaching a Child to Imitate

The instructional tactics used to teach imitative behavior are the techniques described earlier: shaping, reinforcing, prompting, fading, and extinguishing. In preparation for training, the teacher should gain control over the child's attending behavior and should determine which stimuli function as reinforcers for the child to be trained. The reinforcing properties of stimuli should not be assumed; their effectiveness in strengthening the behavior of the child should have been demonstrated. Also in preparation for a training session, the teacher should obtain a data collection form for recording the trial-by-trial responses of the student and should locate a quiet, distraction-free place to conduct the training.

The teacher may use many different motor behaviors in training. In a program developed to teach severely retarded children to imitate, Baer, Peterson, and Sherman (1967) listed 130 behaviors to model. Striefel (1977) listed 25 motor behaviors, such as hand raising, and 25 verbal behaviors that could be imitated. Striefel's program is complete with procedures for establishing functional reinforcers and attending behaviors, as well as imitation. It also includes data collection forms, prompting techniques, and procedures for achieving generalization. Additional programs that teach imitation are

- How to teach through modeling and imitation (Striefel, 1981)
- Parent training curriculum for families of developmentally disabled children (Jensen, Carlson, Saunders, & Hinerman, 1981)

- Teaching developmentally disabled children (Lovaas, 1981)

It is best to start by teaching the child simple one-step motor behaviors:

- place hand on head
- pat table
- raise hand over head
- touch nose with finger
- push toy car
- rub stomach with hand
- place hand on knee
- wave goodbye
- stomp foot
- brush hair
- drop ball
- touch ear
- tap chair
- stand up
- hold nose
- open mouth wide
- cover eyes with hand
- hold arm extended in front
- shake head
- touch floor

The behaviors may increase in difficulty to include using more body parts (e.g., raising both arms), a chain of two or three steps (e.g., picking up a spoon and placing it in a bowl), and imitating verbal items (e.g., "ma," "ba").

A discrete trial format is frequently used in training. The discriminative stimulus includes the teacher saying "Do this" and modeling the behavior. If the child does not respond, the appropriate prompts are used. The child's response is correct if it is similar to the model. Initially, the teacher reinforces all correct responses and ignores incorrect responses. Of course, the teacher must fade any prompts used after the child has learned to imitate the behavior. If, for example, the behavior to be imitated is "clapping hands" together, the teacher says, "*John*, get ready" and waits for the student to look at her, place his feet and hands down, and sit quietly. The teacher then says, "Do this," claps her hands together, and waits 2 to 3 seconds for a response. If John does not respond, the teacher prompts the response by taking hold of his hands, clapping them together, and reinforcing the behavior. After several trials with the full physical prompt, the teacher changes the prompt to a partial physical one by starting the clapping response but dropping the prompt part way through and letting the student complete the clapping

motion independently. The prompt is further reduced until John imitates the model without any additional prompts.

Massed training is sometimes conducted in blocks of trials; with this approach, programs A and B are taught as AAAAA BBBBB. Two other methods of conducting trials have also been shown to be effective, however. Mulligan, Guess, Holvoet, and Brown (1980) suggested that distributed trial training might be more effective and efficient than massed training. With distributed trial training, trials of two or more programs are mixed such that the trials for programs A and B are taught as ABABABABAB. The same discrete trial format can be used with both methods.

Hart and Risley (1975) described a method of instruction entitled "incidental teaching," which is an instructional interaction between the teacher and the student that occurs naturally in an unstructured situation. For example, during a free play period, a child may tug on the teacher's sleeve and point to a truck on a shelf that she wants to play with but cannot reach. If the teacher is working on verbal imitation, he may say to the student, "Do this," and model the word (or sign) "truck," prompt the student if necessary, and reinforce the child for imitating by giving her the truck. The steps of the discrete trial format can also be applied to the incidental teaching approach. For severely handicapped students, incidental teaching may not be appropriate during the initial acquisition of imitation, but it may help to transfer imitative control to natural settings as learning progresses.

Teaching Generalized Imitation

Baer and associates (1967) taught severely handicapped students to generalize their training to new behaviors by modeling many different behaviors. After students began to respond correctly to a new model on the first presentation, some responses went unreinforced. This study showed that two important procedures facilitate generalization: (1) teaching enough examples and (2) delaying reinforcement (Baer, 1981). Therefore, the teacher must have many different behaviors for the students to imitate. At first, every correct response should be reinforced; then, as teaching continues, the schedule of reinforcement should be modified. The teacher can switch from continuous reinforcement to fixed ratio reinforcement in which only every other response or every third response is reinforced. Intermittent reinforcement is finally implemented in order to vary reinforcement and make it unpredictable. In addition, the teacher should select some new responses that are never reinforced in training.

Striefel, Wetherby, and Karlan (1978), as well as Whitney and Striefel (1981), described a matrix training procedure (see Figure 3–3) that can be helpful in achieving generalization not only across new behaviors, but also across other dimensions, such as responding in new nontraining settings and with persons not involved in training. After the child has been taught to imitate correctly, additional behaviors may be introduced with new trainers. In Figure 6–1 there are 16 combinations of persons and behaviors. By using the matrix training procedure, only 7 need be taught. After successfully completing the 7, the student should be able to imitate correctly any new behavior with any of the four persons involved. Other procedures that promote generalization have been described by Stokes and Baer (1977) and Baer (1981).

FOLLOWING DIRECTIONS

Successful teaching depends a great deal on the use of verbal instruction. Much of the teaching that goes on in any classroom involves verbal explanations and directions. Using verbal instructions is easier for a teacher than shaping each new behavior that must be taught and also saves instructional time. Teaching students to follow directions is another step in the process of establishing control. Following directions is a skill typically taught by using shaping, prompting, and fading procedures, along with reinforcement of correct responses. Modeling and imitation are also effective tactics. In addition to these procedures, shadowing and time delay may be used.

Teaching a Child to Follow Directions

The teacher prepares to teach a child how to follow directions by listing several simple instructions. Initially, instruc-

tions should involve behaviors that can be physically prompted, e.g., stand up, sit down, come here, raise your arms, give me a hug, bring me (*name of object*), stop, push the car. The first three instructions are taught separately until each is mastered. Then the teacher presents the three instructions in random order during the same training session(s) until the student meets the necessary criterion (e.g., 100% of the directions followed correctly for two consecutive days). The teacher continues the training by introducing two or three new directions in a session and teaching to criterion. The level of reinforcement is gradually reduced by changing from continuous to intermittent reinforcement.

When the student can follow new directions on the first presentation, the behavior has been generalized across instructions of the same type, i.e., those that involve simple actions. There are many classes of instructions and the child may not be able to follow instructions in other response classes. Additional probes and training may be needed to ensure generalization across settings and persons. The matrix training procedure developed by Striefel and associates (1978) facilitates generalized instruction-following behavior.

Shadowing

A procedure referred to as shadowing may be helpful if a student requires physical prompts to follow directions. Jensen and associates (1980) recommended shadowing in teaching a student to follow a "Come here." command. A second adult stands behind the child and provides physical

Figure 6–1 Matrix Training across Behaviors and Persons

	PERSON 1 (TEACHER)	PERSON 2 (AIDE)	PERSON 3 (VOLUNTEER)	PERSON 4 (PARENT)
BEHAVIOR 1 COMB HAIR	TEACHER MODELS/ COMB HAIR	AIDE MODELS/ COMB HAIR	VOLUNTEER MODELS/ COMB HAIR	PARENT MODELS/ COMB HAIR
BEHAVIOR 2 EAT WITH SPOON (Pretend)	TEACHER MODELS/ EAT WITH SPOON	AIDE MODELS/ EAT WITH SPOON	VOLUNTEER MODELS/ EAT WITH SPOON	PARENT MODELS/ EAT WITH SPOON
BEHAVIOR 3 DRINK FROM GLASS	TEACHER MODELS/ DRINK FROM GLASS	AIDE MODELS/ DRINK FROM GLASS	VOLUNTEER MODELS/ DRINK FROM GLASS	PARENT MODELS/ DRINK FROM GLASS
BEHAVIOR 4 PUSH CAR	TEACHER MODELS/ PUSH CAR	AIDE MODELS/ PUSH CAR	VOLUNTEER MODELS/ PUSH CAR	PARENT MODELS/ PUSH CAR

Exhibit 6–1 Instruction and Data Sheet for Following Directions (Come Here) Goal A, Step 1

Target Behavior: The child will come to the adult within 5 seconds following the cue, "come here," from a distance of 5 feet.
Date Step 1 program begun _____ Date completed _____

Goal A, Step 1
Summary of instructions for teacher/parent:
    Definition: Teacher/parent #1 will give the instructions (the instructor).
               Teacher/parent #2 will act as the person prompting the child (the shadow).
  1. Shadow stands directly behind child.
  2. Instructor stands facing child approximately 5 feet away.
  3. Instructor says, "_____ (child's name), come here."
  4. Shadow, standing behind child, places hands on child's shoulders and assists child in walking to instructor (full physical prompt).
  5. If the child comes without resisting, that means that the child has responded correctly. Give social and tangible reinforcement.
  6. Put a plus (+) on your data sheet.
  7. If the child resists, that means that he didn't respond correctly, shadow implements overcorrection.
  8. Put a minus (−) on your data sheet.
Child may move to next step (A-2) when he achieves 80% correct across 40 continuous trials.

Date: Date: Date: Date:
Parent/Teacher: Parent/Teacher: Parent/Teacher: Parent/Teacher:
Time: Time: Time: Time:

% Correct: % Correct: % Correct: % Correct:

Date: Date: Date: Date:
Parent/Teacher: Parent/Teacher: Parent/Teacher: Parent/Teacher:
Time: Time: Time: Time:

% Correct: % Correct: % Correct: % Correct:

Source: Reprinted from *Parent Training Curriculum for Families of Developmentally Disabled Children*, p. 55, by W.R. Jensen and CBTU staff, with permission of the authors, © 1980.

assistance as needed. The teacher says, "*John,* come here." If the child does not respond, the second adult (the shadow) physically assists the child in walking to the teacher. On succeeding trials, the shadow is faded by gradually reducing physical contact. Jensen and associates (1980) stated that the shadowing procedure makes direction following easier and faster to learn.

Each step of the following directions program developed by Jensen and associates (1980) has a data collection sheet with all of the instructions for the trainers (Exhibit 6–1). The target behavior is stated, along with prompts to be used, directions for scoring, and the criterion for advancement to the next step. The curriculum also includes a following direction-stand up program. Lovaas (1981) has written a program on how to teach a child to follow verbal instructions.

Foxx (1980) described the use of shadowing in connection with graduate guidance and a chain of behavior, such as putting on pants. Full physical guidance is faded until the teacher is not touching the child. At that point, the teacher may keep his or her hands within an inch of the student's hands and shadow (lead or follow) the child's movements.

Shadowing is an additional prompt if physical contact has been dropped too suddenly and the frequency of correct behaviors has decreased.

Time Delay

Control over a new response may be established by pairing a new stimulus with a stimulus that already controls the behavior. Instead of fading the initial controlling stimulus, the teacher inserts a gradually increasing time delay between the new stimulus and the controlling stimulus. The procedure is an errorless learning tactic because the initial control stimulus prompts correct responses and diminishes the likelihood of errors until the new stimulus controls correct responses.

Use of the time delay procedure is appropriate when a student is already under imitative control and the teacher wants the student to respond to verbal instruction. The teacher begins by saying, "*John*, stand up"; immediately says, "Do this"; and models the stand up behavior (the controlling stimulus). After several trials of correct imitation, the teacher inserts a 0.5 second time delay, between saying "*John*, stand up." and modeling the behavior. The time delay is increased from 0.5 second to 1 second, then to 2, 3, 4, and 5 seconds, consecutively. Of course, if the child responds to the verbal instruction prior to the presentation of the controlling stimulus, the modeling procedure is dropped. The time delay procedure has proved very effective with severely handicapped students. Snell and Gast (1981) reviewed the time delay procedure and the relevant research literature in depth.

MATCHING

It is important for children to learn to recognize the similarities and differences in objects. Frequently, severely handicapped students do not attend closely to the characteristics of objects. To teach these children to attend to objects, the instructor should use an activity that is highly reinforcing. For example, the teacher may place two cups on a table, one bright red and one blue, with a piece of candy nearby. After getting the child's attention, the teacher gives the verbal instruction "Watch the *candy*," places the candy under one of the cups, and asks the child to make a response that indicates where the candy is (e.g., "Point to the candy." or "Get the candy."). The concept of object permanence is a prerequisite for this task, since the child must understand that objects exist even when they cannot be seen. The child indicates where the candy is, and the teacher allows the child to eat it as reinforcement. After several correct trials, other objects may be substituted for the candy. When the attending behavior has been sufficiently strengthened, primary reinforc-

ers can be eliminated and the behavior maintained with intermittent praise. Many matching tasks have a relatively high chance factor. In this example, even the student who does not pay attention to the objects and just guesses which cup the candy is under has a 50-50 chance of being correct. Teachers should set the criterion for mastery high enough (e.g., 90%) to ensure that the student has learned the task.

In order to teach a child to match objects, the teacher may collect a group of common toys or other items of interest to the child in matched sets. Each pair of objects must be identical. The first step in the matching program involves only one pair of objects. One of the objects is placed on the table and the second given to the child to match. Lovaas (1981) suggested that a brief verbal statement, "Put same with same," be used as the discriminative stimulus. The teacher does not ask the child to find or match the object by name, rather asks the child to find one that is the same as the sample. Because there are no distracting objects in this first step, an errorless learning situation has been created. If the child fails to respond, prompts are used.

In the second step, the teacher proceeds in the same manner as in the first, but places a second object (a distractor) on the table. The probability of the child making an error in putting same with same can be minimized by initially placing the distractor further away from the child, perhaps off to the side of the table, before the child attempts to match the object. As trials are successful, the teacher gradually moves the distractor closer and closer until both objects on the table are an equal distance from the child. Then the positions of the two objects are switched in random order.

Training should proceed with additional pairs of objects. After the child has mastered the first five or six steps of the training sequence, the teacher should train the child with more than one pair of objects concurrently, adding new examples until the student can match unfamiliar objects with their sample on the first presentation. Following match-to-sample training, a child should be able to select an identical object from an array of other objects when presented an object as a sample. Like imitation, matching is useful only as a generalized skill. Therefore, the generalization procedures outlined in the training of generalized imitation are applicable to the training of generalized matching. Match-to-sample training, again like imitation, can be used as a means for training children in more complex and sophisticated sets of behavior. Such training is helpful not only in teaching language and reading, but also in teaching basic vocational skills, such as sorting and packaging.

After teaching the child to match objects, the teacher should proceed to more abstract tasks, such as matching pictures and then matching pictures to objects. The Lovaas (1981) curriculum includes an 11-step program for teaching children to match visual stimuli. The program lists the necessary materials and outlines procedures for (1) "matching identical three-dimensional objects," (2) "matching identical two-dimensional objects (pictures)," (3) "matching three-dimensional objects with identical two-dimensional representations," (4) "matching objects in classes," (5) "matching generalized two-dimensional objects," and (6) "matching generalized three-dimensional objects to generalized two-dimensional representations" (pp. 71–77).

Successful instruction of children who are deficient in attending, imitation, following directions, and matching behaviors is unlikely to occur without acquisition of these critical prerequisites. It is important for the teacher to bear in mind that although establishing these learning prerequisites can be time consuming, failure to do so, more than likely, renders instruction in more sophisticated tasks futile.

Chapter 7
Modeling Tactics

For hundreds of years, formal education was restricted to aristocrats who could afford live-in tutors. As education became more widely available, group instruction became the predominant teaching mode, and the individual tutorial model was discarded as incompatible with group instruction.

DIRECT TEACHING: A BASIC INGREDIENT OF CLASSROOM INSTRUCTION

Current teaching methods practiced by special education teachers have a closer affinity to the tutorial format than many educators may think. Many teaching activities actually include elements of one-to-one tutoring. For example, seat work activities, discussion groups, or reading circles all incorporate some basics of teacher-child interaction. Even though interchanges with individual students become less frequent when children are grouped together for instruction, the similarities to the tutorial pattern far outweigh the differences.

Teachers tend to consider one-to-one direct teaching a luxury reserved for remedial reading teachers, speech therapists, special tutors, or resource teachers. It is true that these specialists can do more one-to-one teaching with their students than can classroom teachers. Nonetheless, when children are working in small groups, they require the same corrective feedback and assistance that a single child gets from a teacher in a tutoring session. Unfortunately, many teachers dismiss tutoring tactics as impractical with an entire class, in spite of the fact that other teachers organize their classes so that they can use direct individual instruction options frequently and successfully.

Traditional group teaching methods are fine for students who can study and progress through the curriculum without directly interacting with the teacher. When traditional methods fail to bring about educational progress in learners, however, teachers must resort to more direct teaching methods. Individual tutoring provides more support for students who are struggling to learn than can be provided by most traditional group instruction methods.

Many teachers are responsible for 15, 20, or more students at a time. Providing continuous individualized attention for all these children would be a full-time effort; however, such constant attention is quite unnecessary. In summarizing research on a variety of approaches to teaching reading, Chall (1967) suggested that most children learn to read regardless of the teaching approach used. On the other hand, teachers should not use only group instruction techniques simply because a group of students has been assigned to them. Considerable individual attention can be provided while working in the midst of a group of students. For example, the teacher can move from desk to desk asking questions, giving individual feedback, and delivering reinforcement during seat work sessions. This type of teaching has been termed a roving tutorial or group-individualized style of teaching.

The mini-tutoring session is contrary to the traditional concept of tutoring, which included a very structured session in a cloistered setting, often for a duration of 25 to 45 minutes. Many teachers believe that little or nothing can be accomplished in less time, but an intensive 5-minute tutoring session, focused on specifically pinpointed skill deficits, can accomplish as much or more than a longer session in which several topics may be covered. For example, a teacher may use a one-to-one session for (1) informal probing to learn the exact performance level of a student on a specific skill; (2) short, intensive drill or practice on specific items; or (3) teaching new concepts.

MODELING TACTICS

Modeling has been used with a variety of learners, but it is particularly effective for teaching children who are prone to making numerous mistakes while learning a comparatively simple skill. Many teachers believe that children learn best by correcting their own errors. For some children, this adage may be true; for other children, particularly handicapped learners, mistakes may never be discovered with only infrequent corrective feedback or may become so ingrained that "unlearning" becomes increasingly difficult. A pattern of continued failure that causes these children to give up without really trying may develop. Modeling, incorporated into direct teaching tactics, helps to break this pattern because it reduces the chance of errors, while still teaching the skill. Reducing the frequency of errors can decrease frustration for both pupil and teacher. For some children, it provides a rare opportunity for academic success.

In modeling, the teacher provides an exact demonstration of the student response desired. Most teachers model frequently in the course of daily instruction, but they may do so only as a last desperate step to help the child provide the correct response. For example, instruction begins with the teacher asking the child a question. The child does not know the answer to the question, but guesses at the answer. Next, the teacher attempts to help by giving examples of similar problems or providing part of the answer:

Teacher (*holding up a flashcard with the word* cat *on it*): "What is this word?"
  Child: "Cut."
  Teacher: "No, that's not right . . . look at the vowel."
  Child: "Cot?"
  Teacher: "No, no . . . now what sound does the *a* make?"
Child: *a*
  Teacher: "Now, what is this word again?"
  Child: "Cast."
  Teacher: "No! That's still wrong, the word is cat."

Here is another example:

Teacher (*holding up a flashcard with 6 × 2 on it*): "What's six times two?"

Child: "Ten."
Teacher: "No, if six times one equals six, then what is six times two?"
  Child: "Eight."
  Teacher: "Now think! Six times one is six and six times three is eighteen. What would six times two be?"
  Child: "I don't know."
  Teacher: "Yes, you do; it's twelve. What is it?"
  Child: "Twelve."
  Teacher: "Now, why didn't you say twelve in the first place?"

In these examples, modeling was used to provide the answer only after the teacher and the child had both reached the end of their patience. Much valuable time was consumed in a trial-and-error guessing game. This approach is problematic because it assumes that the child really knows the right answer, but cannot remember or is being oppositional. Students usually give a correct response if they are able to do so. This teacher could have used a modeling sequence quite effectively. Instead, the sequence of teacher-child interaction was haphazard and inefficient. Modeling by itself without consideration of other teaching responses or the learner's response will probably be ineffective. In actuality, modeling as a teaching tactic should be a systematic and structured approach.

TYPES OF MODELING PROCEDURES

There are numerous modeling procedures. Three sequences that are well supported by the literature are antecedent modeling, error-dependent modeling, and partial modeling.

Antecedent Modeling

When a model is presented with each item to be taught and precedes the request for a student response, the procedure is called antecedent modeling. The teacher does not wait for an error to occur before modeling the answer. If an appropriate reinforcer is in effect and the student consistently imitates the teacher, learning is virtually errorless. As previously stated, a consistently used teaching sequence is just as critical with this strategy as with any tutoring sequence. The desired sequence for antecedent modeling is

1. model (teacher)
2. request (teacher)
3. correct response (student)
4. praise (teacher)

The procedure is easily applied to a great variety of skills, such as word identification, language development, math, and even social behavior:

Teacher (*holding up a flashcard with the word* where *on it and modeling*): "This word is *where*."
Teacher (*requesting a response*): "What is this word?"
Student (*responding correctly*): "Where."
Teacher (*praising the student*): "That's good reading."

Teacher: "The dog is going *into* the dog house."
Teacher: "Where is the dog going?"
Student: "The dog is going into the dog house."
Teacher: "Great. You said the whole sentence."

Teacher: "Five, ten, fifteen, twenty."
Teacher: "Your turn."
Student: "Five, ten, fifteen, twenty."
Teacher: "That's excellent counting by fives."

Teacher (*handing some marbles to Donny*): "Now I'm going to share some of my marbles with Donny."
Teacher: "Let's see you share."
Student hands some marbles to Donny.
Teacher: "Good sharing, Tony."

Because this procedure makes responding so elementary, many teachers dismiss the tactic as a teaching tool. Part of the beauty of the modeling sequence is that it is uncomplicated, but its potential effectiveness should not be underestimated. The prescribed sequence must be followed carefully and consistently.

Should an error occur, the teacher remodels the correct response and again requests the response:

Teacher (*pointing to the word* shirt *on the chalkboard where the words* send, shirt, *and* slight *are written*): "S, H has a *sh* sound."
Teacher: "Which word has a *sh* sound?"
Student (*pointing to* slight): "Shirt."
Teacher (*pointing to* shirt): "Shirt has a *sh* sound."
Teacher: "Which word has a *sh* sound?"
Student (*pointing to* shirt): "Shirt."
Teacher: "Now, you got it right, good going."

Teacher (*holding up a card with the word* rain): "This word is rain. I think it will rain. Rain is spelled *R-A-I-N*."

Teacher (*laying the card face down*): "Spell rain."
Student: "*R-i-a-n*."
Teacher (*holding up card*): "Rain is spelled *r-a-i-n*."
Teacher (*laying card face down*): "Spell rain."
Student: "*R-a-i-n*."
Teacher: "Perfect."

Teacher (*writing first letter of student's name*, J): "Here is how the first letter is written, *J*."
Teacher: "Now you write *J* on the line below."
Student writes incorrect *J*.
Teacher (*erasing bottom portion of* J *and tracing over, writing the curve to the left*): "Here is how the first letter is written."
Teacher: "Now you write *J* on the line below."
Student writes *J*.
Teacher: "Now, that's a good looking *J*!"

Since student abilities vary widely, the teacher must decide how much can be expected of a particular student in a 3- to 5-minute teaching session, based on the teacher's discretion and professional judgment. Generally, teachers can expect to obtain between 50 and 200 correct responses without tiring the student. The type of skills being taught and the proficiency level of the student must be considered. For example, motor responses (e.g., saying the answer) can be quite rapid and numerous.

Teachers who use this intensive direct teaching tactic find that it allows them to provide quick assistance to a student with only 3 to 5 minutes expended. Therefore, the teacher can give individual attention to several students within one work period, with each student getting immediate assistance at critical learning points.

Error-Dependent Modeling

An alternative to antecedent modeling is error-dependent modeling. With this tactic, the teacher provides a model only when the student makes an error; no modeling occurs when the student response is correct. A frequently used sequence for error-dependent modeling is

1. request (teacher)
2. correct response (student)
3. praise (teacher)
4. request (teacher)
5. incorrect response (student)
6. model (teacher)
7. request (teacher)
8. correct response (student)
9. praise (teacher)

In the following examples, the teacher uses error-dependent strategy and provides models *only* when errors occur:

> Teacher (*placing three triangles of differing sizes on a table*): "Point to the biggest triangle."
> Student points to the biggest triangle.
> Teacher: "Aren't you smart!"
> Teacher (*pointing to the three triangles on the table*): "Point to the smallest triangle."
> Student points to the largest triangle.
> Teacher (*pointing to the smallest triangle*): "No, that's not the smallest triangle. This one is the smallest."
> Teacher: "Now you point to the smallest triangle."
> Student points to the smallest triangle.
> Teacher: "Now you've got it."
>
> Teacher: "What did the boy in the story do after he picked up the ball?"
> Student: "He dropped it."
> Teacher: "He didn't drop the ball after he picked it up, he threw it."
> Teacher: "What did he do after he picked up the ball?"
> Student: "He threw it."
> Teacher: "Good, now you've got it."

Both antecedent modeling and error-dependent modeling ultimately elicit a correct student response. Research comparing these tactics indicates that both are effective. Many teachers prefer to use error-dependent modeling, however, because they have been taught that students should arrive at their own answer. On the other hand, antecedent modeling is considered more effective for certain children because it is virtually errorless and, thus, less frustrating to the child. The type of modeling chosen should depend on the child with whom the procedure is to be used. A child who appears anxious or frustrated after making an error may be a good candidate for antecedent modeling. On the other hand, error-dependent modeling may be a better choice for a rote task, such as math fact drills or sight word drills. Finally, it must be kept in mind that many children do not learn from mistakes; making many errors may, in fact, reinforce inappropriate responding.

Partial Modeling

Teachers who are eager for children to learn as much as they can on their own may choose to provide a partial model rather than an antecedent or error-dependent model. As the name implies, only part of the answer (response) is demonstrated in a partial model. This type of model is useful because it can induce the student to supply the correct answer without having the full answer modeled:

> Teacher (*holding up a picture of an Irish setter*): "What is this?"
> No student response.
> Teacher: "Do . . ."
> Student: "Dog."
> Teacher: "Great, that's good working."
>
> Teacher (*holding up a card with the word* hat *written on it*)
> No student response.
> Teacher: "H . . ."
> Student: "Hat."
> Teacher: "Right, good for you."
>
> Teacher (*holding zipper board*): "Pull up the zipper."
> No student response.
> Teacher grasps the end of zipper as if to pull it.
> Student pulls up zipper.
> Teacher (*giving child a hug*): "Good working."
>
> Teacher (*grasping glass placed in front of student*): "Pick up the glass."
> No student response.
> Teacher reaches for the glass and stops.
> Student picks up the glass.
> Teacher (*rubbing student's shoulder*): "That's very good."
>
> Teacher: "Put on your stocking."
> No student response.
> Teacher picks up stocking, opens it, and hands it to the student.
> Student puts on stocking.
> Teacher: "That's great. You've put on your stocking all by yourself."

If this procedure is to be effectively used, it is important to make a careful decision about how much of the response to model. If the student does not make a correct response after the first partial model, the teacher simply adds more to the model until a correct response is produced. In the sequence for putting on a stocking, the student did not respond to the verbal request. The teacher may begin by modeling the dressing skill and then gradually fading or removing the model when the child begins to respond correctly. If errors persist, the fading procedure may have been too rapid, or one particular step may be an obstacle. For example, children often have great difficulty getting the stocking opening over their toes. The teacher may help by holding one side of the stocking open while the child holds the other side. In this case, the partial model includes physical assistance. Later, after the child gains confidence and some physical control, the teacher assistance may be faded from the sequence, leaving only the verbal cue, "Put on your stocking."

FADING FROM A COMPLETE MODEL

Sometimes it is difficult to get children to stop relying on a model before giving the correct answer. Fading is a procedure for systematically reducing the amount of help being provided by the teacher. The keys to fading are consistency in the amount of help given and aptness of the schedule for removal of the model. It requires adherence to a set of specifications for each fading step; these specifications should include criteria that help the teacher decide when to move down to the next step or back to a previous step.

Table 7–1 is a program of steps for fading the model provided for a child during the teaching sessions of a language program. The ultimate goal of this program is to have the child label a picture with a full sentence when asked "What is this?" Each of the steps is a subgoal that is bypassed as soon as the student masters it. This program gradually reduces the amount of help the child needs to give the correct response.

Fading can be scheduled in several ways. Three common procedures are to fade (1) the amount of the step modeled (see Table 7–1), (2) the type of assistance provided (e.g., physical assistance to partial physical to model to verbal), and (3) the amount of assistance in a given time period (e.g., one prompt per 5-minute session). Fading tactics may be used in

- language development tasks (e.g., fading the model)
- self-help skills, such as toothbrushing and toileting (e.g., fading the type of assistance)
- dressing skills (e.g., fading the type of assistance)
- motor tasks (e.g., fading the type of assistance)
- social tasks (e.g., fading the number of prompts in a given time period)

PLANNING FORMS IN A MODELING PROGRAM

Modeling programs are easily documented on the planning forms. Initially, the main components of the planned program are specified on the Direct Teaching Program Checklist (Exhibit 7–1). The brief notations on the checklist are supplemented by more detailed information (e.g., the exact target, complete analysis, and the precise sequence of targets for individual teaching sessions) on the Preprogram Planner (Exhibit 7–2). Before attempting to begin instruction, the teacher describes the exact teaching procedures to be used on the Teacher Presentation Guide (Exhibit 7–3). Daily instruction plans are updated on the Daily Planner, which shows what remains the same and what is to be changed (Exhibit 7–4). It can be seen, for example, short-term objective (STO) 15.12 was not mastered as rapidly as STO 15.11 and that it was mastered after the teacher changed to a variable ratio schedule of reinforcement. It is also worth noting that only one tactic was changed at a given time.

MODELING PROGRAMS FOR HANDICAPPED CHILDREN

Although many instructional materials include suggestions that teachers model or demonstrate behaviors in some way, some instructional programs developed for use with handicapped children systematically incorporate modeling as part of their teaching strategy. As noted earlier, it is the sequence of events in which modeling occurs, not simply the modeling itself, that facilitates learning.

DISTAR

The Direct Instruction Strategy for Teaching Arithmetic and Reading (DISTAR) programs incorporate a systematic teaching strategy with precise page-by-page instructions to the teacher. The strategy is designed to elicit a unison or choral response from a group of learners for each stimulus presented. Teacher prompting of responses follows a progression from modeled to independent responding. At the model step, the teacher demonstrates the correct response and requests students to imitate the response. For example,

Table 7–1 Fading Program

Step	Teacher Request	Teacher Model	Student Response
1	"What is this?" (shows picture of cat)	"This is a cat." (5 consecutive)	"This is a cat."
2	"What is this?" (shows picture of cat)	"This is a . . ." (5 consecutive)	"This is a cat."
3	"What is this?" (shows picture of cat)	"This is . . ." (5 consecutive)	"This is a cat."
4	"What is this?" (shows picture of cat)	"This . . ." (5 consecutive)	"This is a cat."
5	"What is this?" (shows picture of cat)	No model provided (5 consecutive)	"This is a cat."

Exhibit 7–1 Completed Checklist for a Modeling Program

DIRECT TEACHING PROGRAM CHECKLIST*

(For supervisors use only)

PROGRAM _Spelling – Sally R._

	Approved Date	Verified (For supervisors use only) DATE Initial

TARGET _Spell words from 2nd grade work-_
(What to teach) _book — Task Analysis of conditions_

ANALYZE _Divide missed words into sets of 10_
(What to teach)

ASSESS _Pretest –select missed words, daily Probes_
(How measure)

INTERVENE _Antecedent modeling_
(What Teaching Tactic is used)
with adaptations for spelling

(SEE PRESENTATION GUIDE
ON BACK OF THIS PAGE)

Arranged Event _praise, hall monitor_

Arrangement _every correct, point every 5th correct_

CHECK PROGRESS/ _10 word daily probe_
MASTERY   (How measure)

REDIRECT _modify arrangement of points_
(What back-up teaching tactic may be used)
select another consequent event

(SEE PRESENTATION GUIDE
ON BACK OF THIS PAGE)

*Many of the procedures outlined on this checklist were adapted from the materials developed in the Field Based Special Teacher Education Program at George Peabody College for Teachers of Vanderbilt University.

Exhibit 7–2 Subtask Listing of 57 Words to Be Taught

PREPROGRAM PLANNER*

Name **Sally R.**   Service Program _____

Long Term Goal # **15.0 Spelling**   Instruction Schedule **10:30 – 10:40**

Short Term Objective **15.1 Orally spell 240 words from second grade workbook list with 100% accuracy.**

Initial Assessment: **10 word daily probe of 57 words incorrect on pre-test**

Sub-Skill Objectives: (Please number each one)

S.T.O. No.	Conditions:	Behavior:	Criterion:
15.11	10 word cards	Orally spell	100% correct, 3 consec. days
15.12	"	"	"
15.13	"	"	"
15.14	"	"	"
15.15	17 word cards	"	"
15.16	57 word cards (randomly sampled)	"	"

---

learners may be asked to respond to a signal by saying the sound *a* following the teacher's model (Exhibit 7–5). If all students respond correctly and on time, the teacher may praise the response and move to the independent step, requiring learners to respond to a signal without a preceding teacher model (test). If any one of the group responds incorrectly or not on time, the teacher undertakes a correction procedure that uses a "model-lead-test" strategy and requires the learner(s) to say it with the teacher.

The DISTAR and direct instruction programs have been shown to be highly effective. They are widely used in special and regular education programs throughout the United States. Adherence to the teaching procedures is crucial to the success of the program.

Corrective Reading

Engelmann, Becker, Hanner, and Johnson (1978) designed the Corrective Reading Program for upper elementary and adolescent children who have experienced difficulty in learning to read. Two of the program's daily activities involve teaching strategies similar to those employed in DISTAR. For example, the same model, lead, independent sequence of teaching activities is included. The first activity is a "boardwork" activity in which the teacher uses modeling to provide phonic word attack practice (Exhibit 7–6). In the second activity, the teacher employs the modeling strategy to correct errors and to integrate the earlier phonics drills into the oral reading of individual learners.

Exhibit 7–3 Specifications for Modeling Tactics

TEACHER PRESENTATION GUIDE

INTERVENE:

Setting/Materials	Teacher Says/Does	Child Says/Does
First 10 spelling word cards (randomly alternated)	holds card up	
	"This word is (chair)"	
	"This chair is brown"	
	"Chair is spelled c-h-a-i-r"	
	lays card down	
	"Spell chair"	"chair"
	(if correct) "nice spelling"	"c-h-a-i-r"
	—point every 5th word—	
	(if in error — repeat sequence)	

REDIRECT:

Setting/Materials	Teacher Says/Does	Child Says/Does
"	provide a privilege point	"
	for 1 out of 5 correct	
	response on the average	
	change privilege from	
	hall monitor to calling roll.	

Exhibit 7–4 Daily Record of Modeling Procedures

DAILY PLANNER*

Planning		Instructional Tactics					Measurement	
Ⓐ	Ⓑ	Ⓒ	Ⓓ	Ⓔ	Ⓕ	Ⓖ	Ⓗ	Ⓘ
	Sub-Objective	Materials	Presentation Mode	Child Response	Arranged Event	Arrangement	Progress Checking Tactic	Child Mastery/ Non Mastery
3/4	15.11	32	40	50	60,61	72,74	81	90
3/5	"	"	"	"	"	"	"	90
3/6	"	"	"	"	"	"	"	91
3/7	15.12	"	"	"	"	"	"	90
3/8	"	"	"	"	"	"	"	90
3/11	"	"	"	"	"	"	"	90
3/12	"	"	"	"	"	72,73	"	90
3/13	"	"	"	"	"	"	"	90
3/14	"	"	"	"	"	"	"	91
3/15	15.13	"	"	"	"	"	"	90
3/18	"	"	"	"	"	"	"	90
3/19	"	"	"	"	"	"	"	91
3/20	15.14	"	"	"	"	"	"	90

KEY

Ⓐ **Date:** date for which planned

Ⓑ **Sub-Objective:** (number from Program Plan Sheet - up to 30)

Ⓒ **Materials:**
30 = no materials
31 = published materials
32 = teacher made
33 = other

Ⓓ **Presentation Mode:**
40 = modeling
41 = questioning
42 = physical assistance
43 = prompt
44 = other

Ⓔ **Child Response:**
50 = oral
51 = motor/gestural
52 = written
53 = other

Ⓕ **Arranged Event:**
60 = social
61 = token
62 = consumable (edible)
63 = activity (e.g., free play)
64 = other

Ⓖ **Arrangement:**
70 = variable interval
71 = fixed interval
72 = continuous
73 = variable ratio
74 = fixed ratio
75 = other

Ⓗ **Progress Checking Tactic**
80 = criterion-referenced test
81 = daily record
82 = normative test
83 = other

Ⓘ **Child Data:**
90 = non-Mastery
91 = Mastery

*Many of the procedures outlined on this checklist were adapted from the materials developed in the Field Based Special Teacher Education Program at George Peabody College for Teachers of Vanderbilt University.

Exhibit 7–5 Modeling within the DISTAR Strategy

SOUNDS

TASK 1   Teaching a as in and

a. Point to a. You're going to learn this sound.
b. My turn. When I touch it, I'll say it. I'll keep on saying it as long as I touch it.
c. (Pause.) Touch a and say: aaa. Lift your finger.
d. Again. Touch a for a longer time and say: aaaaaa. Lift your finger.
e. Again. Touch a for a shorter time and say: aaaa. Lift your finger.

TASK 2   Children identify a

a. Point to a. Your turn. When I touch it, you say it. Keep on saying it as long as I touch it.
b. (Pause.) Get ready. Touch a. The children say aaa. Lift your finger.

To correct	1. Say the correct sound immediately. aaa.
	2. Say it with me.
	3. Point to a. Get ready. Touch a. Say aaa with the children.
	4. Again. Repeat step 3.
	5. Repeat a and b.

c. Again. Repeat b two times.

Source: From DISTAR® Reading I, *Teacher's Guide,* p. 14, by Siegfried Engelmann and Elaine C. Bruner. © 1974, 1969, Science Research Associates, Inc. Reprinted by permission of the publisher.

Exhibit 7–6 Example of Modeling Employed in *Corrective Reading*

EXERCISE 8   Opposites
The next Thinking Operation is Opposites.
1. **If something is not going up, it's** (pause; signal) *going down.*
   To correct:
   a. **My turn. If something is not going up, it's going down.**
   b. **Your turn.** Repeat step 1.
2. **If something is quiet, it's not** (pause; signal) *noisy.*
   If something is not empty, it's (pause; signal) *full.*
   Repeat step 2 until firm.
Individual test
Call on individual students to do step 1 or part of step 2.

Source: From *Corrective Reading, Series Guide,* p. 17, by S. Engelmann, W. Becker, S. Hanner, and G. Johnson. © 1980, 1978, Science Research Associates, Inc. Reprinted by permission of the publisher.

Project MORE

Other programs that systematically employ modeling in their teaching strategy are the independent living skills packages developed by the Mediated Operational Research in Education (MORE) Project. These training packages, which can be administered by paraprofessionals, are designed for use with moderately handicapped learners. The packages focus on daily living skills, such as toothbrushing, hairbrushing, showering, and hanging a shirt on a hanger. The teaching strategy is designed to employ the least amount of prompting necessary to obtain a correct response on a given program step (Figure 7–1).

The basic steps of the teaching strategy are

1. no help
2. verbal assistance
3. verbal assistance plus demonstration
4. verbal assistance plus physical help

Each step employs progressively heavier prompts. For instance, when the student makes an error at the no help level

Figure 7–1 Project MORE Teaching Strategy

The Teaching Strategy

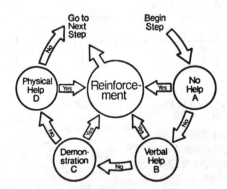

Demonstration [C]— show your student how to do the step as you say the step title. You can demonstrate either by pointing to an item or body part, by gesturing, or by modeling the step for the student; however, do not touch him/her at this level of help. After your demonstration, arrange the supplies to be just as they were before your student needed help, and make sure your student is in the same position as before. This will prevent the student from having to repeat earlier steps already done correctly. Ask your student to do the step on his/her own. If the step is done correctly after a *Demonstration*, reinforce your student, go to the next step, and again provide *No Help.*

Source: From *Showering* by Project MORE. Copyright © 1978 by George Peabody College for Teachers, Vanderbilt University. Reprinted with permission of the publisher, Hubbard.

(e.g., "Brush your teeth."), the trainer provides vocal assistance (e.g., "Pick up the toothbrush."). If the learner still does not respond or responds incorrectly, the trainer demonstrates or models the response (e.g., trainer says "Pick up the toothbrush," picks up the toothbrush, and puts it down). Modeling is one of a series of prompting behaviors used in these programs and is generally the pivotal point of the program. Learners who cannot imitate a model generally have difficulty making progress in the Project MORE programs.

Training for Independence

A series of self-contained packages, Training for Independence (Hofmeister, Gallery, & Hofmeister, 1977) is distributed by Developmental Learning Materials. The packages, which focus on a variety of self-help skills, include in the teaching strategy a modeling step similar to that in Project MORE. For example, one program developed to teach use of zippers, buttons, shoes, and socks includes a "tell, show, help" teaching sequence. The show step includes a model (Figure 7–2).

Figure 7–2 Training for Independence Modeling Procedure

SHOW: If the learner is still having difficulty, *show* him how to complete the step. Then have him do it by himself, and praise him.
Example:

   I: Watch me hold the button.

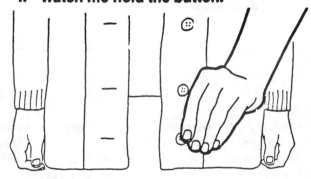

   Now you do it.

L: (Holds the button.)

I: You did a good job holding the button.

Source: Reprinted from *Training for Independence (Zippers, Buttons, Shoes and Socks)*, p. 11, by A. Hofmeister, M. Gallery, and J. Hofmeister. © 1977, Developmental Learning Materials, with permission of the publisher.

Functional Speech and Language Training for the Severely Handicapped

Guess, Sailor, and Baer (1976) developed a program to train the severely handicapped in functional speech and language. This four-part series includes instructions for systematic modeling as part of the training and correction procedures. Step 1 teaches item labeling (Exhibit 7–7) and employs a response-dependent modeling procedure. Step 4 teaches the learner to ask a question by means of an antecedent modeling procedure (Exhibit 7–8). In some steps (e.g., Step 2), no modeling is used. Later in the program (Step 20), verbal interaction between two trainers is modeled (Exhibit 7–9).

In early trials, learner approximations (e.g., partial words or phrases) of the complete response are reinforced. Modeling and other prompts are systematically faded from the teaching procedure within a step as progressive trials are completed.

RESEARCH ON MODELING AND IMITATION

Modeling and imitation paradigms have been shown to be extremely effective as teaching procedures with children (Baer, Peterson, & Sherman, 1967; Brown & Sontag, 1972; Guess, Sailor, Rutherford, & Baer, 1968; Jobes, 1975; Lovaas, Berberich, Perloff, & Scheffer, 1966; Schumaker & Sherman, 1970; Smith, 1973). These procedures have been used with children who had handicapping conditions ranging from minimal handicaps to severe mental retardation and severe emotional disturbance. The instructional tasks taught via this method have been diverse. Brown and his associates used modeling to teach a number of reading, math, and spelling skills (Bellamy & Brown, 1972; Brown, Bellamy, & Gadberry, 1971; Brown, Hermanson, Klemme, Haubrich, & Ora, 1970; Goodman, Bellamy, & Pierce, 1972). Spelling was the instructional target when Jobes (1975) used this technique. She coupled the modeling strategy with an observational learning system adapted from the extensive literature on social learning research led by Bandura (1965, 1968, 1969). Results of Jobes' study demonstrated that learning occurred under both conditions, but students learned more under direct instruction. Modeling has been similarly successful with nonacademic instructional goals.

Cooke and Apolloni (1976) used peer models to teach children appropriate social interactions. Another study incorporated modeling tactics with discussion procedures to train children to engage in social interaction behaviors. This experiment was a systematic replication of the study conducted by Cooke and Apolloni (1976), who had found that

Exhibit 7–7 Use of Modeling to Teach Labeling

Trainer	Student
Trial 1	
(Shows ball to student)	
WHAT'S THAT?	"Car"
LET'S TRY AGAIN. THAT IS A BALL, BALL. (Scores [-] on Scoring Form)	
WHAT'S THAT?	"Ball"
VERY GOOD! THAT IS A BALL!	
Trial 5	
(Shows ball to student)	
WHAT'S THAT?	(No-response; student is silent more than 10 seconds)
THAT'S NOT RIGHT. BALL.	
(Scores [NR] on Scoring Form)	
WHAT'S THAT?	"Ball"
GOOD TALKING! THAT IS A BALL.	

Source: Reprinted from *Functional Speech and Language Training for the Severely Handicapped,* Part 1, p. 13, by D. Guess, W. Sailor, and D.M. Baer. © 1978, H & H Enterprises, with permission of the publisher.

social interaction patterns established during a training session generalized to a free play setting. The second study focused on both the teacher-student interactions during the training periods and students' interactions with peers in a subsequent free play setting. Results of this study indicated that the direct instruction of social interactive behaviors increases the use of these behaviors during the training sessions, regardless of the specific teaching procedures. It did not show the spontaneous use of interactive responses as Cooke and Apolloni had originally shown, however. Population differences between the minimally handicapped group used by Apolloni and Cooke and the severely emotionally disturbed children in this study may account for the discrepancy between the two studies. Both studies indicate that with

a child who has a response within his or her repertoire, the modeling tactics are effective in generating a high rate of responses.

Although studies have indicated the strength of an imitation paradigm in teaching children a variety of tasks, little work has been done with concurrent measurement of teacher and learner behavior. Shores and Stowitschek (1976) conducted several studies for the purpose of extending and replicating research in the area of modeling and imitation across children's academic and social behavior, adding the element of teacher behavior measurement. Sight word reading, math fact recognition, and language development were the instructional targets used to examine the effects of both antecedent and contingent modeling paradigms. Results of

Exhibit 7–8 Use of Modeling to Teach Questioning

Trial 3

SAY, WHAT'S THAT?	"Wha at"
I THINK YOU CAN DO BETTER. (Scores [-] on Scoring Form for Phase II)	
LET'S TRY AGAIN. SAY, WHAT'S THAT?	"Wha dat"
GOOD, THAT WAS MUCH BETTER.	

Source: Reprinted from *Functional Speech and Language Training for the Severely Handicapped*, Part I, p. 32, by D. Guess, W. Sailor, and D.M. Baer. © 1978, H & H Enterprises, with permission of the publisher.

Exhibit 7–9 Use of Modeling to Teach Verbal Interaction

Trainer	Second Trainer (model)	Student
Trial 1		
(Holds up cookie)		
WHAT DO YOU WANT ME TO DO?		"I want eat cookie"
THAT'S NOT QUITE RIGHT, DICK. (Scores [-] on Scoring Form)		
MARY (second trainer), WHAT DO YOU WANT ME TO DO?	I WANT YOU EAT COOKIE.	
GOOD TALKING MARY, THAT WAS RIGHT!		
(Eats cookie)		
(Holds up another cookie)		
DICK, WHAT DO YOU WANT ME TO DO?		"I want eat cookie"

Note: In this example, the second trainer modeled a response which also included the item label (cookie). This was done since the student included the item label in his initial (although incorrect) response. The second trainer also correctly stressed the pronoun "You" in her response.

Source: Reprinted from *Functional Speech and Language Training for the Severely Handicapped*, Part II, p. 40, by D. Guess, W. Sailor, and D.M. Baer. © 1978, H & H Enterprises, with permission of the publisher.

the academic studies showed that both antecedent and contingent modeling were effective teaching procedures, but that errors occurred less frequently in antecedent modeling procedures.

Another study involving modeling indicated that pinpointing and contingent reinforcement are prerequisites to the successful use of a direct teaching procedure. A multimedia training procedure on the use of a modeling tactic was assessed with pre-service special education teachers (Stowitschek & Gable, 1978). Four teachers completed the training package while they were carrying out teaching practice with upper primary age learning-disabled children. All teachers used the modeling tactic to criterion performance (90% of observed teaching instances). No difference in the children's math performance (calling out answers to math facts) or reading performance (calling out answers to sight word cards) was observed following the teacher's completion of the modeling package. This finding suggests that modeling is an ineffective strategy. It was surmised that the lack of instructions for pinpointing or for measuring learner performance in the training package may have been a contributing factor to the results. Informal examination of the teaching content selected by the teachers revealed that they presented stimuli (words or math fact problems on cards) from the entire pool given them (90 to 100 items) and did not restrict instruction to a set of 5 or 10 stimuli at a time. In addition, reinforcement techniques provided by the package were restricted to contingent praise. Teachers varied considerably in the consequent events provided for correct responding, although not in the consequent events provided following attempts at correct responding. The empirical determination of a reinforcer may be a necessary prerequisite for the successful employment of appropriate consequent events.

Research to date has supported the effectiveness of the modeling strategy when used in a specific pattern; however, the effectiveness of the strategy becomes questionable when teachers do not employ it systematically. This particular area of research should surely be included in future analyses of teacher use of modeling strategies.

Chapter 8

Questioning Tactics

E very school day in classrooms across America teachers are asking questions, many questions. A typical elementary school teacher may ask as many as 350 questions each day. As much as four-fifths of a secondary school teacher's instructional interaction with students may be comprised of questioning. In 30 minutes, a social studies teacher commonly makes over 60 inquiries. A science lesson is seldom finished until the teacher has posed 180 questions. In classrooms and other instructional settings for exceptional learners, this pattern is repeated. Despite a wide variety of teaching experiences and educational backgrounds, the classroom behavior of teachers has at least one common denominator—frequent, indeed very frequent, questioning.

QUESTIONS: KINDS AND FUNCTIONS

Questions asked by teachers may be intended to gain information, assess mastery, check progress, increase knowledge, promote thinking, test memory, stimulate discovery, and initiate or maintain interaction. Often, the intended purpose of a given who, what, when, where, how, or why question is never realized, however. Many teachers do not wait for an answer to one question before asking another; others supply the answer before students have had time to deliberate. On the other hand, many questions are repeated or reworded so often that it is impossible to determine whether the objective of the original questions has been met. Too frequently, teachers appear to be asking questions at random. A student's response to a question may be logged mentally or outright forgotten by a teacher in the process of asking the next question. In such instances, the instructional merit of the question is certainly marred, if not eradicated.

Fortunately, most teachers can dramatically improve the instructional utility of their questions and questioning strategies with minimal effort.

Kinds of Questions

Questions have been classified traditionally as lower order or higher order. Lower order questions require simple recall or factual memory. These questions, typically wh-questions (who, what, when, where, but not why), are answered frequently with a yes or no, a single word, or a short phrase. Higher order questions require higher thought processes. Questions containing such words as *why, predict, compare, discuss, justify,* and *evaluate* are considered higher order questions. Numerous systems for classifying questions have been developed. Unfortunately, these systems often consist of poorly defined, overlapping categories and conflicting terminology. Most important, teacher use of questions based on a hierarchy has not been consistently shown to affect student performance directly and positively.

Rather than study classification systems and use them as a basis for instructional decision making, the special educator must take a straightforward approach to the task of using questions in the classroom. As with any other teaching approach, the first step is to select the most appropriate educational goals and objectives for each student. After an instructional objective has been operationally defined, the teacher must decide which teaching tactic is most appropriate and most efficient in helping the student reach that objective. Questions and questioning strategies should be selected only after the educational objective has been determined.

A number of different question types and questioning sequences have been shown to have beneficial effects on student learning. Oftentimes, teachers need to formulate their own questioning sequences and construct the strategy that most appropriately meets the demands of a given instructional objective. Once such questioning strategy has been designed and tried, the teacher can adjust it, implement it again, classify it according to the ease with which it helped students reach the objective, and file it for future reference.

Instructional Purposes of Questioning

The universality with which teachers employ questions in one-to-one interactions, small-group discussions, and large-group presentations indicates the many and varied functions that questions serve. A single question may provide information ranging from the level of a student's attention to a precise reading difficulty. Questioning strategies can lead students to mastery of new material and provide useful models for resolving problems students encounter when the teacher is not present. Questions can be employed directly to promote acquisition, mastery, and generalization of academic skills, language development, social skill development, as well as self-help and daily living skills.

Questioning strategies may function as (1) diagnostic tools, (2) instructional tactics, or (3) feedback mechanisms for evaluating the effectiveness of other teaching strategies. They may be simple or fairly complex. Questions may be one component of an instructional tactic, or they may be the entire instructional tactic. They can be used as general setting events, e.g., leading questions, or as specific antecedents to student responding. Questions may be employed effectively as general feedback or as corrective feedback. With relative ease, questioning strategies used with individuals can be modified for group teaching situations. By designing and carefully assessing their own questioning strategies, teachers can enhance their instructional efficiency exponentially.

SELECTION FACTORS

In selecting the most appropriate teaching tactic and format, e.g., modeling versus questioning and small-group instruction versus group-individualized instruction, the teacher should consider at least four factors: (1) What is the particular teaching utility of this strategy? (2) What preliminary considerations are needed with regard to this strategy? (3) What special teaching demands does this strategy present? and (4) What is the primary instructional purpose of this strategy?

Utility for Teaching

The teacher must carefully assess the utility of any questioning strategy for teaching specific tasks or skills before choosing questioning over another direct teaching tactic. Questioning strategies appear to be especially well suited for (1) teaching fairly complex skills, (2) conducting follow-up drill and practice activities, and (3) quickly pinpointing student trouble spots.

Complex skills, such as reading and listening comprehension, verbal reasoning in mathematics, creative writing, logic, and interpretation of symbols, require students to discriminate between closely related stimuli and respond differentially to those stimuli. A simple mathematical word problem, for example, requires numerous skills. Students must be able to read the problem and determine its solution. In deciding how to reach that solution, students must state operations and set up equations. In the process, they must recognize printed words indicating the operation required, e.g., subtraction, and differentiate those words from phrases indicating other operations. Finally, they must set up an equation so as to arrive at the correct answer.

Questioning strategies are effective in determining if the student has learned to make the necessary discriminations for solving complex problems. Such strategies can be used to probe the student's understanding of specific concepts, e.g., subtraction versus addition, within the general problem. If the student's concept or computation is incorrect, questioning strategies can be used to focus the student's attention on a particular area or to restrict the amount of information provided so that the student has an opportunity to recognize and correct the error. Wh-, either-or, yes-no, and multiple choice questions can be sequenced to help students differentiate between closely related stimuli and respond correctly when fine grain discriminations are needed.

Questioning strategies are also very effective in follow-up teaching tactics. After a reading exercise aimed at increasing comprehension skills, for example, questions can be presented to assess student knowledge, orient the student to new interpretations, and expand existing concepts and knowledge. Response-dependent questions may be used effectively as follow-up teaching strategies.

Pinpointing and correcting errors that occur are critical to effective teaching. Most teachers do not have time to work individually with students for assessment or intervention over long periods of time. On the other hand, teachers often function as roving tutors, moving around the room, observing and questioning students individually as they work independently. The diagnostic questioning procedure is one of the most efficient mechanisms available to the teacher for assessing student classroom performance on a daily basis. By using a preestablished questioning sequence, the teacher can pinpoint student errors precisely (e.g., the student does not differentiate between present progressive and future progressive tenses), give appropriate feedback, and move on to assist another student.

Preliminary Considerations

Different teaching strategies have different behavioral prerequisites. Before employing any questioning strategies, teachers should assess the developmental levels of their students and the types of responses already in their students' repertoires. It is important for the teacher wishing to use questioning strategies to ascertain that the student is capable of making simple discriminations and conditional responses, e.g., can answer yes-no questions correctly.

Teaching Demands

All strategies place constraints on the teacher. The teacher must consider the effect of any strategy on planning time, classroom instruction time and behavior, and recordkeeping. In effect, the teacher must determine how practical the strategy will be in the classroom. If the teacher has planned or is able to plan for short tutorial sessions with students, questioning strategies are excellent for one-to-one interaction. During one-to-one sessions, teachers can simultaneously instruct and assess the development of skills; however, the teacher must apply questioning strategies with consistency and proficiency, which requires practice and concentration.

A questioning strategy should never be used as the sole tutorial approach, since it is not always the most effective strategy for teaching any given skill. In addition, teachers need to recognize when a questioning strategy that has been successful in the past is no longer effective and have a backup strategy, such as modeling, planned. Backup strategies are frequently needed for students who are first acquiring a skill. For the teacher wishing to obtain a quick estimate of a student's skill level, questioning may be the most appropriate strategy. When questioning tactics are used to assess student errors, the roving tutorial format is most effective and appropriate.

Primary Instructional Purpose

If the primary purpose of instruction is either to gather information on the kinds, frequency, and patterns of student errors or to build new responses, questioning strategies may be used. As noted earlier, quick assessment and pinpointing of errors are possible with diagnostic questioning sequences, while new responses can be acquired by students tutored in one-to-one and small-group teaching sessions.

GENERAL GUIDELINES FOR USING QUESTIONS

Throughout the instructional day, teachers use questions as prompts, cues, and feedback. Many of these questions occur spontaneously; others are planned components of questioning sequences. In either case, there are several guidelines to improve general teacher questioning:

1. Ask one question at a time.
2. Wait for a response. Allow enough time for students to formulate their answers.
3. Correct student errors consistently and immediately.
4. Praise frequently and give positive feedback when student responses are correct.
5. Evaluate the questions. Are they properly worded? Are terms used within the student's vocabulary?
6. State questions as clearly and concisely as possible; avoid verbal bloat.
7. Avoid random questioning. Plan how and with whom questions are to be used.
8. Avoid rephrasing questions as a matter of course. Rephrase questions in response to student error or misinterpretation only.
9. Do not rely exclusively on questions requiring only yes or no answers.
10. Challenge student correct responses on occasion.
11. Do not limit instructional objectives to recall and memory questions if the aim is problem solving.
12. Use age-appropriate language when questioning adolescents and adults.
13. Ask questions that are specific, relevant, and directly related to the curriculum and instructional materials being used.
14. Make the objective of the question clear to the student.

Student achievement and learning are tied closely to well-organized, intentional instruction. Excellent questioning is excellent teaching (Belch, 1975).

DIRECT QUESTIONING TACTICS

After an instructional objective has been written, teacher and student behavior has been described in observable terms, and a basic student progress measure has been designed or selected, the teacher is ready to use direct questioning tactics. These tactics are used primarily with an individual student or with a small number of pupils. Some sequences are specific to a particular content area (e.g., oral reading feedback sequences), while others appear to be applicable across skill areas (e.g., response-dependent and diagnostic questioning sequences).

Basic Question-Answer Sequence

The simplest and most commonly used question-answer sequence can be described temporally and structurally as a teacher-child-teacher interaction. The "ideal" question-answer sequence begins with a teacher question (antecedent event), is followed by a correct student response (answer), and ends with an appropriate teacher consequence behavior (subsequent event). The majority of all simple question-answer sequences begin with a wh- question, since such a question is often the focal point of an instructional objective. Typically, the function of wh- questions in the classroom differs from that of wh- questions outside the classroom. For example, when a teacher asks, "What time is it?" the teacher is probably asking a question directly related to an educational objective (e.g., The student will state orally the correct time in hours and minutes 9 of 10 times when asked to do so during the school day for 5 consecutive days.).

Lead Questions and Response-Dependent Questions

A number of questioning tactics may be employed to help students as they learn to respond to a specific question or

Exhibit 8-1 Lead Question to Focus Student Attention on Time Telling

PROGRAM __Time Telling__

TARGET __Tell time in hours and minutes__

INTERVENE __Lead Questions__
(What teaching tactic is used)

Teacher Antecedent/ Consequent Behavior	Child Response
(Clock with movable hands on display)	
Lead question: "Do you see this clock?"	"Yes."
"Good." Sets hands to 9:17.	
Key wh- question: "What time is it?"	"Nine seventeen."
"Excellent, it is 9:17!"	

Exhibit 8-2 Lead Question to Focus Student Attention on Expressive Language

PROGRAM __Expressive Language__

TARGET __Say action words in sentences__

INTERVENE __Lead Questions__
(What teaching tactic is used)

Teacher Antecedent/ Consequent Behavior	Child Response
(Picture of dog chasing ball on display)	
Lead question: "Do you see the dog?"	Points to the dog
"Right, that's the dog."	
Key wh- question: "What is the dog doing?"	"Dog is chasing ball."
"Good talking! The dog is chasing a ball."	

problem in a skill area. Teachers may ask questions that provide little or no prompting in order to test the students' response under conditions of ultimate performance—lead questions. Also, following an incorrect response, teachers may ask questions that help the students arrive at the correct response—response-dependent questions. Lead questions and response-dependent questions may be used in the same instructional sequence or in separate sequences.

Lead questions generally, but not always, take the form of a question. They may precede a wh- question, e.g., "What time is it?". Lead questions have two primary functions: (1) they focus the child's attention on the topic or experience to be discussed (Exhibits 8-1 and 8-2), and (2) they introduce and teach new knowledge and concepts (Exhibit 8-3).

Assessment of a student's mastery of a specific educational objective may include assessment of the number and kinds of lead questions the student needs to respond correctly. Student "answers" may be verbal, nonverbal, or both.

Exhibit 8–3 Lead Question to Introduce New Information

PROGRAM __Pre-math: Sorting__

TARGET __Sort big and little objects__

INTERVENE __Lead Questions__
(What teaching tactic is used)

Teacher Antecedent/ Consequent Behavior	*Child Response*
Lead question: "See? These are little houses."	Nods head
Lead question: "Do you see? These are big houses."	Nods head
Key wh- question: "Where does this house go?"	"Goes there." (places house with other little houses)
"Right! That's a little house. It goes with the little houses!"	

If lead questions do not produce the desired student response, the teacher may formulate other questions to cue the child or restrict the response alternatives available (Exhibit 8–4). These are called response-dependent questions. Response-dependent questions should be ranked by the teacher according to the level of support they provide. The goal of instruction is not only to obtain a correct answer to the lead question, but also to provide fewer and less restrictive response-dependent questions.

In Exhibit 8–4, the lead question, "Where is the dog?" oriented the child to the picture and set the stage for the next question, "What is the dog doing?" When the child did not respond after 5 seconds, the teacher provided a response-dependent question, "Is the dog chasing?" This question is more specific and may be answered with a yes or no response. The objective, student use of an action word, has not been achieved if the sequence of questioning is allowed to stop at this point, however. In order to obtain a response that fits the objective, another question is required (Exhibit 8–5).

In Exhibit 8–5, the teacher asks the response-dependent question, "What is the dog chasing?" Because chasing is a subset of doing, the question classifies and restricts the child's answer. In the alternative question given in Exhibit 8–5, the child must first judge the semantic correctness of the subsets "chasing" and "chewing." If the child responds correctly to the question, "Is the dog chewing or chasing?" the teacher can use the next question to cue the child to answer in a complete sentence, e.g., "What is the dog chasing?"

In some instances, perhaps because of time constraints, the teacher may not wish to persist in trying to evoke the desired response on a specific item. Instead, the teacher may ask other response-dependent questions that require a simpler discrimination by the child. For example, the teacher may ask, "Is the dog chewing?" This question requires a negative response. If the child says, "No, the dog's not

Exhibit 8–4 Teacher-Child Interaction Sequence with Both Lead Question and Response-Dependent Question

PROGRAM __Expressive Language__

TARGET __Say action words in sentences__

INTERVENE __Response-Dependent Questions__
(What teaching tactic is used)

Teacher Antecedent/ Consequent Behavior	*Child Response*
(Picture of dog chasing ball on display)	
Lead question: "Where is the dog?"	Points to dog
"Right, that's the dog."	
Key wh- question: "What is the dog doing?"	No response
Response-dependent question: "Is the dog chasing?"	"Yes."

Exhibit 8–5 Alternative Response-Dependent Questions

PROGRAM __Expressive Language__

TARGET __Say action words in sentences__

INTERVENE __Response-Dependent Questions__
(What teaching tactic is used)

Teacher Antecedent/ Consequent Behavior	Child Response
Response-dependent ques- tion: "What is the dog chasing?"	"Dog chasing ball."
"Good. The dog is chasing the ball!" (OR)	
Response-dependent ques- tion: "Is the dog chewing or chasing?"	"Dog chasing."
Response-dependent ques- tion: "What is the dog chasing?"	"Dog chasing ball."
"Very good!"	

chewing," the child has used an action verb. Furthermore, the teacher still has the options of waiting for further clarification by the pupil or of repeating the key wh- question, "What is the dog doing?" The teacher may ask a question that requires a positive response, e.g., "Is the dog chasing something?" The child must evaluate this question and still has an opportunity to say the complete response correctly. "The dog is chasing a ball, isn't he?" requires a mere affirmation, but it does close the instructional interaction between teacher and child in a positive manner.

In developing response-dependent question sequences, the teacher should begin by ordering the questions that are to be used if the child responses are incorrect. Usually, questions are ordered so that a student's answer alternatives are increasingly restricted, i.e., more prompting and support are provided with each consecutive error by the student.

Response-Dependent Questioning Sequences

Presented contingent on pupil error responses, response-dependent questioning sequences are essentially feedback tactics. They are remedial tactics that may be used with individual students or with small groups of students. They provide evaluative information that can be used as feedback on both pupil performance and questioning effectiveness.

Response-dependent questioning sequences consist of a series of question types designed to gain certain responses from students. Question types are usually arranged in order from those questions that request a complete answer from the student with little prompting to more and more restricted questions that provide heavier prompting, and target only one part of the response. Generally, when response-dependent questioning is used to teach a skill, more heavily prompting or restrictive questions are required in the early stages of acquisition to obtain correct responses. Later, less restrictive, more open-ended questions lead to correct responses.

Response-dependent questioning sequences are most likely to be used by teachers in a corrective manner in the classroom. Indeed, until a student approaches mastery of a skill, it is likely that response-dependent strategies will comprise the bulk of a teacher's questioning techniques.

Mathematics

One response-dependent questioning strategy of demonstrated efficacy in teaching verbal reasoning in mathematics (Armstrong, 1977; Stowitschek & Armstrong, 1978) consists of five questions used sequentially, beginning with the least supportive question and ending with a question type that greatly restricts student alternative responses:

1. opening question (OQ). This question immediately follows the reading of a problem by the subject or by the teacher, e.g., "What is the equation?" The student then writes and solves the entire equation before proceeding to the next problem.
2. constructed response (CR). This question is intended to produce a single phrase from the pupil, e.g., "Which words tell us what we need to find out?" It is more restricted than the opening question, but still requires the student to construct a response. *This is the first question in the remediation series.*
3. multiple choice (MC). The student is given a choice of two responses, one of which is the correct response, e.g., "Do we multiply or divide?" The MC question follows an error on the CR question.
4. restricted alternative (RA). This question eliminates the incorrect alternative provided in the MC question, but does not provide a model, e.g., "We don't multi-

ply, so what do we do?'' This question follows an error on the MC question.

5. complete model (CM). The complete model is given if the student errs on the RA question. The teacher then proceeds to the next problem if the student correctly imitates the model.

A correct response at any question level moves the instruction to the next stimulus (e.g., problem or portion of a problem).

There are four basic components to finding the answer to a word problem in mathematics: (1) restating the problem, (2) determining the operation, (3) identifying the first and second numerals of the operation, and (4) solving the equation. During instruction, the teacher supplies the student with a number of word problems and an answer sheet that includes spaces for filling in parts of the equation to be solved:

The response-dependent questioning sequence can be used to help the student complete each of the four problem-solving components that are necessary to answer a simple word problem, such as the following:

> If there are 20 apples in a basket, and 5 boys want to share the apples equally, how many apples will each boy get?

The opening question is used only once, at the beginning. If the student errs on the opening question, the teacher begins the series of remedial questions until a correct response is obtained. In the sample questioning sequence shown in Exhibit 8–6, it is assumed that the student does not answer correctly until the last question in the sequence.

Response-dependent questioning has been shown to be effective for teaching verbal reasoning skills in mathematics, an area that usually presents difficulty for special learners. In addition, repeated exposure in the classroom accustoms students to this sequence of questions, and they may begin to ask themselves the same questions as a decision sequence. In this way, the independent problem-solving skills of students may be enhanced.

Reading Comprehension

It is likely that reading comprehension could be taught by means of this or other carefully delineated response-dependent questioning sequences. The acquisition of reading comprehension skills may be divided into distinct categories, such as fact information, vocabulary information, and inference information. Adaptations of this questioning sequence should reflect the skill level, age, and special learning characteristics of the student.

Exhibit 8–6 Sample Response-Dependent Questioning Sequence

FIRST STEP: To restate the problem

CR 1—Which words tell us what we need to find out?
MC 2—Do we find out how many apples each boy will get, or how many boys want to share apples?
RA 3—We already know how many boys want to share apples, so what do we need to find out?
CM 4—Say, we need to find out how many apples each boy will get.

After any correct response, the teacher should underline the words in the problem that tell what is to be found out and proceed to determining the operation.

SECOND STEP: To state the operation

CR 1—What is the operation?
MC 2—Do we multiply or divide?
RA 3—Not multiply, so what do we do?
CM 4—Say, we divide.

After any correct response or at the end of the sequence, the child puts the appropriate sign in the box and proceeds to writing the equation.

THIRD STEP: To state the equation (the first numeral)

CR 1—What is the equation?
MC 2—Is the number that tells us how many objects are to be divided 20 or 5?
RA 3—Not 5, so what is it?
CM 4—Say, 20 objects are to be divided.

FOURTH STEP: To state the equation (the second numeral)

CR 1—What is the equation?
MC 2—Does the number 5 tell us how many groups we have or how many objects are to be divided?
RA 3—It's not how many objects are to be divided, so what is it?
CM 4—Say, 5 tells us how many groups we have.

After a correct response or at the end of the sequence, the child writes the appropriate number in the second blank and the teacher proceeds to solving the problem.

FIFTH STEP: To solve the problem

CR 1—What is the answer to the equation? (gives student time to compute)
MC 2—Is it $20 \div 5 = 3$ (teacher reads incorrect equation) or is it $20 \div 5 = 4$ (teacher reads correct equation)?
RA 3—$20 \div 5$ does not equal 3 (incorrect), so $20 \div 5 =$ what?
CM 4—Say, $20 \div 5 = 4$.

After saying the correct response, the child writes the answer in the third blank, and the teacher proceeds to the next problem.

Exhibit 8–7 Response-Dependent Questioning Sequence to Teach Outcome Prediction in Reading

PROGRAM __Reading Comprehension__

TARGET ____Predict (say) outcomes from reading selections____

INTERVENE _____Reponse-Dependent Questions_____
(What teaching tactic is used)

Teacher Antecedent/ Consequent Behavior	*Child Response*
Opening question: "What will Mr. Gibbs do?"	No response
Multiple choice: "Will he move to Montreal, stay in Chicago, or go to the farm?"	No response/incorrect
Restricted alternative: "Mr. Gibbs has no friends at the farm and fears moving so he will . . ."	No response/incorrect
Complete model: "Mr. Gibbs has no friends at the farm and fears moving so he will stay in Chicago."	"Mr. Gibbs will stay in Chicago."
"Yes, very good."	

Exhibit 8–7 shows a series of response-dependent questions used to teach "prediction" to secondary school students. In this hypothetical situation, the students have just read a short story and are "making predictions" on a follow-up basis. This teacher did not use the constructed response question and gave three (rather than two) choices to the student at the multiple choice question level and thereafter. It is likely that the teacher had already worked with the student at the two-question level. As a follow-up to this response-dependent questioning sequence, the teacher might ask a why question to underscore the reason for arriving at the conclusion. For example, the teacher might ask, "Why do you think Mr. Gibbs will stay in Chicago?" or "Why don't you think Mr. Gibbs will move to Montreal?"

Exhibit 8–8 illustrates response-dependent questioning used to teach the reading comprehension skill of sequencing events. Again, the teacher may close the entire sequence with a question that requires the student to tie the sequence of events together logically and in accordance with details of the story, e.g., "Why did Mr. Way steal the car before he went to work?" or "Why did Mr. Way go to work after he had stolen the car?" The teacher should be prepared to assist the students if they have difficulty answering the follow-up question(s).

Exhibit 8–8 Response-Dependent Questioning to Teach Sequencing of Events

PROGRAM __Reading Comprehension__

TARGET ____Sequence (say) the order of 3 events in the stories____

INTERVENE _____Response-Dependent Questions_____
(What teaching tactic is used)

Teacher Antecedent/ Consequent Behavior	*Child Response*
Opening question: "Tell me in order what Mr. Way did that day."	Incorrect
Multiple choice: "Did Mr. Way go to work, steal the car, and rob the bank?"	Incorrect
Restricted alternative: "Mr. Way did not go to work, steal the car, and rob the bank. What did he do?"	Incorrect
Complete model: "Mr. Way robbed the bank, stole the car, and then went to work."	"Mr. Way robbed the bank, stole the car, and then went to work."
"That's right!"	

Language

Response-dependent questioning approaches are extremely helpful for teaching language and early concepts to young handicapped children. Two questioning tactics that have been shown to be effective in this area are the full model-open question sequence and the open question-full model sequence (Hendrickson & Stowitschek, 1980). The actual responses targeted by the teacher, of course, vary with each objective and each child, and the types of questions employed to teach expressive language may differ from those used to teach verbal reasoning.

During the open question-full model sequence, a series of progressively more restricted questions is used:

1. open question. This type of question (or statement) is intended to obtain a single word, short phrase, or complete sentence response, e.g., "Tell me about this."
2. multiple choice. This type of question presents alternative responses that include the correct response, e.g., "Is it a *cat*, or is it a *cow*?" (More alternatives may be added.)
3. restricted alternative. This type of question eliminates the alternative incorrect response without presenting a complete model of the correct response, e.g., "It's not a cow. What is it?"
4. full model. This may be a question or a statement followed by a direct model intended to obtain a correct imitative response. The teacher asks the student to imitate the answer, e.g., "Say, it's a cat." The teacher follows a correct child response with praise and then repeats the original open question, i.e., "Tell me about this."

If the student does not successfully imitate the full model, a partial model, i.e., a limited number of the words in the target response, should be provided. For instance, the teacher may direct the child to "Say, it's a." After the child repeats, "It's a," the entire model (e.g., "It's a cat") is given again.

The full model-open question is a reverse procedure. The same questions are employed, but in the opposite order. This sequence appears to lead to more rapid acquisition of expressive language skills in young handicapped children and students with severe deficits. It may also be more enjoyable for teachers of children with limited repertoires, since the children respond correctly earlier in each question sequence and, therefore, more frequently in the total training session. Higher functioning students and their teachers, on the other hand, appear to prefer not to use the model before the student responds (Shores & Stowitschek, 1977).

Children are not exposed to all question types as frequently in the full model-open question sequence, since most children succeed after the answer has been modeled. Therefore, teachers may wish to alternate sequences once the student's response repertoire has been built to a level that permits the student to respond correctly in the open question-full model sequence. In this way, students develop skill in answering various question types. In addition, when a teacher has multiple objectives for students in each teaching session, e.g., to answer in complete sentences *and* to answer a variety of question types correctly, the open question-full model sequence may be more appropriate. A teacher may also select the open question-full model strategy for older students or students who have spontaneously displayed the desired behavior. The open question-full model strategy is more appropriate for students who would benefit from minimal support, such as those who are about to be mainstreamed.

Spelling

Response-dependent questioning strategies may be applied effectively to teach spelling, partly because they go beyond modeling techniques of simply providing the correct spelling before or after the child has responded. In a typical questioning sequence, the error made by the child can be brought to his or her attention through a question that itself may lead to self-correction (Exhibit 8–9).

The teacher inserts the spelling rule with the complete model. To close the sequence, the teacher may want the student to repeat the rule.

DIRECT TEACHING STRATEGIES THAT EMPLOY QUESTIONS

Mand-Model Strategy

In promoting language development, the mand-model strategy can be a primary direct teaching tactic or a secondary tactic used to facilitate generalization (Rogers-Warren & Warren, 1980). This strategy increases the rate of a child's verbalizations and their complexity, i.e., from simple labels to complex sentence forms. The mand-model strategy is an attempt to capitalize on spontaneous teacher-child interactions and the interest of the child at that time. Teacher-child interactions remain informal, for the most part.

The interactive sequence begins when the teacher asks the child a simple wh- question (Exhibit 8–10).

The function of the question in the mand-model strategy is to open the interaction sequence with an utterance that requires a response from the child, and, in turn, leads the child to verbalize. The child's answer is functional for the child, since it helps the child acquire a desired object. In the mand-model sequence the question asked at the beginning of the

Exhibit 8–9 Response-Dependent Questioning to Teach Spelling

PROGRAM	Spelling

TARGET ___ Spell words following the "ie" rule with a long "a" sound ___

INTERVENE ___ Response-Dependent Questions ___
(What teaching tactic is used)

Teacher Antecedent/ Consequent Behavior	Child Response
Open question: "How do you spell weigh as in I weigh 200 pounds?"	W-i-e-g-h
Constructed response: "What is the ie rule?"	No response
Multiple choice: "Is it w-e-i-g-h or w-i-e-g-h?"	W-i-e-g-h
Restricted alternative: "It's not w-i-e-g-h, so what is it?"	No response
Complete model: "Weigh is w-e-i-g-h; i before e except after c or when it sounds like a as in neighbor and weigh."	W-e-i-g-h
"Good spelling!"	

Exhibit 8–10 Mand-Model Strategy

PROGRAM	Expressive Language

TARGET ___ Single-word utterances in play setting ___

INTERVENE ___ Mand-model strategy ___
(What teaching tactic is used)

Teacher Antecedent/ Consequent Behavior	Child Response
Question: "What do you want?"	No response/points
Mand: "Tell me what you want."	Points
Model: "Say puzzle."	"Puzzle."
Praise: "Great talking! Here's the puzzle."	

interaction is never a yes or no question. The question is stated so that it requires a substantive verbal response. The mand is simply a request for a verbal reply, and the model is a complete demonstration of the desired behavior.

Communicative Interactive Model

In the communicative interactive model, the teacher acts as a facilitator by saying or doing things to evoke commu-

nicative behavior (Allen, 1980). It is a process for maintaining dialogue. The teacher-child verbal exchange process itself becomes the center point of the instructional objective. To maintain the interaction, the teacher says or does whatever is likely to evoke a child response and lead to a child initiation (Exhibits 8–11 and 8–12).

In the communicative interactive model, questions may vary, seemingly from topic to topic, as the child's attention shifts. The teacher asks questions in a nonthreatening, though directive, manner. An instructional objective, for instance, may be to increase the duration of teacher-child interactions or the number of child initiations.

Generative Question Modeling Strategies

Teaching children to respond with new linguistic forms or to make other generative responses may be feasible through use of simple question-modeling strategies (Clark & Sherman, 1975). At first, the teacher may need to model every answer the child gives. Later, once the answers are under the stimulus control of the questions, new examples of the

Exhibit 8–11 Communicative Interactive Model for Single-Word Utterances

PROGRAM __Expressive Language/Social Behavior__

TARGET ___Maintain dialogue, single-word utterances___

INTERVENE ___Communicative interactive model___
(What teaching tactic is used)

Teacher Antecedent/ Consequent Behavior	*Child Response*
(Child by toys with teacher nearby)	1. Points
2. "You want ball? Say ball."	3. Nods, makes sound "ba."
4. Gives ball	

Exhibit 8–12 Communicative Interactive Model to Maintain Dialogue

PROGRAM __Expressive Language/Social Behavior__

TARGET ___Maintain dialogue___

INTERVENE ___Communicative interactive model___
(What teaching tactic is used)

Teacher Antecedent/ Consequent Behavior	*Child Response*
(Child at easel)	1. "See my picture?"
2. "Look, you used red and . . ."	3. "and some blue."
4. "Yes, it's a beautiful blue."	5. No response
6. "What color is her face?"	7. "Red face, no hands."
8. "Oh, what happened to her hands?"	9. Laughs
10. Laughs. "She is funny."	11. "Funny."

trained forms may occur spontaneously. A sample teaching sequence follows:

Teacher:	He is a *baker*.	(Statement including stimulus form)
Teacher:	What did he do yesterday?	(Question—past tense)
Child:	Yesterday he *baked*.	(Answer—stimulus item with /t/ inflection)
Teacher:	He is a *baker*.	(Statement including stimulus form)
Teacher:	What will he do tomorrow?	(Question—future tense)
Child:	Tomorrow he will *bake*.	(Answer—stimulus item with no specific inflection)
Teacher:	He is a *baker*.	(Statement including stimulus item)
Teacher:	What is his job?	(Question)
Child:	His job is *baking*.	(Answer—stimulus item with /ing/ inflection)

(Clark & Sherman, 1975, p. 323)

Other Functions of Direct Questioning

As a complete teaching tactic or as a component of a larger teaching technique, direct questioning functions in ways too numerous to enumerate completely. Among the situations in which questions may have particular instructional merit, however, are the following:

- Questions and questioning sequences may be especially useful for teaching multiple skills to a child; for example, the rate of verbalization may pertain to a social objective as well as to a language objective.
- Questioning tactics are extremely useful for teaching different skills to a small group of students who are engaged in similar tasks. For example, while students are putting pieces of separate puzzles together, the teacher can inquire about shape, size, function, or quantity, as each pertains to individual student objectives.

- Questions may be presented to a large group in a drill format. The teacher can increase student response rates and total practice time if all students are actively involved in drill and practice exercises. By supplying each student with a set of flash answer cards and asking questions that require true-false or yes-no answers, the teacher literally is able to "see" the response of each student. Students simply flash their answer to the teacher.

- Response-dependent sequences can be used in a diagnostic manner. If a teacher uses response-dependent questioning while acting as a roving tutor, the questioning sequence may be considered a diagnostic questioning sequence (Armstrong, 1977).

- Peers are a valuable resource in any classroom. They can be taught to use questions to initiate and maintain socio-linguistic interactions, assist in drill and practice exercises, and participate as language models in group teaching sessions.

TEACHER-DESIGNED QUESTIONING STRATEGIES

Many teachers adapt or modify questioning strategies to meet their own needs. Teachers may design their questioning sequences in a variety of ways.

Teaching spelling often entails preview, practice, testing, and additional practice on words that were spelled incorrectly. Often students are instructed to write words that they missed on their spelling test 10 times, for example, as their review. During spelling bees, the student who has made a mistake is usually eliminated from the game and must wait to hear another student spell the word correctly. The questioning sequence presented in Exhibit 8–13 is a procedure that focuses the student's attention on the error immediately after it has been made. If the student is writing the word, the teacher can simply point to the misspelled word and follow the identical sequence.

In Exhibit 8–13, the teacher begins with the lead question, "How do you spell apple?" If the student errs, the teacher repeats the error as a question. If the student repeats the mistake, a multiple choice question and, if necessary, a full model are given. Even in a spelling bee, this strategy could be used. A new word could be presented to the next student, and the word *apple* put back in the pool of words.

Teachers may wish to follow guidelines for teaching in specific content areas, such as oral reading, that have been established by educational researchers. Hansen and Eaton (1978) described a corrective feedback hierarchy that consists of seven steps. A teacher may employ their hierarchy to establish a questioning sequence to correspond with each step (Table 8–1). As with other response-dependent tactics,

Exhibit 8–13 Teacher-Designed Questioning Sequence to Teach Spelling

PROGRAM _Spelling_____

TARGET ____Spell names of 5 types of fruit_____

INTERVENE _____Questioning sequence (teacher-designated)_____
(What teaching tactic is used)

Teacher Antecedent/ Consequent Behavior	Child Response
Lead question: "How do you spell apple?"	"A-p-e-l"
Repetition of error: "A-p-e-l?"	"A-p-l-e"
Multiple choice: "Do you spell apple, a-p-l-e or a-p-p-l-e?"	"A-p-l-e"
Full model: "You spell apple, a-p-p-l-e."	"A-p-p-l-e"

if the teacher uses the adapted tactics consistently, the students will learn the sequence and are likely to employ it in the resolution of problems they recognize. The teacher may even consider teaching the questioning (self-questioning) sequence directly.

Zetlin and Gallimore (1980) reported a general three-step questioning sequence, experience-text-relationship, that has been used to order questions for teaching listening comprehension. The teacher begins by asking questions about students' experiences as they relate to the story that will be read, e.g., going shopping, having a friend, riding the subway. These experience questions function as lead questions. After reading a short section of the story, the teacher asks questions that focus on literal picture or story details; these questions are typically wh- questions. Finally, in the same session or after a number of listening sessions, the teacher asks questions that bring students' experience and knowledge together with details of the story. In preparing for these sessions, teachers must plan the questions they intend to ask.

Table 8–1 Hansen and Eaton's Seven-Step Hierarchy with Possible Teacher Questions

Step	Question
1. Purpose of question: Cue the student that he has read a word incorrectly.	1. What is the word after "army." How do you pronounce the last word in the sentence?
2. Purpose of question: Have student finish sentence and guess the word.	2. Can you reread the sentence correctly?
3. Purpose of question: Have the student break the word into parts and pronounce each one.	3. Do you see any smaller words in that word? What does "b-a-t-t-l-e" spell?
4. Purpose of question: Provide student with aided visual cue to decrease the stimuli.	4. What word do you see if you cover "b-a-t-t-l-e" with your finger?
5. Purpose of question: Provide student with a phonic cue to indicate location of his error.	5. If you cover all the letters but "b-a," what sound(s) do you have?
6. Purpose of question: Provide the student with a choice of the correct word and incorrect word.	6. Is the word "cattleship" or "battleship"?
7. Purpose of question: Provide the student with the correct word.	7. The word is "battleship." Read the word and the complete sentence.

Source: Hierarchy from Hansen and Eaton (1978, p. 73).

A corrective or response-dependent questioning strategy for dealing with incomplete or incorrect responses is essential. When the teacher is using this strategy with a small group, the session may be tape-recorded so that the fidelity with which the strategy was followed can be assessed.

As simple information-seeking questions are mastered, students are introduced to comprehension questions. There are five levels of comprehension questions, which are presented in a hierarchical manner:

1. Questions require simple detail recall.
2. A simple interpretation is required.
3. Questions deal with interrelationships among details or sequence of events.
4. The student is asked to integrate elements of the story that were not necessarily presented, e.g., predict the story's outcome, justify that prediction.

5. Questions are designed to reveal the students' understanding of the story and events and to change their ideas on the basis of new information.

Whether teachers use empirically validated questioning sequences, strategies that include questions, or design their own questioning strategies, it is essential that they apply the chosen strategy consistently if its effect on students is to be ascertained. Teachers must be particularly observant of their own questioning behavior. Only appropriate practice can improve a teacher's effectiveness in the use of questioning strategies.

CURRICULAR APPLICATIONS OF QUESTIONING STRATEGIES

Questions dominate teacher-student verbal interaction. Although they are used in many curricular materials, few of these instructional materials use questioning strategies in a consistent and structured manner. Even fewer use validated questioning sequences. While most publishers suggest that teachers question students regarding this or that lesson or objective, few detail the manner in which questions should be presented or student errors should be treated. Only the most structured materials, e.g., DISTAR (Engelmann & Osborn, 1973), provide teachers with specific instructions on asking questions.

DISTAR Language III

When using DISTAR Language III (Engelmann & Osborn, 1973), teachers present highly structured lessons to their classes daily. The Teacher's Guide contains detailed descriptions of teaching procedures and general teaching tactics. Teachers are advised to be prepared fully each day before beginning their lesson. A Teacher Presentation Book is used daily in the presentation of new concepts and language-related objectives. The daily lesson consists of three structured parts: (1) an oral presentation to the class, (2) independent written activities, and (3) a work check and reteaching period (Exhibit 8–14). DISTAR provides the teacher with much more information, general guidance, and specific instruction than do most curricular materials.

DISTAR Arithmetic

Engelmann and Carnine (1970) designed DISTAR Arithmetic I and II to teach children basic arithmetic concepts. In the Teacher's Guide, seven points that characterize good teaching are presented. One of these points is that teachers need to separate thinking operations from the repetition of statements, i.e., the goal is to teach students concepts, not

Exhibit 8–14 Sample Lesson from DISTAR Language III

Teacher-Directed Oral Activity

Task: Synonyms and Opposites

- We're going to do synonyms and opposites. First we're going to do synonyms.
  1. Everybody, what's a synonym for **unhappy?** Wait. Yes, **sad** is a synonym for **unhappy.**
  2. What's a synonym for **little?** Wait. Yes, **small** is a synonym for **little.**
  3. What's a synonym for **big?** Wait. Yes, **large** is a synonym for **big.**
  Repeat items 1 through 3 until all children's responses are firm.
- Now we're going to do opposites.

Teacher-Directed Workbook Activity

Task: Synonyms and Opposites

- Everybody open your workbook to lesson 19. Wait. Find part A.
  1. Everybody read the instructions for the first item out loud. *Write a synonym for each word.*

  Everybody read the first word out loud. Wait. What's a synonym for **unhappy?** Wait. Yes, **sad.** Write it in the blank. Check a few children's work.

  Read the second word out loud. Wait. What's a synonym for **little?** Wait. Yes, **small.** Write it in the blank. Check their work.

Teacher-Directed Textbook Activity

Task A: Writing Stories about Pictures

- Everybody open your textbook to lesson 19. Wait. Read the instructions for part A out loud. *Use a sheet of lined paper. Write two sentences about the picture. In the first sentence tell what you see in the picture. In the second sentence tell how the boy feels.* Everybody look at the picture in part A.
- Let's make up two sentences about the picture. The first sentence will tell what you see in the picture. The second sentence will tell how the boy feels. What will the first sentence tell? Wait. Yes, what you see in the picture. What will the second sentence tell? Wait. Yes, how the boy feels. Repeat these questions until all children's responses are firm.

Source: From DISTAR® Language III by Siegfried Engelmann and Jean Osborn. © 1973, Science Research Associates, Inc. Reprinted by permission of the publisher.

---

sentences. To prevent students from responding rotely, a two-step questioning tactic is employed. First, the students are asked to answer a question with a single word or phrase. Next, they are asked to respond with the full sentence:

Teacher: What is four plus one?
Children: Five.
Teacher: Say the whole thing.
Children: Four plus one equals five.

or

Teacher: Six minus *how many* equals two?
Children: Four.

Teacher: Six minus *how many* equals two? Say the whole thing.
Children: Six minus *four* equals two.

The DISTAR arithmetic program also gives specific instructions regarding error correction. In one lesson, a correction box in the Teacher Presentation Book illustrates use of a simple setting event question to focus the children's attention on the task should they make a mistake (Exhibit 8–15).

In another typical oral activity, the skill—object counting—is presented with a number of questions used throughout the teaching activity. The basic question, e.g., How many objects are there? is repeated after various activities are presented by the teacher (Exhibit 8–16).

In DISTAR arithmetic symbol identification, questions are used in a slightly different manner. First, an opening wh-question is asked. Next, several setting event questions are asked prior to the presentation of a picture with seven objects. Following the presentation of that picture, the children are asked to answer two specific yes-no questions and a question that calls for demonstration of mastery of the skill (Exhibit 8–17).

Project MATH

Cawley, Fitzmaurice, Goodstein, Lepore, Sedlak, and Althaus (1977) designed a comprehensive mathematics program, called Project MATH, for use with exceptional learners. The materials are divided into four levels and four major strands: (1) numbers, (2) measurement, (3) geometry, and (4) fraction. One of the main purposes of Project MATH is to provide the teacher with a range of options for presenting different skills and concepts so that various handicaps to learning may be circumvented. The scope and sequence of

Exhibit 8–15 Correction Procedure in DISTAR Arithmetic

---

d. Everybody, what's the first thing you do when you work a minus problem? (Pause and signal.) *Write the minuses.* Yes, write the minuses. Then what do you do? (Pause and signal.) *Count backward for every minus.* Yes, count backward for every minus. Repeat until firm.
e. Look at the side with the ring around it. (Pause.) Write the minuses. *(The children write four minuses under 4.)* Check responses.
f. Now what do you do? (Pause and signal.) *Count backward for every minus.*

| To correct | When you work a minus problem, first you write the minuses. Then what do you do? (Pause and signal.) *Count backward for every minus.* |

Source: From DISTAR® Arithmetic I by Siegfried Engelmann and Doug Carnine. © 1970, Science Research Associates, Inc. Reprinted by permission of the publisher.

Exhibit 8–16 Counting Events and Objects: Touching and Counting Objects

Exhibit 8–17 Counting Events and Objects: Counting Objects Group Activity

22

TASK 4 COUNTING EVENTS AND OBJECTS Touching and Counting Objects

Emphasize words in **boldface.**

  a. Hold up your presentation book. Point to the row of objects.
     Look at this row of objects.
  b. You will touch the objects at one-second intervals as the children count. **Count the objects.**
     Every time I touch an object, you count. (Pause.) **Get ready. Touch.** *1, 2, 3, 4, 5, 6.*
  c. What number did we end up with? (Signal.) *6.*
     So how many objects are there? (Signal.) *6.*
     Repeat *b* and *c* until the responses are firm.
  d. Call on individual children to touch and count the objects. You will clap at one-second intervals to signal the responses.
     You're going to touch and count. Every time I clap, you touch an object and count it. (Pause.) **Get ready. Clap.** *(The child touches and counts the objects.)*

To correct	If touching and counting cannot be coordinated, physically help the child touch and count the objects. Stamp your foot as the signal to count the objects.

     How many objects are there? (Signal.) *6.*

16

TASK 3 COUNTING EVENTS AND OBJECTS Counting Objects Group Activity

  a. Hold up your presentation book and point to the row of objects. **Look at this row of objects.**
  b. You will touch the objects from left to right at one-second intervals as the children count. **Count the objects. Every time I touch an object, you count.** (Pause.) **Get ready. Touch.** *1, 2, 3, 4.*

To correct	If the children make counting mistakes, count with them. Repeat until the response is firm.
	If any children count before you touch an object, or if any children count after the others have counted, tell them: **Let's try it again. You have to watch my finger. When I touch an object, you count.** (Pause.) **Get ready. Touch.** *(The children count as you touch the objects.)* Repeat until the response is firm.

  c. What number did we end up with? (Signal.) *4.*
     So how many objects are there? (Signal.) *4.*
  d. You will touch the objects at one-second intervals as the children count. **Count the objects again.** (Pause.) **Get ready. Touch.** *1, 2, 3, 4.*
  e. What number did we end up with? (Signal.) *4.*
     So how many objects are there? (Signal.) *4.*
     Repeat *d* and *e* until the response is firm.
  f. You will touch the objects **from right to left** as the children count. **Let's start at the other end and see if we end up with the same number.** (Pause.) **Get ready. Touch.** *1, 2, 3, 4.*
  g. What number did we end up with? (Signal.) *4.*
     So how many objects are there? (Signal.) *4.*
     Yes, there are four objects.
     Repeat *d* through *g* until the response is firm.

Individual Test
  Call on several children for *b* and *c*.

activities in Project MATH develop mathematical skills and tie them to everyday social use; however, the program does not provide instructions regarding teacher behavior at the level of detail that programs such as DISTAR do.

The entire Project MATH curriculum is underpinned by the concept of learning as an interactive process. Each lesson is presented visually so that the teacher can identify immediately the input-output mode of the teacher and student, the major strand and area of instruction, and an abbreviated objective. Although the lessons include types of questions a teacher may ask (Exhibit 8–18), it is the teacher's responsibility to sequence the questions in relation to specific behavioral objectives.

To address the question of social utility of learned mathematics concepts and skills, Project MATH provides Social Utilization Units (SUUs) with ideas for learning projects and experiences that will help students recognize the relationship between mathematics and daily living (Exhibit 8–19). The

Exhibit 8–18 Sample Lesson in Project MATH

LEVEL 3   **M366**

Project MATH Instructional Guide

STRAND	Measurement
AREA	Graphing
CONCEPT	Graph

OUTPUT

BEHAVIORAL OBJECTIVE	⟨illegible⟩ Presents picture graphs.	**LEARNER** States what the picture graphs show.

ACTIVITIES

1. Reading a Picture Graph. Present the learners with a picture such as the one illustrated. Say, "This is called a picture graph. It tells us something about the boys and girls whose names are on it. Each circle stands for one day absent during the month of September. Joe was absent 4 days during September. How many days was Mary absent?" Then ask these questions: (a) Who was absent the most during September? (b) Who had the best attendance record? (c) Did any two have the same record? (d) Who has the better record, George or Alice? (e) What two students have the best records?

JOE	O O O O
MARY	O O O O O O
GEORGE	O
ALICE	O O O
MARK	O
CHRIS	O O O O O

2. On Your Own. Present the learners with a picture graph representing the number of glasses of milk drunk by various learners in one day. (See illustration.)

Call on different learner to answer the following questions:
(a) How many glasses of milk did Edward drink?
(b) Who drank the most milk in one day? (c) Which two drank the same number of glasses of milk?
(d) Who drank the least amount of milk? (e) Who drank more milk, Melanie or Jean?

ALICIA
JACK
JONATHAN
JOHANNA
JEAN
MELANIE
EDWARD

SUPPLEMENTAL ACTIVITIES M366: a, b, c.

MATERIALS Picture graphs as illustrated.

EVALUATION

Present a picture graph of learners who have done homework assignments. Ask appropriate questions, and have the learner answer them by referring to the graph.

© 1977 EDUCATIONAL DEVELOPMENT CORPORATION

Source: Reprinted from *Project MATH, Instructional Guide,* by J. Cawley, A. Fitzmaurice, H. Goodstein, A. Lepore, R. Sedlak, and V. Althaus with permission of the publisher. © 1977, Educational Development Corporation.

Exhibit 8–19 Social Utilization Unit: Travel and Vacations

Social Emphases

1. Net cost factor of various forms of travel
2. The relationship of cost and time when travel and vacation plans are made
3. Planning for acquisition and expenditure of resources for travel and vacation

Necessary Skills

1. Reading maps, mileage charts, and/or time tables
2. Computing costs in terms of dollars and cents to the sums less than tens of thousands
3. Operations on whole numbers, including addition and subtraction of five-digit columns, division of two-digit by three-digit numbers (Instructor should assist where necessary.)

Introduction

This SUU may be introduced by one or both of the following activities.

(1) Have the learners indicate vacation preferences. List these on the chalkboard. Elicit a list of vacations that the learners have taken. Examine the relationship between preferences and actual vacations that have been taken. Indicate that learners should value their ideas about vacations because they will ultimately reach an age when they will make decisions on vacations and travel.

(2) Obtain a few brochures or advertisements on travel plans. Suggest that although it isn't possible to visit these places now, the group could simulate such visits in class. The group could select three of four places to visit (Caribbean, Washington, Alaska, Europe). Elicit discussion as to reasons why some of these are preferred. Discuss accordingly, highlighting some major factors.

Procedure

Suggest that the learners select three or four ideal vacation spots and develop a plan to simulate and examine them. The learners could select vacations in areas or regions that are quite different from one another (e.g., Caribbean and Alaska in wintertime). Suggest two activities. The first activity is an actual simulation of the vacation. The second activity is an actual plan for the vacation in terms of cost and time.

One set of learners could assume responsibility for Alaska, another for Washington, and so forth. The format of the chart may vary.

Probe Questions

Which of the various locations require commercial forms of travel (i.e., Caribbean—boat or plane) and which allow you private means of travel (i.e., Alaska—drive)? Which combination of travel to each place is the cheapest, fastest? Are there combinations of travel that make the combination of time and cost better deals? What is the total cost of a trip to one or more places? Which aspects of the vacation cost the most (travel, food, and lodging)? Does this combination vary (i.e., if you go by car and have to eat and stay over)? What is the value of certain kinds of travel for one person versus four persons? Can you afford a vacation? What type? Will you save your money for a vacation after you begin to work?

Procedure II

One of the major factors to be considered in vacation planning is the "off season." Discuss the concept of "off-season" travel, and repeat the analysis in the previous chart with this in mind. Consider also the possibility of travel packages where one price includes most of the costs.

Probe Questions

Why are the rates cheaper during "off-season" than during the height of the season? Does a place such as Washington have an "off-season" such as a resort in the Caribbean? What about foreign travel? If you live in New York, for example, can you go to Europe as cheaply as you can go to California? What are some of the reasons why you might go one place in spite of the cost? Are there places nearby that provide many of the same activities and advantages as those studied? How much can be saved in time and money by going closer to home?

Extension

This SUU may be extended by having individuals report on cultural, historical, or other aspects of a certain place. Written reports can be prepared and a brochure designed for members of the group.

		Caribbean	Alaska	Washington, D.C.
Distance from present location				
Means of travel				
Length of travel time	(one-way/ round trip)			
Cost of travel				
Lodging				
Food				
Other expenses				
Other				

Source: Reprinted from *Project MATH. Instructional Guide,* by J. Cawley, A. Fitzmaurice, H. Goodstein, A. Lepore, R. Sedlak, and V. Althaus with permission of the publisher. © 1977, Educational Development Corporation.

activities are also intended to promote generalization of learned skills. Many of the SUUs contain probe questions that can be used to question various kinds of skills, but they do not include specific suggestions for presenting the questions. Ordering and grouping of questions and corrective procedures are left to the teacher. Similarly, the teacher must evaluate the activity.

Understanding Questions: Supportive Reading Skills

One of few efforts to use questions as a means for reaching specific objectives is the Understanding Questions: Supportive Reading Skills kit (Boning, 1974). This kit is accompanied by a Teacher Manual and set of pre- and post-tests that have been designed expressly to teach students the function and meaning of different questions and question words. Multiple choice questions are presented in sequential lessons (student booklets), from least difficult to most difficult in terms of such elements as vocabulary, type of question, length of the question, and number of answer choices. Exhibit 8–20 presents sample questions from an initial and advance lesson.

RESEARCH ON TEACHER QUESTIONING

The educational significance of teacher questioning is well documented (Adams, 1964; Armstrong, 1977; Aschner, 1961; Gall, 1970). Numerous educational researchers (Belch, 1975; Borg, Kelley, Langer, & Gall, 1970; Loughlin, 1961; Zahorick, 1974) have suggested that proficiency in the use of questions and questioning tactics is closely tied to overall teacher competency. Until recently, teacher questions have been assessed in terms of the *kinds* of questions asked, i.e., higher or lower order questions (Gall, 1970), rather than in terms of the *functions* of those questions in helping students to master educational objectives.

Research on the kinds of questions teachers ask reveals that as many as 70% of all questions are wh- questions (Belch, 1975). Investigations have also confirmed the informal observation that the frequency of questions asked in teacher-student interactions in regular classrooms (Floyd, 1960; Moyer, 1966; Schreiber, 1967; Stevens, 1912) and special education settings (Fine, Allen, & Medvene, 1968; Lynch & Ames, 1972) is high. Ultimately, research has indicated that the type of question a teacher asks may not be nearly so critical as the manner in which the teacher applies the question. Indeed, it has been shown that selective, sequenced, and response-dependent questioning improves the performance of both handicapped (Armstrong, 1977; Belch, 1978; Hendrickson & Stowitschek, 1980; Hillman, 1960; Stowitschek & Armstrong-Iacino, 1978) and gifted learners

Exhibit 8–20 Sample Exercises from Understanding Questions

Source: Reprinted from *Understanding Questions: Supportive Reading Skills,* by R.A. Boning, with permission from the publisher. © 1974, 1981 Barnell-Loft Company.

(Gallagher, Aschner, & Jenne, 1967) and may be the key to effective use of questioning by teachers.

To date, the majority of investigations on the effects of teacher questions on student performance have been correlational; investigators have studied teacher responses and student responses separately. The results have been conflicting and inconclusive (Okey & Humphreys, 1974). Relatively few attempts have been made to determine directly and systematically the functional relationship between teacher questioning behavior and subsequent student responding. The need to validate questioning tactics and to clarify the relationship between teacher questions and pupil performance is as great today as it was when Stevens observed teacher questioning behavior in 1912 (Gall, 1970).

There have been efforts to validate the use of diagnostic questioning tactics in one-to-one interactions with children (Borg et al., 1970; Hendrickson & Stowitschek, 1980; Stowitschek & Armstrong-Iacino, 1978; Stowitschek & Hofmeister, 1974). Researchers have found that a number of student behaviors can be modified in a positive manner with the careful and systematic implementation of diagnostic questioning sequences as remedial tactics. This approach provides ongoing evaluative information both on the student's progress and on the effectiveness of the tactic itself. Unlike most teaching tactics, questioning tactics can enable the teacher to pinpoint errors precisely and apply further remediation immediately. In addition, questioning sequences can be learned by teacher-trainees with relative ease, and it is one of the tutorial formats used most readily in the classroom once it has been learned (Stowitschek & Hofmeister, 1974).

Given the conflicting results of research on questioning tactics, the advice of Gall (1970) may be as pertinent to teachers as any research "evidence." Gall (1970) suggested that, instead of trying to teach by using several categories of questions, teachers should simply (1) define the educational objective and (2) delineate questions and questioning sequences to meet the objective. Furthermore, given the lack of validation data on questioning tactics, it behooves every teacher to evaluate the effectiveness of each questioning tactic he or she employs. Although remedial tactics have been the recent focus of researchers and educators, the potential instructional worth of setting event questions should not be overlooked by teachers. Because teaching is an interactive process (Flanders, 1960) and questions are a primary means by which teachers initiate and maintain interaction with students, it is wise for all teachers to learn to design and use effective questioning tactics.

Chapter 9

Small-Group Applications of Direct Teaching

The teaching format or framework of instruction clearly affects any teaching tactic employed. Most teaching with children occurs outside the one-to-one format. Possible formats include whole class discussions, small-group exercises (e.g., reading circle), group-individualized activities (seat work or desk work), and other less typical formats, with the group-individualized format predominating in many special education classrooms (Shores, 1977). The basic elements of successful teacher-child interaction are consistent across these formats, but there are some critical differences in their application under group and group-individualized formats: differences in logistical organization, management of (problem) behavior, pacing, and presentation tactics.

Many graduates of special education training programs have found great difficulty in applying what they practiced in pre-service practica to the in-service classroom (Shores & Stowitschek, 1975). In practica, the pre-service teacher-trainee often teaches a "program" to an assigned child. Once in student teaching, the trainee may do little more than adopt the presentation mode (whether systematic or not) already established by the supervising teacher and may not be able to practice prescribed tactics across teaching formats.

The following two representative classroom situations illustrate what may happen in small-group teaching formats and how these events may affect the participating children, especially in terms of (1) the amount of time that the children are allowed to engage in appropriate practice and (2) the amount of time that the teacher spends on events where children are not engaged in appropriate practice.

10:20 A.M.   Mr. Zzidd says, "It's time for group reading. I only want six at a time." The teacher is sitting down. Some of the eight participating children are still working to complete the worksheet assigned during the previous period, while others are scooting chairs across the room to the group circle and still others are getting books out of desks, talking, and so on. Mr. Zzidd begins to chastise children for being late. The children are shuffling from one chair to the next, since they are permitted to sit in different places each day because the teacher does not want to stifle individuality of choice. The teacher has begun describing the lesson.

10:28 A.M.   As usual, Mr. Zzidd calls on the first child on his left (Johnny) to read. He asks Johnny to read two pages while the other children are to follow along in the book. Six of the eight children are beginning to fidget. Some are reading ahead; two are flipping through the book, looking for pictures; and the two on the far right of the circle are engaged in an elbow prodding match. Sally, who is sitting next to Johnny, is following along at the same place in the reader. The teacher stops Johnny and tells the children to "listen up."

10:36 A.M.   Mr. Zzidd says, "Johnny, you had better read more carefully next time; you mispronounced at least seven of the last fifteen words." He then proceeds to ask Johnny a series of comprehension questions. The children's attention wanders, and they return to fidgeting. The teacher shushes the children repeatedly, saying "It's Johnny's turn, wait your turn." and "Sally, you especially had better pay attention because your turn is coming up next."

10:42 A.M.   The teacher calls on Sally to read, and a similar sequence of events occurs; however, now Johnny is busily engaged in pulling out his lower lip, trying to examine it. His reader has slipped off his lap.

11:10 A.M.   Mr. Zzidd says, "It's time to return to your desks for spelling." and talks to Casandra (the fourth child in the circle) "Casandra, we'll have to start with you next time, so long as my memory holds. The rest of you had better show me some improved behavior next time." Before he has finished the last sentence, half of the children have begun shuffling their chairs and moving back to their desks.

In the entire 50-minute period, only three of the eight children had had the opportunity to participate in exercises directly related to the purpose of the reading circle (oral reading fluency, reading comprehension). One child, Sally, who may have been engaged in an analogous response (silent reading) was not reinforced, but was cautioned to do what she was already doing. At this rate, assuming that no children were absent, each child would be able to practice the intended reading responses less than twice per week. Eight of the 50 minutes were lost in "preparations," which also diminished the opportunity for practice. The children who engaged in appropriate practice did so in a continuous time block; therefore, their oral reading may or may not have been spontaneous, since they knew what part they would read and had the opportunity to read ahead. The remaining children practiced fidgeting, possibly undesirable reading behaviors, and misbehaviors. The general threat would probably have no positive effect.

Ms. Zatts had the good fortune to acquire the help of a reliable volunteer. She viewed this as a boon, because now she could give more individual attention, not necessarily in a one-to-one format,

but in a small-group format. She placed into a small group four children who needed extra practice in phonics and began teaching.

Ms. Zatts: "Today we're going to work on blending sounds as a group. Sometimes I will ask all of you to answer me at once. Other times I will ask each of you to give me an answer. Ready?" (*writes several consonant-vowel blends on the board and places her finger beside the first sound*). "Tersell, look at the board. Class, what's this sound?"

Sammy: "*sp*"
Jane: "*sp*" (*½ second later*)
Tersell: "*sh*"
Angela: No response
(The group responds over a period of 2 seconds).

Ms. Zatts: "Good answer. Can you say the next sound?" (*runs her finger under the next sound blend*)

Sammy: "*sk*"
Jane: "*sp*"
Tersell: "*ks*"
Angela: (*slides down in chair*)

Ms. Zatts: "Angela, don't slump in your chair." (*holding Angela's arm*) "Sammy, what's that sound?"

Sammy: "*sk*"
Ms. Zatts: "Jane, what's this sound?"
Jane: "*sk*"
Ms. Zatts: "Right. Tersell, what's this sound?"
Tersell: "*sk*, like my skates."
Ms. Zatts: "Good. Angela . . . back in your seat, Tersell . . . Angela, what's this sound?"
Angela: "*sk*"
Ms. Zatts: "Well, I'm glad you're all getting it right and doing so well. Here's the next sound."
Tersell: "*sn*"
Ms. Zatts: "Right, Tersell. What is it, group . . . answer, group."
Sammy: "*sn*"
Tersell: "*sm*"
Jane: "*sn*"
Angela: (No response)
Ms. Zatts: "Say it a little louder, Jane. The next sound is *sl*. Now . . ." (*places her palm underneath the word on the board*)
Tersell: "*sl*"
Ms. Zatts: "Good, Tersell. That's right, but everybody's not saying it together. C'mon, turn around."
Class: "*sl*"
(Some say it sooner, some later; Angela watches Tersell's lips and imitates.)

Ms. Zatts: "Good thinking, Angela. Jane, how do you say this one?" (points to *st*)

Class: *"sn"* (Jane: *"st "*)

Ms. Zatts: "No. First Jane. Jane, what's this sound?"

Jane: *"st"*

Ms. Zatts: "Sammy, turn around and sit up straight. Okay, everybody, what's this one?"

Sammy: *"st"*

Jane: *"st"*

Tersell: *"st"*

Angela: "It's the hissy one."

Ms. Zatts: "Jane . . . Quiet, Angela . . . Jane, what's that sound?"

Jane: *"st"*

Ms. Zatts: "Now you are getting it, Jane."

This pattern of dialogue continues throughout the 20-minute period with the exception that the children become increasingly fidgety and Ms. Zatts becomes increasingly reprimanding.

In this phonics practice session, Ms. Zatts attempted to obtain responses from the group, as well as from individuals. Some children responded to the stimuli (sound blends) written on the board; other children did not respond at all, imitated other children, or made incorrect responses. All this took place almost simultaneously. In many instances, all responses may have been rewarded. Children who responded early (e.g., Tersell) were praised, possibly for not responding with the group, and children who responded late were praised, possibly for responding late. Because the children did not all respond at the same time, the teacher could not easily discern whose response was correct, whose was incorrect, and whose was imitated. Children who responded incorrectly, as well as those who responded correctly, were praised. Teacher time was spent getting the children to sit up, turn around, look at the teacher, and speak loudly, because they had not been informed in advance what behavior was expected of them. If the teacher's questions varied in type or in timing, the children often responded at different times. Also, the teacher's requests for responses were consistently different, which reduced their potential for cueing the children to respond at a specific point. Individual responses were requested either from the child who had already responded correctly (Jane) or from each individual in the group, regardless of that child's response.

Teaching children individually can be either helpful or a waste of time, particularly if the teacher does all the talking and gives the child little opportunity to respond. Direct teaching in a group can multiply this waste if the group is not managed well. On the other hand, efficient small-group teaching can multiply the benefits obtainable from teaching each child individually. The gains made in, say, five indi-

vidual tutoring sessions, each lasting 20 minutes, can be made in a single session lasting 20 minutes.

GROUP CIRCLE AND GROUP RESPONSE FORMATS

In the group circle format, 5 to 10 children are seated in a semicircle in front of the teacher, and the teacher calls on one child at a time to respond, selecting the child at random or as hands are raised. In the group response format, 3 to 12 children (usually 3 to 5) are seated in front of the teacher in one or two semicircular rows, and children respond simultaneously, although they are occasionally asked to respond individually.

Table 9-1 illustrates the similarities and differences of group circle and group response formats in reference to their basic instruction attributes. The selection of either a group circle format or a group response format is dependent on the type of skill to be taught. If the intent is to provide practice on chain responses, problems that can be solved orally, or responses that can vary in wording or rate (e.g., reading fluency, silent reading paired with answers to comprehension questions, reading and solving math story problems), a group circle format may be appropriate. If the intent is to teach simple, rote responses or concept formation discrimi-

Table 9-1 Instructional Attributes of Systematic Group Circle and Group Response Formats

Attributes	Group Circle	Group Response
Grouping children	X	X
Focusing on the task (the children do the responding)	X	X
Rules for behavior	X	X
Rules for responding		X
Signals for responding		X
Consistency of presentation wording	X	X
Choral responding		X
Teaching to the child who performs at the lowest skill level	X	X
Reinforcing correct responding	X	X
Pacing		X
Correcting errors	X	X

nations (e.g., phonic or phonemic unit practice, counting, math combinations, labeling pictures), a group response format may be appropriate.

Grouping Children

In both formats, it is important to place children who are at similar skill levels in the same group. Proper grouping makes it unnecessary for children who perform at higher skill levels to wait for other children to reach the same level of performance. It also avoids placing children who perform at lower skill levels in a situation where they must struggle constantly to keep up with the others. When a group response format is selected, it is crucial that the children who are performing at about the same skill level be grouped together. Otherwise, the lower performing children may delay the progress of the higher performing children. If, after a day or two of teaching with a group of children, it becomes obvious that there are two or more distinct levels of performance, it is strongly recommended that the group be split into two separate groups or that children who perform at one or the other level be recombined with another more similar group of children.

Focusing on the Task

Although focusing on the task is a genuine concern of all systematic instruction, it warrants particular attention in reference to group teaching. Teachers may "steal the show," and children may spend a great deal of time not engaged in task responding. In fact, many of the other attributes stem from this basic concern (cf. Engelmann, 1970).

Rules for Behavior

In order to avoid behavior problems, teachers may state the rules for behavior before they begin teaching. Rules for behavior are particularly important in group teaching formats, because the opportunities for misbehaving are greater in group teaching than in one-to-one teaching and the time wasted in handling behavior problems is multiplied by the number of children in the group. Besides the teacher stating three or four rules, such as "sit tall," "hands to yourself," "look at the teacher!" it is often useful to have them posted in a visible location (e.g., on the blackboard) and, for the first few sessions, to have the children orally repeat the rules. Later, a simple reminder of the rules may be all that is necessary to maintain order when an occasional disruption occurs. Verbal praise for good behavior can be helpful when specific rules that were followed can be cited by the teacher. Once children begin responding in the group, the need to cite the rules diminishes because the engaged response time tends to replace the occurrences of disruptive behavior.

Rules for Responding

Group teaching is more efficient when the children know how and when to respond early in the teaching sessions. Often, by establishing rules for responding, the teacher can avoid potentially frustrating or negative interactions that result from misunderstandings about what is expected. Depending on the group format and the task demands, three or four rules, such as "talk loudly, wait your turn, stop at the end of the sentence," can help prevent unnecessary interruptions or delays in children's responding to the task.

Signals for Responding

This feature is also unique to the group response format. Because it is essential that children know when to respond and that they respond in unison at certain times and individually at other times, consistency in the use of signals for responding is paramount. The signal may be a finger placed on the board, a finger tap on a page, or a hand lowered. Signals are usually preceded by a "get ready" statement. Typically, group response formats, such as that used in DISTAR Reading, include signals for cueing different practice responses (e.g., saying sounds separately, then together). When the use of signals becomes "second nature" to teachers, not only is the efficiency of their teaching improved, but also the "mechanistic" appearances of group responding often vanish.

Consistency of Presentation Wording

Many teachers play "pick a cue" games (Day, 1979) with children, albeit unwittingly. Adults have been encouraged not only to repeat a statement or question when other adults do not understand it the first time, but also to paraphrase it. Many teachers seem to have extrapolated this into the notion that it is good teaching to present something in several different ways *before* the child is required to respond. It seems that the less readily a child responds, the greater the number and variety of cues for responding thrown at the child, and the more bewildering it is.

Inconsistency in the wording of teacher cues may make the students uncertain about the exact task that is related to the instructional cues presented by teachers. Hence, students are faced with the dilemma of trying to decide which response is desired. One consistently worded cue for responding is all that should be used, particularly in the early stages of instruction. In any case, the set of statements or questions employed to cue a response should be (1) consistently worded in the same way, (2) closely related to the types of cues the children are confronted with in other situations, and (3) tested to make sure the children understand what response is expected.

Choral Responding

In the group response format, children typically respond in unison for the majority of the teaching session. Otherwise, there would be little reason to place children in a group rather than conducting one-on-one tutorial sessions. Although some educators consider this attribute of the group response format "dehumanizing" or "mechanistic," they do not generally object to it when its purpose is to improve musical abilities (e.g., choral singing, class sing-alongs) or recreational abilities (e.g., tug-of-war, rally sprints). Why should it be objectionable when it is used for reading, math, or language development? When used properly, group response formats are combined with other teaching formats for multiple levels of exposure and responding for a given skill. Typically, group responding is intended to instill in children's repertoires the desired responses at levels that will maximize the chances of success when these responses are required under varied conditions.

Choral responding can maximize teaching efficiency, because the number of responses obtainable in a group session is multiplied over the number obtained in an individual session by the number of children who participate; for example, if 150 child responses can be obtained in a 10-minute individual session, 750 responses can be obtained in the same amount of time with a group of five children.

Teaching to the Lowest Performing Child

If the object of small-group teaching is to provide individualized instruction within a group, then no member of the group should be experiencing failure in performing the task. As mentioned earlier, children should be grouped according to similarities in performance. When a child makes an error, the error should be corrected immediately and the child should make the correct response with the rest of the group before proceeding. In this way, all children in the group proceed at similar rates. If some children continue to err frequently over time, regrouping of children should be considered.

Reinforcing Correct Responding

Verbal praise contingent on correct responses is an integral element of systematic group teaching formats (see Chapter 5). The opportunity for praise is great in group formats. However, praising can quite rapidly become routine and ineffective if it is not varied considerably in the type of teacher comments made, the enthusiasm exuded, and the proportion (schedule) of praise to correct responses. Authors of programs that employ group response formats often suggest that teachers use pointed praise, verbalizing the task

performed correctly, as well as commending the performance.

Pacing

Although verbal praise for correct responding and attending to task is an extremely important motivation technique, the rate at which presentations are made is also important in this regard. For most teaching formats, particularly for the group response format, fast-paced presentations and changes in the tempo, verbal stress, and intonation all help to maintain interest and increase the opportunity to respond. Pacing is often the difference between "going through the motions" of group teaching and proficient group teaching.

Correcting Errors

When a child responds incorrectly in the group circle format, the correction may be as simple as a reminder and a request that the child repeat the task correctly. Detecting individual errors in group response formats is somewhat more difficult than it is in other formats, but it is more easily done when the group responds at exactly the same moment. Typically, error correction involves modeling, requesting an individual response, and, once a correct response has been obtained, having the group return to an earlier part in the program and repeat the entire task.

GUIDELINES FOR GROUP CIRCLE TEACHING

Systematic applications of group circle teaching have certain basic tenets in common:

1. *The entire group should participate.* Although children typically respond one at a time in a group circle, the teacher must avoid spending too much time with one child. It is often tempting to dwell either on a correct response that shows a particular child's brightness or on an error response that shows another child's need for more help. Succumbing to these temptations is probably the most significant cause of management and instructional problems in group circle teaching, because the rest of the children in the group are tempted to engage in other activities that may be counterproductive. As a rule (although it varies with the content of instruction), a teacher should spend no more than 15 to 20 seconds with a given child.
2. *Initially, stimulus presentations and corresponding responses by children should be divided into the shortest (smallest) meaningful units.* Instead of having one child read entire pages or passages aloud, the teacher

should ask each child to read no more than one or two sentences. With a math story problem, one child can read the problem, another child can construct the equation, and another child can solve the constructed equation. Dividing the stimulus presentation and response into the shortest meaningful units gives more children an opportunity to participate and keeps the other children effectively attending to what the called-upon child is doing.

3. *The teacher should call on children at random.* If there is no pattern that tells children when they are to be called upon, they will pay more attention. This alertness gives every child an equal chance to engage in the responses necessary to learn the instructional task. It also helps the teacher avoid constantly calling on "the good student" or on "the poor student" and, thus, does not single out one student as superior or inferior to the rest of the children in the group.

4. *All children should know what they should be doing when they have not been called upon.* For instance, if one child in a reading circle has been called upon to read a sentence aloud, the other children should read the sentence silently to ensure that they are attending to the task at hand. Teachers should vary the point at which they call upon another child to read, because this encourages all the other children to follow along with the called-upon child (e.g., call on a child to pick up the reading in the middle of a sentence at one time, another child after two sentences, and another child after one sentence, but do this at random).

5. *The planned activity should be interspersed with opportunities for child-initiated responding.* Variety in the teaching session heightens the children's interest and broadens response applications. For example, when oral reading is the planned activity, the teacher may ask any student who wishes to respond to explain or make inferences about the content of a passage that has been read aloud.

The following is an example of a group circle format systematically applied:

As the hands on the clock indicate 10 o'clock, five of the children in Ms. Rousette's class remove their readers from their desks and take their usual seats around a circular table. The remaining children in the class stay at their desks, open the reading workbook to the page indicated on the blackboard, and begin individual work. Ms. Rousette praises the class for "getting ready on time" and sits down at the table with the five children: Billy, Jose, Shauna, Judy, and Krista. Presenta-

tion materials had been prepared the previous afternoon and are at the table, ready for immediate use.

Ms. Rousette: "All right, children, we are going to read the story in the series together, but first let's review the rules for group circle. Judy, what is the first rule?"

Judy: "Hold my reader on the top of the table."

Ms. Rousette: "Good, Judy. Krista, what is the second rule?"

Krista: "Quietly wait my turn to read."

Ms. Rousette: "Jose, what is the third rule?"

Jose: "I forgot."

Ms. Rousette: "Children, help Jose out."

Children: "Follow along with my finger."

Ms. Rousette: "Everybody say it once more."

Children: "Follow along with my finger."

Ms. Rousette: "Good. Jose . . . and Billy, the last rule?"

Billy: "Stop at the end of a sentence."

Ms. Rousette: "That's great. Now, everyone, repeat them with me."

(Ms. Rousette and the class read the rules.)

Ms. Rousette: "Let's begin with Krista reading the first sentence."

(Krista reads the first sentence fluently.)

Ms. Rousette: "That's just fine, Krista. Billy . . ."

(Jose begins to put his head under the table.)

Ms. Rousette: "I really like the way Judy, Shauna, and Billy are following along in their books while someone else reads."

(Jose begins to follow along. Billy reads the first sentence, but continues beyond it.)

Ms. Rousette: "STOP." (*calls on Judy*)

(Judy reads the next sentence.)

Ms. Rousette: "Good reading, Judy. What is a corral?"

(Judy answers correctly.)

Ms. Rousette: "That's an on target answer. Billy, please read the next sentence."

(Billy reads the next sentence fluently and stops at the end.)

Ms. Rousette: "Good stopping at the end of the sentence, Billy. Jose, you're really on track now. Shauna?"

(Shauna reads, but skips a word.)

Ms. Rousette: "Go back and try that sentence again, Shauna."

(Shauna reads the sentence and inserts the incorrect word. The children raise their hands.)

Ms. Rousette: "What word should Shauna use?"

(The children answer. Shauna rereads the sentence correctly.)

Ms. Rousette: "Shauna, why were the horses afraid?"

(Shauna answers correctly.)

Ms. Rousette: "Great, you got the point of the story right away, Shauna."

This process of calling on children at random, inserting single comprehension questions, and verbally commending correct responses continued for approximately 20 minutes (until the end of the story). During that time, each child had the opportunity to respond orally at least eight times and answer at least five questions. The indicator behavior of following with their fingers in the book while another child was reading continued throughout the session but was dropped in later sessions. Jose disrupted the session only once.

Instructional Programs Using Group Circle and Group Response Formats

Among the published materials that have incorporated group circle and group response teaching approaches, the Direct Instruction Model (Engelmann, 1970) is the most prominent. These programs contain not only group teaching presentation formats, but also other teaching strategies and systematically sequenced, step-by-step curriculum materials.

DISTAR Reading, Arithmetic, and Language

The first of the published instructional programs to employ systematic group teaching tactics was the Direct Instruction System for Teaching Arithmetic and Reading (DISTAR; Engelmann & Bruner, 1974; Engelmann & Carnine, 1975; Engelmann & Osborne, 1976). The principal teaching approach is the small-group format. Generally, students respond in unison, but there are individual turns. Errors made by a student are corrected immediately, and correct responding by that student is worked back into the group response format. Each lesson is tightly scripted as to both the teacher's and the student's actions and verbalizations (Exhibit 9–1). Teachers provide a verbal signal ("Get ready."), alerting students that a response is expected, followed by a visual hand signal (e.g., finger touching the presentation booklet or hand dropped).

When requesting either group or individual responses, three principal modes of cues are presented: model, lead, independent (test).

Type of Cue	Teacher Verbalization
Model	"My turn: a a a."
Lead	"Say it with me. Get ready: a a a."
Independent	"Now you say it. Get ready."

Exhibit 9–1 Sample Script for Group Teaching

SOUNDS

TASK 1 Teaching a as in and

a. Point to a. You're going to learn this sound.
b. My turn. When I touch it, I'll say it. I'll keep on saying it as long as I touch it.
c. (Pause.) Touch a and say: aaa. Lift your finger.
d. Again. Touch a for a longer time and say: aaaaaa. Lift your finger.
e. Again. Touch a for a shorter time and say: aaaa. Lift your finger.

TASK 2 Children identify a

a. Point to a. Your turn. When I touch it, you say it. Keep on saying it as long as I touch it.
b. (Pause.) Get ready. Touch a. The children say aaa. Lift your finger.

To correct	1. Say the correct sound immediately. aaa.
	2. Say it with me.
	3. Point to a. Get ready. Touch a. Say aaa with the children.
	4. Again. Repeat step 3.
	5. Repeat a and b.

c. Again. Repeat b two times.

Source: From DISTAR® Reading I, *Teacher's Guide*, p. 14, by Siegfried Engelmann and Elaine C. Bruner. © 1974, 1969, Science Research Associates, Inc. Reprinted by permission of the publisher.

Of course, these cues occur in varying combinations and differing orders. In some instruction sequences, the lead prompt is used only as part of a correction procedure. The verbal statements themselves change to fit the task. Specific instructions for initiating and continuing the program are included in a teacher's guide, often in the form of steps, as for grouping children (see Exhibit 9–2). The basic teaching protocol is supported by the teacher's guide, which provides both rules and rationale, such as "Pace tasks appropriately" (see Exhibit 9–3).

In the DISTAR program, teachers must achieve control over their own presentation behavior in order to teach efficiently and effectively. Thus, each potential problem area is treated in the guide (e.g., Exhibit 9–4) and emphasized in the DISTAR training workshops, which are routinely held.

The DISTAR language and arithmetic programs, although adjusted to fit the particular curricula, follow the same basic teaching approach (Exhibits 9–5 and 9–6).

Corrective Reading Program

Engelmann and associates developed the Corrective Reading Program for middle and upper elementary school-aged children and for older children who have failed to acquire adequate reading, decoding, and comprehension skills. The 1975 version, which is still in use, consists of three components: (1) small-group word attack skill practice, (2) indi-

Exhibit 9–2 Instructions for Grouping

1. Place all the children who make no errors in one group.

2. Unless the group is too large, add to it all the children who make one error. This is your top group.

3. Rank all the children who score two or more errors.

4. Place the five or six children who made the highest number of errors in one group. This is your lowest performing group.

5. Place the remaining children in the middle group.

Your initial grouping of the children should follow these rules:

1. Avoid dividing the class into more than three small groups.

2. Make the lowest-performing group the smallest.

3. The highest-performing group should be the largest.

Source: From DISTAR® Reading I. *Teacher's Guide.* p. 6, by Siegfried Engelmann and Elaine C. Bruner. © 1974, 1969, Science Research Associates, Inc. Reprinted by permission of the publisher.

Exhibit 9–3 Pacing Instructions

5. Pace tasks appropriately. Pacing is one of the more difficult presentational skills to master. Pacing is the rate at which different parts of the task are presented. All portions of a task should not be presented at the same rate.

Different pacing is specified throughout the manual. Many of the formats contain instructions "pause one second," or "pause three seconds."

Note that all signals are paced with the same timing. The children learn that the signal will follow one second after you stop talking in a task. Keep this interval constant.

Source: From DISTAR® Reading I. *Teacher's Guide.* p. 8. by Siegfried Engelmann and Elaine C. Bruner. © 1974, 1969, Science Research Associates, Inc. Reprinted by permission of the publisher.

vidual oral reading practice in a group circle format, and (3) individual study and oral reading to an assigned checker. Basically, the direct instruction strategy used in DISTAR is followed in the word attack skills component, with some variations; for example, the teacher may write the stimuli on the board (Exhibit 9–7).

In the group circle story reading activity, children respond individually; they take turns reading parts of the story and answering comprehension questions. Many of the direct instruction principles are retained. For example, there are explicit rules for behavior (Exhibit 9–8). One notable change from DISTAR is that the Corrective Reading Program includes a contingency system based on the awarding of points that may be exchanged for reinforcing events (Exhibit 9–9).

The 1978 edition of the program contains some rather significant changes from the first edition. First, three levels of decoding instruction in group response formats are presented in separate books. Second, the instruction focused on reading comprehension is expanded to include instruction in underlying concepts (Thinking Basics), thinking operations (Comprehension Skills), and the comprehension of written material (Concept Applications). The first two books of the comprehension series use a group response format, while the third book uses a group circle format.

Other Group Response Programs

Other programs that use a group response format are *Morphographic Spelling and Spelling Mastery* (Science Research Associates, 1980), *Corrective Mathematics* (Engelmann & Carnine, 1980), and *Mathematics Modules* (Engelmann & Steely, 1980). The Spelling Mastery Program is heavily teacher-directed at first, but it gradually allows the student to assume more independence in completing exercises. The remainder of these programs include group response instruction.

Since the Direct Instruction Model contains several instructional elements that may be considered generic, variations have been successfully employed to supplement existing curricula and programs. For example, the *Management System for Sullivan Programmed Reading* (Rosen, 1976) was designed to render the program more useful with reading-deficient children. Activities correspond to each of the programmed reading books in the series. One of the activities provides practice in reading aloud the sounds and words contained in the corresponding pages of the reading book. This activity is done with the children as a group, or it may be adapted by the teacher for use with one child at a time (Exhibit 9–10). Once criterion performance has been reached, the children practice reading sounds and words independently before they go on to the corresponding pages of the programmed reader. This supplement extended the life and utility of an instructional program that is found in many classrooms. The supplement updated the program and compensated for what many teachers had criticized as deficiencies or gaps in instruction.

Exhibit 9–4 Example of Potential Teacher Problem with DISTAR

Correct signal-violation mistakes by saying (if it is **a** Sounds or Sound-It-Out mistake):

You're early. Watch my finger.
Return your finger to the pointing position.
Get ready. Child responds again.
You're early. Watch my finger.
Let's try it again. Get ready. Touch.
Child responds as you touch.
Great! Now let's try it again.
Return to the beginning of the task.

Only if you consistently return to the beginning of the task after each signal-violation correction will the children learn to attend to your signal. Once they learn that you will repeat the task until they are all responding on signal, they will attend much more closely to the signal.

How to Point
■ Hold your finger about an inch from the page, just below the sound.
■ Be careful not to cover the sound—all the children must be able to see it.
■ Say "Get ready."
■ Hold your finger in the pointing position for at least *one second.*
■ Look at the sound to demonstrate to the children that they too should be looking at it.

Common Pointing Errors
■ Touching the sound
■ Not saying "Get ready"
■ Covering the sound
■ Pointing for less than one second

How to Touch
■ At the end of the one-second interval, move your finger quickly away from the page, then quickly and decisively touch the page just below the sound.
■ The instant your finger touches the page, look at the low-performing child in the group. See if he responded the instant you touched the sound.
■ Hold the touch for two seconds, then quickly and decisively pull your finger away from the page.

Common Touching Errors
■ Touching the sound before the one-second interval
■ Touching the sound indecisively
■ Covering the sound while touching it
■ Failing to look at the low performer the instant you touch the sound
■ Touching the sound for less than two seconds
■ Indecisively pulling your finger away from the page

Source: From DISTAR® Reading I, *Teacher's Guide.* pp. 9, 13, by Siegfried Engelmann and Elaine C. Bruner. © 1974, 1969, Science Research Associates, Inc. Reprinted by permission of the publisher.

Exhibit 9–5 Sample

TASK 4   Identity Statements
We're going to talk about these things. When I touch something, you tell me about it.

d. Point to the shoe.
   Everybody, what is this? Touch. *A shoe.*
e. Say the whole thing. Touch. *This is a shoe.*

Let's do that again.
f. What's this? Touch. *A shoe.*
g. Say the whole thing. Touch. *This is a shoe.*
   Repeat until all children responses are firm.

a. Point to the ball.
   Everybody, what is this? Touch. *A ball.*

Error
Children say the entire sentence.
Correction
1. Stop. My turn. What is this? Touch. *A ball.*
2. Your turn. What is this? Touch. *A ball.*
3. Now say the whole thing. Touch. *This is a ball.*
4. Repeat steps 2 and 3 until all children respond correctly.
5. Repeat a.

b. Say the whole thing. Touch. *This is a ball.*

Let's do that again.
c. What's this? Touch. *A ball.*
   Say the whole thing. Touch. *This is a ball.*
   Repeat c until all children's responses are firm.

h. Point to the dog.
   Everybody, what is this? Touch. *A dog.*
i. Say the whole thing. Touch. *This is a dog.*

Let's do that again.
j. What's this? Touch. *A dog.*
   Say the whole thing. Touch. *This is a dog.*
   Repeat *j* until all children's responses are firm.

Source: From DISTAR® Language I. *Teacher's Guide*, p. 20, by Siegfried Engelmann and Jean Osborn. © 1976, 1972, 1969. Science Research Associates, Inc. Reprinted by permission of the publisher.

The *Behavior Analysis Phonics Primer* (Becker & Jackson, 1974) was developed initially for use in the Behavior Analysis Follow Through Project. It focuses on phonetic skills that children need in order to begin work in programmed reading (Sullivan Associates, 1973). It also provides instructional activities to facilitate the transition into programmed reading. The *Primer* uses a group response teaching format, and there is a distinct emphasis on supplementing contingent teacher attention with a token economy approach (Exhibit 9–11).

RESEARCH ON SMALL-GROUP FORMATS

The empirical base for small-group teaching has been steadily increasing. Research has been conducted on elements of direct instruction, the Direct Instruction Model, and supplemental applications of the group response format.

Some of the most impressive research findings in education today are contained in program evaluations of the Direct Instruction Model. Stevens and Rosenshine (1981) identified four characteristics of effective instruction: "(1) it takes place in groups, (2) it is teacher directed, (3) it is academically focused, and (4) it is individualized" (p. 1). In their discussion of instruction conducted in groups, they pointed out that students who work in groups receive more demonstration and feedback from teachers than do students who work alone. They also noted that, although there is some contrast in the findings on group responding, the Oregon Direct Instruction Follow Through Program—which relies heavily on choral responses—has been the most successful of the Follow Through programs.

The impact of the Direct Instruction Model was reported in a national study of eight Follow Through models (Abt Associates, 1976, 1977). When the results of the Direct Instruction Model were compared with the results of control models, statistically and, possibly, educationally significant

Exhibit 9–6 Sample

TASK 1 ROTE COUNTING   Counting by One—New Numbers

Words spelled with extra letters should be held when they are said.

Group Activity

a. My turn. I'm going to count and end up with twelve.
    What number am I going to end up with?(Signal.) *12.*
    Yes, twelve.

b. Listen.Quickly count to 8.   Nniiinne, 10, 11, 12.
    Listen to the hard part. Nniiinne, 10, 11, 12.

c. When I drop my hand, say the hard part.Raise your hand.
    Nniiinne.Drop your hand and count with the children:
    10, 11, 12.

| To correct | If the children answer early or late, stop them immediately. Tell them to watch your signal. Repeat c. |

Repeat from "Raise your hand" as many as ten times if
the children need practice. After each series say: Again.

d. Now let's start counting with one and end up with twelve.
    (Pause.)   Get ready. Count.
    Count with the children on 10, 11, 12,
    (The children count from 1 to 12.)
    Repeat from "Get ready" several times if the children
    need practice. After each series say: Again.

e. All by yourself. Count and end up with twelve.(Pause.)
    Get ready. Count.*(The children count to 12.)*

| To correct | Count with the children on the difficult part of the series until they can do it alone. |

Repeat from "Get ready" as many as ten times if the
children need practice. After each series say: Again.

f. Good counting. You ended up wiiith (signal) *12.*

Individual Test

Call on several children for *e* and *f*. Concentrate on the
children who are having problems.

---

differences in achievement, cognitive, and affective tests supported the use of the Direct Instruction Model. In reference to reading, one conclusion contained in the report was that "the Direct Instruction Model is the only model which consistently produces substantial progress" (p. 155).

Citing this evaluation, Becker (1977) discussed the components of the model that may have contributed most to these findings. He considered the amount of teaching time devoted to a given subject area with specified teaching procedures a critical factor and referred to Rosenshine's (1977) conclusions that the Direct Instruction and Behavior Analysis Model showed more academic-engaged time than in other programs. As extended support for the direct instruction model, Becker and Gersten (1982) concluded from longitudinal follow-up research that, although the graduates of their program lose ground, they often perform significantly higher than do similar children in the community.

The Direct Instruction Model has also been successfully used outside the United States. Maags and Maags (1979) described nearly a decade of research and application of direct instruction in Australian regular and special education programs. They summarized their findings in the statement that "there is no other major output of acceptable educational research in Australia that has shown the results obtained by this body of Direct Instruction Research" (p. 32).

There have been several studies comparing group and individual instruction or comparing differing group makeup. For example, Biberdorf and Pear (1977) examined the differential effects of alternating presentations between two subjects and presenting the same stimuli to one subject. They reported that the "group" teaching was more efficient than the individual teaching and that each of the subjects in the teaching group learned some of the other subject's words in the picture naming task.

Exhibit 9–7 Board Exercise

Exercise F: Build-ups with **op**

1. (Write on the board: **op**.)

2. (Point to **op**. Pause.) WHAT WORD? (Signal.) (Correct mistakes.)

3. (Add **r** to beginning: **rop**. Point to word. Pause.) WHAT WORD NOW? (Signal.) (Correct mistakes.)

4. (Add **d** to beginning: **drop**. Point to word. Pause.) WHAT WORD NOW? (Signal.) (Correct mistakes.)

5. (Erase **dr** and add **sh** to beginning: **shop**. Point to word. Pause.) WHAT WORD NOW? (Signal.)

6. (Erase **sh**. Repeat steps 2-5 until firm.)

Source: From Corrective Reading Program. *Teacher's Management and Skills Manual*. p. 31. by Siegfried Engelmann et al. © 1975. 1973. Science Research Associates. Inc. Reprinted by permission of the publisher.

Exhibit 9–8 Rules for Responding

Exercise G: Teacher introduces rules for story reading

EVERYBODY, WE'RE GOING TO READ A STORY TOGETHER. EVERYBODY'S GOING TO
HAVE A FEW TURNS. I'LL CALL ON THE PEOPLE TO READ.
HERE ARE THE RULES THAT YOU ARE TO FOLLOW.

RULE 1: YOU FOLLOW WITH YOUR FINGER THE WORDS THAT ARE READ.
RULE 2: YOU READ LOUDLY WHEN THE TEACHER CALLS ON YOU.
RULE 3: YOU STOP AT THE END OF EACH SENTENCE.
RULE 4: YOU RAISE YOUR HAND WHEN YOU HEAR A MISTAKE.
RULE 5: YOU SAY NOTHING UNLESS THE TEACHER CALLS ON YOU.

ANY QUESTIONS? (Answer questions.)

Source: From Corrective Reading Program. *Teacher's Management and Skills Manual*. p. 48. by Siegfried Engelmann, et al. © 1975. 1973. Science Research Associates. Inc. Reprinted by permission of the publisher.

The importance of pacing and teacher proficiency in using a group presentation procedure was demonstrated in a study by Carnine (1976). In comparing a "slow-rate" presentation (e.g., pauses between presentations to look at lesson plans) with a "fast-rate" presentation (less than 1-second pause between presentations), Carnine found that not only was students' off task behavior less frequent under the "fast-rate" condition, but also the percentage of correct responses was higher.

The evaluation reports on the Direct Instruction Model and the current summation of advanced research on direct instruction (Stevens & Rosenshine, 1981) suggest that the small-group format applications of direct teaching tactics show the greatest promise for effective and efficient teaching. Based on the data at hand, wise teachers of mildly or moderately handicapped persons should seriously consider adopting small-group instruction as a mainstay of their classroom arsenal.

Exhibit 9–9 Error Data and Point Chart

Name _____

Error-Data and Point Chart No. _____

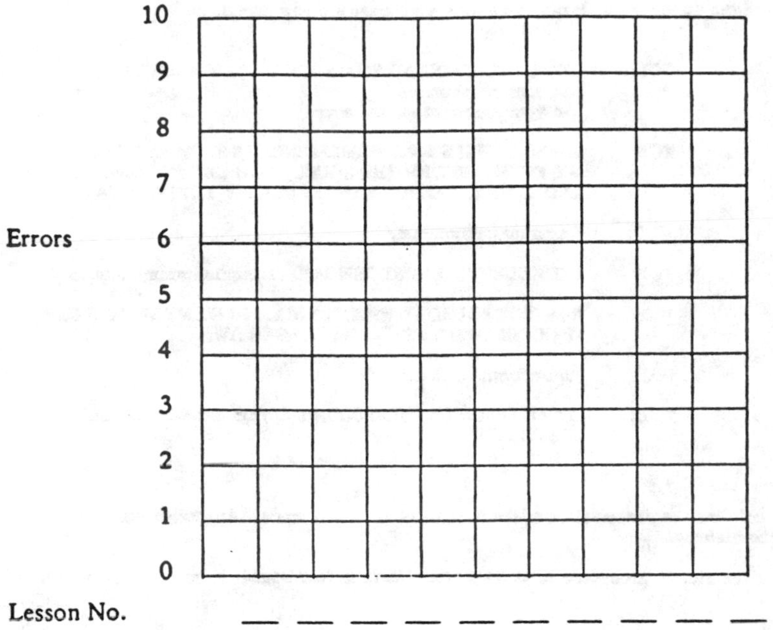

Errors

10
9
8
7
6
5
4
3
2
1
0

Lesson No.   _ _ _ _ _ _ _ _ _ _

Lesson No.									
Word Attack									
Group Reading									
1st Read Reading									
2nd Reading									
Bonus									
Total									

WEEKLY TOTALS

Total points for week	= _____	Total points for week	= _____
Total errors for week	= _____	Total errors for week	= _____
Divide errors by 5.----5⌐		Divide errors by 5.----5⌐	
Average errors for week	= _____	Average errors for week	= _____

Source: From Corrective Reading Program, *Teacher's Management and Skills Manual*, p. 6, by Siegfried Engelmann et al. © 1975, 1973, Science Research Associates, Inc. Reprinted by permission of the publisher.

Exhibit 9–10 Example of Small-Group Instruction Techniques

⟹ PRESENTING A NEW SOUND: Complex procedure

Here is an example of the dialogue that takes place when you present a <u>new</u> sound.

<u>MODEL</u>	1.	TCH:	LISTEN TO ME READ THIS SOUND. THIS SOUND IS /mmmmmmmmmmm/ (put your finger under the sound)
	2.	TCH:	SOUND IT WITH ME. REMEMBER, AS SOON AS I PUT MY FINGER UNDER THE SOUND, YOU GET IT GOING AND KEEP IT GOING UNTIL I PULL MY FINGER AWAY.
<u>LEAD</u>	3.	TCH&GRP:	/mmmmmmmmmmm/
	4.	TCH:	EXCELLENT! EVERYONE SAID /mmmmmmmmmmmmm/.
	5.	TCH:	NOW YOU SOUND IT WITHOUT ME. REMEMBER TO KEEP IT GOING UNTIL I PULL MY FINGER AWAY.
<u>TEST</u>	6.	GRP:	/mmmmmmmmmmm/
	7.	TCH:	GOOD SOUNDING. YOU SOUNDED /mmmmmmmmmmm/ CORRECTLY.

Use this procedure only for the presentation of the first three or four sounds. After that you can eliminate some of the dialogue.

See the next page for the simple procedure to be used after the first four sounds have been presented.

⟹

WORK SEQUENCE RECORD

In order to use this Management System it is assumed that teachers will be familiar with <u>PROGRAMMED READING</u> or that they are currently using the material.

The WORK SEQUENCE RECORD serves as a checklist so that both the teacher and students can monitor the student's progress within each sub-unit of work. More specifically, the WORK SEQUENCE RECORD helps to:

1. Provide the student and teacher with a systematic sequence for completing the performance objectives for each unit of work.

2. Provide a record of the date when each step of the unit is completed.

3. Train the student to work independently. By checking the WORK SEQUENCE RECORD the student can readily start a new days work without asking the teacher, "What am I supposed to do?"

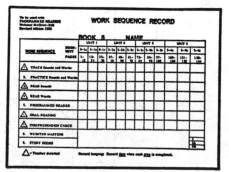

> ✳ <u>Helpful Hint</u>
>
> This Work Sequence Record can be taped or pasted on the front of a student's individual work folder.
>
> Keep the Reading Rate Graph and the PRACTICE Sounds and Words record sheet in this folder.

Exhibit 9–11 Example of Direct Instruction Techniques Used in Supplemental Programs

Feedback: Telling the child if his response is correct.

> *Examples:* Correct response—"Yes, Mary, the sound is **mmm**."
> Incorrect response—"This is the sound **aaa**. John, you said **mmm**. Can you tell me what sound this is?

Praise: A verbalization that shows approval.

> *Examples:* Accompanying feedback for a correct response: "Great," "Beautiful," "Fantastic," "Cheri, that was terrific."

Tokens + Praise: A token is an object which is given to a child as tangible evidence of the teacher's approval. It is always accompanied by praise and is exchangeable for desirable items or activities.

> *Example:* After a correct response the teacher says, "Beautiful job (token given to child), Mary."

Model: Demonstration of the exact behavior required of the child.

> *Example:* As the teacher points to the letter m she says, "This is the sound **mmm**."

Prompt: A verbalization by the teacher that elicits a response from the child.

> *Example:* Phrases like, "Say this word when I point" and, "Say it with me" are prompts. Telling the child the first sound of a word to help him finish a blend is also a prompt. A pointing finger, when it indicates to a child that a response is desired, becomes a prompt.

Source: From *Behavior Analysis Phonics Primer* by J. Becker and D.A. Jackson with permission of the publisher. © 1974, Jill Becker and Student Behavior Laboratories.

Chapter 10

Group-Individualized Applications of Direct Teaching

Sarah Rule and Charles Salzberg

B ecause the practical reality in education is that many children must share a single teacher, ways must be found for groups of children to be taught simultaneously. Several children can learn together in the small-group instructional format, but this format does not satisfy all the educational needs that are likely to arise in the classroom. First, the small-group format requires relatively homogeneous skill grouping, which is not always possible. Moreover, some teachers are reluctant to risk the labeling that invariably accompanies homogeneous grouping. Second, because small-group instruction is teacher-paced and teacher-directed, its exclusive use as a mode of instruction precludes the children's opportunity to learn more independently.

Fortunately, there is a well-developed instructional process that overcomes these difficulties, while making it possible for many children to be directly taught at the same time. This process is group-individualized instruction. Within this framework, children in a class may learn to work independently at their own skill level, proceed at their own pace, and assume growing responsibility for their own skill development. To the casual observer, group-individualized instruction may look like common seat work. After all, children are seated at their desks, working independently on their own materials. Important differences become apparent under closer scrutiny, however. Successful group-individualized instruction results from the systematic integration of carefully selected materials, environmental design, criterion-referenced placement, and progress monitoring systems, as well as the skilled use of direct teaching techniques.

Like most teachers, Mrs. Short faces an instructional challenge; she must teach reading to a class whose skills vary widely. Ellen, for example, knows at least 200 sight words and can sound out words with short vowel sounds; Mark, however, knows only the letters of the alphabet. In between are 10 other children, including Bill, who knows consonant sounds; Cyndi, who can blend some vowel-consonant sounds; and Rita, who can read 25 words, but has limited phonics skills. Instruction in a teacher-paced group would bore Ellen and lose Mark in lessons beyond his comprehension. Mrs. Short decides to use the group-individualized instruction format.

Mrs. Short places the children in reading materials at their own skill levels. They rarely work on the same book page, and many are in different books. When it is time for reading, the children get their instructional packet. Most children are working in Sullivan Programmed Reading materials (Buchanan & Sullivan Associates, 1963) or modified Sullivan materials that introduce new concepts sequentially from simple to complex. Each new concept (sound, blend, or word) is followed by many examples. Thus, the child practices reading the new word frequently before another is introduced. Having learned a single new concept, the child can work independently of the teacher, reading alone and applying that concept. The materials, not the teacher, provide the stimuli as the children work at task mastery. There are regular tests to assess mastery. Because the format in the materials is fairly similar from day to day, many children can go right to work with few instructions from Mrs. Short. She may remind the children working on tests or checkout pages that they should raise their hands when their work is to be checked, however.

Usually, Mrs. Short does a brief (3- to 5-minute) phonics drill with Mark, Rita, and two other children who need to learn the basic phonetic skills that would allow them to read at least some words independently. The content of the drill is matched to the reading materials. Before the children reach a particular sound in the books, they practice it during the drill.

Mrs. Short's behavior is focused on maximizing the frequency of her contacts with individual students. From her drill station, she praises other children as they work. After the drill, she circulates among the children, giving help when needed, praising students who are working, evaluating students' skills at predetermined checkpoints, and giving short (1- to 2-minute) minilessons as students encounter problems or new concepts. The children who are just learning phonetic skills are encouraged to read their individual materials quietly, but loud enough for Mrs. Short to listen to their reading as she circulates. She has marked the first presentation of each new word in the book and has instructed readers to raise a hand when they reach the marks. She listens as they sound out the new words to prevent wrong guesses and rehearsal of errors. Sometimes, several children raise their hands at once. When this happens, the children waiting for Mrs. Short may begin to fidget. One child, Sandy, sometimes gets out of her seat or bothers other children. Mrs. Short is prepared to cope with these children.

Mr. Edd uses the group-individualized instructional format in physical education, even though the only written materials used in this class are individual student progress charts. The students can work at their own pace to master physical activities. Among other things, the students perform the Royal Canadian Air Force Exercises (1962), involving some 48 different exercises. Each student has a wall chart that shows which exercises he or she must do and the number of required repetitions. As the student advances through the program, the exercises become more difficult. When students finish their individually planned day's program, they record their own progress and proceed to the team sports area. Like Mrs. Short, Mr. Edd circulates among students, giving help, feedback, and encouragement, as needed. Students work at their own pace, and strive to improve their own skills. Mike, who is overweight, does not have to sit on the sidelines and watch while first-string basketball player Jinny works out, nor does she have to do exercises that are much too easy for her because she is more physically fit than Mike.

The group-individualized format has also been adapted for teaching a variety of skills in classes of severely retarded students (Sasser, 1978). Students each have a box containing several written and/or manipulative tasks, such as tracing their name or stringing beads. The tasks are different for each student. To work independently, students must learn where their boxes are, when to bring them to their tables, and what their daily job is—to complete each task in the box. After a student has completed a task to a predetermined criterion (for example, independent completion for 3 consecutive days), a more difficult task is substituted. As in the other classes, the teacher circulates among students, praising those who are working, prompting those who need help, and recording the level of help each student needs to complete a given task. A task is mastered when performed independent of help. The progress monitoring system in this use of the group-individualized format is simply a sequential list of tasks.

CRITICAL FORMAT FEATURES

The following are critical features of materials (and programs) appropriate for use in a group-individualized teaching format:

1. a curriculum, be it materials, exercises, or tasks, that is sequenced from simple to complex
2. materials (or directions) that permit students to work fairly independently (i.e., complete a series of responses without a question or direction from the teacher)
3. a method for assessing the students' skills in order to place them at appropriate levels in the materials
4. frequent checkpoints to assess students' mastery of skills as they move through the program
5. remedial procedures (such as supplementary materials or tutorial or small-group lessons) for students who do not master the skills initially, as evidenced by their performance at checkpoints

Some commercially available materials contain many or all of these features. Others can be adapted by providing checkpoints, finding or creating supplementary materials for remediation or practice, or altering the sequence of concepts presented (Stowitschek, Gable, & Hendrickson, 1980).

The extent to which materials must be adapted depends on whether the group-individualized format is to be used to help students acquire new skills or simply to provide the practice in skills necessary for proficiency. If group-individualized instruction is to be used in the skill acquisition phase, careful attention must be paid to when and how new concepts (skills) are introduced. If concepts are simple and are presented one at a time with many practice examples (or applications), it may be feasible to teach them to children one at a time in brief lessons as the teacher circulates. If the concepts are complex, involving several steps or the application of many skills, it may be easier to "preteach" the concept to small groups of students before they use it in the group-individualized format. Furthermore, the teacher must plan for children who do not master the skills; there must be supplementary materials, tutoring, or other remediation procedures.

Other types of materials or program adaptations may be required when the group-individualized format is used for the practice of skills. The teacher's manual for the Corrective Reading Program (Engelmann, Wesley, Carnine, Meyers, Becker, & Johnson, 1973) contains suggestions for using a group-individualized format to develop reading proficiency. Teachers, aides, or volunteers (called checkers) designate material already read in group lessons for independent student reading. Checkers listen to individual students reading aloud. They monitor errors and reinforce accurate reading. Training of volunteer checkers is explained in the manual.

Certain materials are not readily adaptable to the group-individualized format. Materials that rely primarily on verbal responses to teacher questions or other teacher-presented stimuli, such as the DISTAR reading and language programs (Engelmann & Bruner, 1974), do not lend themselves to this approach, although later versions include individual practice supplements. Materials that present concepts with few opportunities to practice their application or require unique learner responses on every page are not readily adaptable to group-individualized instruction. For example, the primer of the 1976 Addison Wesley math series (Eicholz, O'Daffer, & Fleenor, 1976) presents 9 different concepts in the first 14 pages. Each page requires only 3 or 4 student responses and nearly every page requires new instructions. To adapt the primer to the group-individualized format, the teacher would virtually rewrite it.

MAINTAINING QUALITY

It is always a challenge to provide high-quality instruction, and the challenge is never greater than when each child in a class is working on a different concept, in a different material, at a different rate, and with different kinds of problems. The management of so many different instructional programs demands a system to monitor children's progress and ensure that the criteria used to assess that progress reflect skill development.

Monitoring Individual Progress

Quality control in group-individualized instruction begins with a reliable record of each child's daily progress. If individual progress is not carefully monitored, some children almost always get "lost between the cracks," and a child may go for weeks or months without learning and may even be practicing errors. If programs are set up in sequential units, monitoring progress can be quick, simple, and enjoyable for the children.

Exhibit 10–1 is a chart used to help John Doe keep track of his progress in an arithmetic program. Every day, when he got out his books, he also got out his folder with the progress chart. The math program was divided into sequential skills, which are reflected on the vertical axis in the chart. At the end of each math session, John colored in the square that corresponded to the skill on which he had been working. When he completed a skill unit and met the mastery criteria, he moved up one square (row). Each math session moved him one square (column) to the right. Thus, the flat places on the chart reflect periods in which he was working on the same skill unit.

Children enjoy marking their progress chart each day (Salzberg, 1972) and are proud to show it to their parents when they come to visit. These charts allow teachers to see each child's progress at a glance and make it very easy to spot a child who is beginning to have difficulty in a particular unit. Although most children can readily learn to mark their own progress chart, it is important that the teacher check their accuracy.

Monitoring Group Progress

Often, a teacher needs to examine the progress of the whole class at one time. Because it is inconvenient to use individual progress charts for this purpose, a group progress record is needed. Exhibit 10–2 reflects the progress of seven learning-disabled students who attended a special summer class for mildly handicapped children (Salzberg & Rule, 1973). Again, each column reflects one day and contains a tally mark for each child in the class. These marks reflect the quarter book unit in which each child was working that day. The first column indicates that children were intially placed in five different books. At the end of 9 school days, it could be seen that all children had advanced, albeit some more than others. The heavy line shows the curriculum placement of the median (fourth) child. This median line allows the teacher easily to see the general curriculum progress of the entire class. In addition, by scanning the sheet the teacher can assess the progress of individuals and readily spot those

Exhibit 10–1 Daily Individual Progress Record: Arithmetic

John Doe	9/10	9/11	9/12	9/13	9/14	9/17	9/18	9/19	9/20	9/21	9/24	9/25	9/26	9/27
15. Subtraction, three digits, no regrouping														
14. Subtraction, 3 digits, 2 digits no regrouping														
13. Subtraction, 2 digits, 2 digits, no regrouping														
12. Subtraction, 2 digits, 1 digit, no regrouping														
11. Subtraction, basic facts														
10. Advanced Column Addition														
9. Column addition, 3 digits, regroup														X
8. Add 3 digits and 3 digits, regroup													X	
7. Column addition, 2 digits										X	X	X		
6. Add 2 digits and 2 digits, regrouping							X	X	X					
5. Add 3 digits, no regrouping						X								
4. Add 1 digit and 1 digit and 1 digit					X									
3. Basic addition facts			X	X	X									
2. Count 1-100		X												
1. Less than, greater than	X													

Days

who are having problems. Group progress charts can also be constructed for large programs (Exhibit 10–3). (For a more complete discussion of the use of progress monitoring charts, see Bushell, 1978.)

Checking Mastery

Children should be allowed to move to the next unit *only if* they have mastered the skills required in the current unit. Each progress unit should have a corresponding test or mastery check that directly assesses the skills that the unit was intended to teach. Some commercially available programs have unit tests, but these tests do not always address all the relevant skills. For example, the tests in the McGraw Hill Sullivan Reading Program (Buchanan & Sullivan Associates, 1964) call for circling, underlining, or other written responses. The teacher would do well, particularly in the early stages of the program, to test oral reading as well as written responses. Only then can the teacher be sure that the children are acquiring essential decoding skills.

Placing Students Correctly

Mastery tests developed for each unit of an instructional program can also be used as a placement inventory. The teacher has new students work through each unit test until they reach the point at which they can no longer perform to an acceptable criterion level. The criteria that control movement to successive units in a program must be set at a level that equates curriculum progress with learning, but the precise level can be determined by the professional judgment of the teacher.

Several factors must be considered in establishing a criterion level. If the skills that are taught in successive units of a program are highly redundant, mastery criteria can be relatively low. In these cases, children have opportunities for additional practice after they move to the next unit, thereby gaining proficiency. On the other hand, if the skills taught from unit to unit are distinct so that children receive little or no further instruction on a particular set of skills after they leave the unit, the criterion level for passing on to the next

Exhibit 10–2 Progress of a Group of Children Recorded on a Single Chart

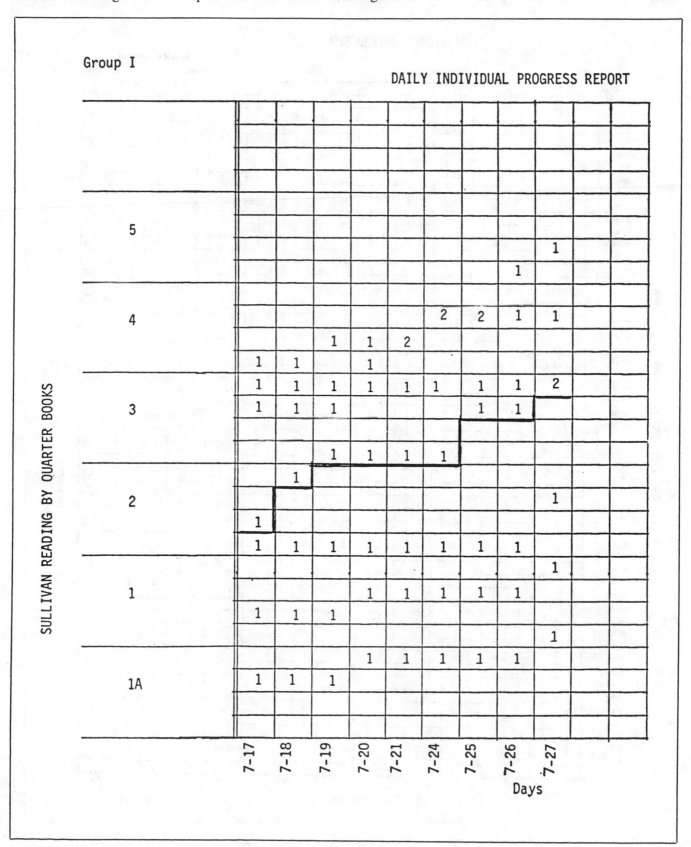

Exhibit 10–3 Form for Monitoring the Progress of a Large Group

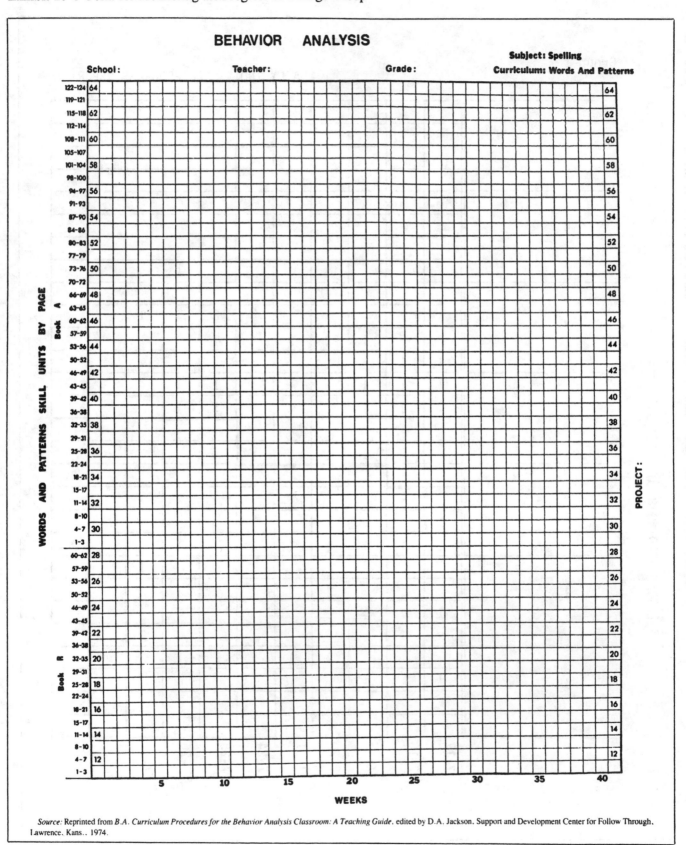

Source: Reprinted from *B.A. Curriculum Procedures for the Behavior Analysis Classroom: A Teaching Guide,* edited by D.A. Jackson. Support and Development Center for Follow Through, Lawrence, Kans., 1974.

unit should be higher. Setting the criterion level too high can be as damaging as setting it too low. If the criterion level is set at 100% correct, for example, children may work on the same unit for many weeks, even though their knowledge of the skills is adequate. In this situation, children acquire relatively few new concepts.

Encouraging Accuracy

Criterion-referenced instructional strategies help children learn to be accountable for their own instructional progress. There are various techniques that teachers use to help children increase accuracy in their day-to-day performance. In praising children for working, teachers can direct attention to accuracy as well (e.g., "Johnny, you've done all these problems exactly right. That's great!"). Teachers can also check the children's papers before the end of the work period and require the children to correct their errors before they can move to another assignment. When a child's pattern of errors suggests carelessness, the teacher may assign additional work to be done at home or in the study hall. Thus, accurate work can be encouraged by a criterion-referenced progress system, by descriptive praise for accurate work, by routine error correction each day, and by the assignment of extra work for careless performance.

CONDUCTING INSTRUCTION

Under optimal conditions in group-individualized instruction, children work at their own desks or chairs, each productively engaged in individually prescribed materials that allow maximum skill growth. The challenge in conducting group-individualized instruction successfully is keeping all the children working with sufficient consistency and independence. There are a variety of techniques that can be brought into play for this purpose.

Teacher Attention

Teachers must carefully time the attention given to each child as they circulate around the room. If a teacher keeps instructional contacts (e.g., praise, direction, assistance) short, preferably 40 seconds or less, children are more apt to attend to the task than if the teacher prolongs instructional contacts (Scott & Bushell, 1974; Stevens & Rosenshine, 1981).

The teacher's ability to scan the entire group while giving instruction to one child is important for success in group-individualized instruction. The way in which the teacher circulates among the children while engaged in group-individualized instruction is also important. Some patterns are much better than others. If the teacher goes from one child to the next in a circular pattern around the table, for example, each child may stop working after the teacher has gone to the next student and resume only when the teacher is all the way around the table. It is best to circulate among the children in an unpredictable pattern. While circulating, the teacher should visually scan the groups and praise children in various places for working.

Establishing a number of rules may also help the group-individualized lessons go more smoothly. Children may be taught to get their own work out of their own folders, to sharpen at least two pencils before each lesson so that they do not have to run back and forth to the pencil sharpener frequently, and to raise their hand when they need help instead of calling out. These rules help to maintain a quiet productive atmosphere. When a child's hand is raised, it is important that the teacher acknowledge it (i.e., "Susy, thank you for raising your hand. I will be with you in a minute"), especially if it will be a minute or two before the teacher can help that child.

For some teachers, the most difficult teaching skill to learn is not to pay attention to children who are not working. When children are daydreaming, teachers generally tend to tell them to get back to work or to ask them what is wrong. Paying attention to unproductive behavior only strengthens it, however. Dawdlers should be cued to get back to work without paying direct attention to them. When a student is daydreaming, for example, the teacher should praise other children around the dawdler for working. When the dawdler returns to work, the teacher should be sure to praise him or her.

Use of Combined Questioning and Modeling Tactics

When students are unable to proceed with independent work because they are faced with new or difficult concepts, the teacher must be prepared to give immediate assistance directed to individual needs. Questioning and modeling techniques can be combined to provide a minilesson to a child who is unable to proceed independently. First, the teacher uses diagnostic questioning to determine if assistance is needed, then shifts to modeling if a minilesson is needed.

Mr. Daggott notices that Sally is sitting and staring at her reading comprehension exercise page. On this exercise, she is to determine the type of question and answer it.

Mr. Daggott: "Sally, do you know what the question asks you to do?"

Sally: "I don't think so."

Mr. Daggott: "Let's see. What are you to ask yourself about the question?"

Sally: "I don't know."

Mr. Daggott: "What kind of question is it?"

Sally: "A real hard one."

Mr. Daggott: "Does it ask about a word or a fact?"

Sally: "A word?"

Mr. Daggott decides on a short minilesson to refresh Sally's memory.

Mr. Daggott: "This one asks about what happened, so it asks about a fact."

Mr. Daggott removes from his pocket some prepared 3 by 5 cards, each of which contains a written sentence and a question.

Mr. Daggott: "Sally, read the sentence and the question, then I will model the answer."

Sally: "The Appaloosa horse had a blanket with brown and black spots. What part of the horse had brown and black spots?"

Mr. Daggott: "It's a fact question. What kind of a question is it?"

Sally: "A fact question."

Mr. Daggott: "Good, the blanket has spots. What part of the horse has spots?"

Sally: "The blanket."

Mr. Daggott: "That's fine."

After presenting more cards, Mr. Daggott has Sally return to the exercise page. He checks to see that she can identify and answer the next question, then moves on. (Time: 1 minute, 40 seconds.)

Misbehavior

Some children go beyond daydreaming. They become disruptive by pushing, shoving, or making distracting noises or rude comments. On these occasions, the teacher must stop them, but in such a way that the misbehavior is not reinforced by teacher attention, even inadvertently. There are many carefully investigated procedures applicable in these situations. They include such simple solutions as moving a child's chair away from the group, as well as the use of fines, reinforcement contingencies for nondisruptive diligent work, contingent observation techniques, a variety of time-out procedures, and overcorrection procedures (Bushell, 1973; O'Leary & O'Leary, 1972; Sulzer-Azaroff & Mayer, 1977).

TROUBLE-SHOOTING

When a group-individualized system of instruction is first implemented, there are usually problems to solve. The most obvious indicator of a problem is a sea of hands raised by children who are waiting for the teacher's help. There are several potential solutions to this problem. First, the academic placement of children in the curriculum materials should be reexamined. Many children may have been placed at levels that are too difficult for them to work on independently. These children should be given mastery tests for the earlier units until a level is found at which they can work with greater independence. A second approach, particularly useful when materials are not sufficiently programmatic, is for the teacher to conduct a short lesson before children approach new concepts. These minilessons allow children to work more independently and, thus, relieve the teacher from the constant press for attention. Sometimes, the lack of independence in group-individualized instruction reflects a problem with a particular child rather than with the general routine or the materials.

Dependency

Some children are overly dependent; these children do not do any work unless the teacher stands right next to them. One teacher invented a careful process to solve this problem; she called it the "red line" procedure.

At the beginning of the year, Cyndi asked for help constantly. When Mrs. Morales helped her, Cyndi would finish that problem, but not do another one until Mrs. Morales helped her again. Mrs. Morales gave Cyndi a page of problems that she knew Cyndi could do. She put a red line after the second, fourth, and sixth problems. She told Cyndi, "I'll help you when you get to the red line, Cyndi, but don't raise your hand until you've worked all the problems up to the line." Cyndi worked one problem and raised her hand. Mrs. Morales gave Cyndi's paper a sidelong glance and saw that Cyndi had not worked up to the red line. Thus, Mrs. Morales proceeded to praise Joe, who sat in front of Cyndi, for working so well all by himself. Cyndi sat with her hand up for several minutes. Finally, she worked the second problem and raised her hand. Mrs. Morales checked Cyndi's work right away and praised her accurate, independent work. After Cyndi had finished the sixth problem, Mrs. Morales put red lines after the ninth, twelfth, and fifteenth problems. Mrs. Morales gradually increased the amount of work between the red lines until, by the end of 2 weeks, Cyndi was working ten problems all by herself before raising her hand. Subsequently, Mrs. Morales gradually moved her up to more sophisticated arithmetic problems.

Teacher Assistants

Another approach to the problem of having too many children waiting too often is to increase the instructional resources in the classroom. For example, children may assist the teacher during instructional periods. Peer helpers can be used as checkers, as roving contingency managers; they can be taught to drill their classmates in rote skills, or they can learn to give instructional feedback and reinforcement (Engelmann et al., 1973; Greenwood, Sloane, & Baskin, 1974).

Pretraining

Some children have more serious problems than a lack of independence. These children may not know that they should raise their hands when they need help. They may simply stop working or, worse, may continue to make errors. Knapczyk and Livingston (1974) used a simple prompting procedure to teach two mentally retarded students to ask for help when they needed it. Before they began independent work and, occasionally, during work time, the teacher or aide reminded the students to raise their hands whenever they encountered something they did not understand or needed help. The teacher and aide were careful to provide assistance whenever the students raised their hands. When these students learned to ask questions, their time on task and accuracy of reading comprehension increased.

FORMAT EFFECTIVENESS

The achievement of students taught primarily through a group-individualized format has been examined on both a large and a small scale. Economically disadvantaged students across the United States participated in the Behavior Analysis Model of the Follow Through Program, which relies on group-individualized instruction as its primary teaching format (Bushell, 1978). Over a 6-year period, the reading progress of these children was superior both to that of a matched control group and to the U.S. norms on the Wide

Range Achievement Test. When Bushell (1978) used data from the Abt Associates' evaluation of Follow Through kindergartners to compare scores on the Wide Range Achievement Test with those on the Metropolitan Achievement Test in listening, reading, and number skills, the performance of the Follow Through sample children was found to be superior to that of the comparison samples (mean scores of 10 different Follow Through sponsors).

Because the Behavior Analysis Follow Through Model includes several other components, the effects of the group-individualized instructional format alone cannot be determined. Achievement gains of other students who had been taught with the group-individualized format corroborate the Follow Through findings, however. Salzberg (1972) investigated the effects of group-individualized teaching coupled with individual contingencies for satisfactory test performance on mathematics achievement in elementary school students. The curriculum was adapted from Suppes' *Sets and Numbers* (1962). Students working under the group-individualized format progressed through the program at rates well above those normally expected. Their quiz performances indicated mastery of the concepts.

In the Summer Learning Project (Salzberg & Rule, 1973), group-individualized teaching formats were used in reading, math, art, and physical education for mildly handicapped students. Students' performance on the Wide Range Achievement Test showed that, after 6 weeks of intensive instruction, the 32 students gained an average of 4.2 months in reading and 2.2 months in math. Moreover, of the 32 children enrolled, 31 children reported that they liked summer school. Twenty-three told the independent surveyor that they liked the summer school more than their regular school. All 32 felt that they had learned a great deal, and 21 said they learned more than in their regular school.

Stevens and Rosenshine (1981) cited additional evidence supporting the efficacy of individualized work when teacher feedback is available. They discussed studies that reported a positive relationship between achievement, students' working behavior, and teacher interaction during seat work. Like Scott and Bushell (1974), they emphasized the necessity for short instructional contacts when using the group-individualized format.

Part II

Supervision in Support of Direct Teaching

In the past few years, striking advances have been made in training teachers to use direct teaching tactics. One of the more notable efforts is the series of projects conducted over the last 10 years at George Peabody College for Teachers of Vanderbilt University. The Interdisciplinary Special Teacher Education Program (InStep; Shores & Stowitschek, 1975), for example, was a federally funded teacher training program that focused on developing generic teaching competencies through supervised practice. The evaluation system included a survey of graduates' impressions about their level of skill once they had begun classroom teaching. Significant discrepancies were noted between teachers' ratings of their proficiency in applying a teaching competency and their need to use that competency. At the time, the InStep training program followed a typical pattern in which didactic instruction in teaching competencies was conducted in course units that did not include opportunities to practice the competencies. Thus, in many cases, competencies that were introduced didactically may not have been practiced in training, and vice versa.

The Prototype Model for Developing Empirically Based Teacher Competencies (Shores & Stowitschek, 1977) was a research and development project funded by the Bureau of Education for the Handicapped. Its goals were to empirically identify teacher behaviors that had predictable and demonstrable effects on the educational performance of handicapped children and to develop appropriate training materials. It became apparent from this project that (1) the combinations and sequences in which teacher behaviors were applied were critical in producing persistent positive effects with handicapped children and (2) the level of supervision needed to apply a given set of teacher behaviors

successfully far exceeded the levels that are typically applied in practica, student teaching, and other practice situations.

The Field-Based Special Teacher Education Program (Shores, Stowitschek, Salzberg, & Kerr, 1979) evolved from the activities and findings of these two projects. It contained four major guiding features: (1) a close relationship between didactic (course work) instructional activities and supervised practice, (2) demonstrations of the use of a competency across multiple instructional situations, (3) verification of competency attainment in terms of an observed criterion level of use and demonstrable changes in the educational performance of handicapped children in association with the use of the competency; and (4) weekly supervision, including observation and feedback. The Field-Based Program was in operation over 8 years and graduated over 240 teachers. Examples of the competencies demonstrated and results obtained with handicapped children are depicted in Tables II–1 and II–2. Many of the procedures and forms described in this book were adapted from this program. The supervision procedures described in Chapter 12 are a composite of the procedures used in the program.

It is evident from these projects that the attainment of teaching competence requires a great deal of effort on the part of the trainee and the supervisor of training. In view of the potential gains or losses to the education of children, however, this effort appears not only reasonable, but demandable.

Teachers and prospective teachers of handicapped children must realize the importance of practice, and so must their supervisors. The rules for the successful practice of teaching are the same as the rules that apply to children for the successful practice of their lessons. Massed practice

Table II–1 Direct Instruction: 1977–1978

TACTIC	USED		CHILD MASTERED		CHILD NOT MASTERED	
	Freq.	%	Freq.	%	Freq.	%
Analysis:						
Task Analysis	505	55.0	407	81.0	98	19.0
Concept Analysis	56	06.0	44	79.0	12	21.0
Criterion Referenced	197	22.0	139	71.0	58	29.0
Is-Does Plan	64	07.0	43	67.0	21	33.0
Observation	56	06.0	39	70.0	17	30.0
Other	37	04.0	25	68.0	12	32.0
Non-reported	0	0	0	0	0	0
Total	915		697		218	
Use of Materials:						
Teacher-Made	445	49.0	363	82.0	82	18.0
Commercial	151	16.0	115	76.0	36	24.0
Adapted	238	26.0	165	69.0	73	31.0
Other	81	09.0	54	67.0	27	33.0
Non-reported	0	0	0		0	
Total	915		697		218	

Table II–2 Pupil Mastery and Non-Mastery of Subobjectives in Curricular Areas: 1976–1977

Curriculum Area	Fall		Spring	
	Mastery	Non-Mastery	Mastery	Non-Mastery
Reading	82	30	118	23
Math	22	1	54	11
Spelling	10	3	0	0
Writing	0	0	51	39
Language	0	0	28	26
Motor	32	10	36	22
Social	0	0	47	15
Self-Help	17	15	85	1
Total	163	59	419	137
	72.4%	26.2%	75.2%	24.5%
	(Non-reported = 3)		(Non-reported = 1)	

without supervision or feedback is not productive. Distributed practice (spaced over time) with supervision and feedback may ensure the acquisition of a direct teaching tactic. Familiarity with a teaching tactic should not be confused with proficiency in its use. Familiarity is gained by taking a course or workshop on the tactics. Proficiency is gained only by repeatedly practicing the tactics with children over an extended time and using supervisory feedback to reanalyze their effectiveness.

This section is for the supervisor of direct teaching, but it is also for teachers who, with the aid of their colleagues, may mutually attempt to improve their teaching skill.

Chapter 11

Organization and Observation of Direct Teaching Practice

Would a surgical intern be permitted to perform her first operation unsupervised? Should a driving instructor supervise a novice by watching from the parking lot? Is there a reason why a pilot-to-be must earn the privilege of flying solo? The answers are obvious. Although the consequences of unsupervised teaching are not usually as serious as those of unsupervised surgery, driving, or flying, the effects on a child's functioning can be long-lasting. Appropriate supervision procedures can ensure that practice teaching is as safe for the child in school as practice surgery is for the patient in a hospital.

This chapter focuses on supervised practice for direct teaching tactics. The findings of a major pre-service teacher training program (Shores, Stowitschek, Salzberg, & Kerr, 1979) suggest that supervised application of direct teaching competencies plays a key role in determining whether the competencies are successfully developed. Similar supervi-

sion procedures were also described for training in-service teachers (Cavallaro, Stowitschek, George, & Stowitschek, 1980). Direct teaching practice experiences should be supervised systematically, as in the supervision model shown in Figure 11–1. Because its purpose is not to solve all teaching problems, but to facilitate the acquisition of direct teaching tactics, the model concentrates on practicum supervision activities. Classroom observations and inspection of records reveal what teacher-trainees are doing in their assigned instruction programs. Feedback and redirection procedures, which are based on the observation and inspection information, are intended to help trainees modify their teaching so that tactics result in positive changes in children's behavior. Verification is the end result of supervision. It has powerful implications for the competency testing problems faced by institutions and certification programs involved in teacher training.

Figure 11–1 Components of a Direct Teaching Supervision Model

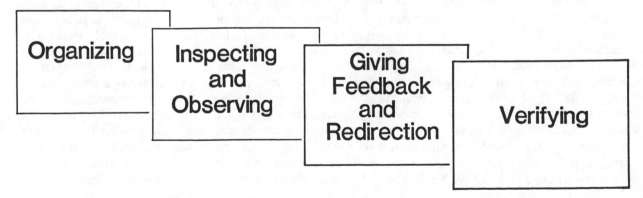

ORGANIZING DIRECT TEACHING PRACTICE

The task of supervision is made manageable by careful preparation. Establishing a suitable site for the practice experience and planning appropriate direct teaching practice programs are two crucial activities of this task.

Establishing a Practice Site

The preparations needed to begin direct teaching supervision vary according to the conditions under which supervision is to occur. For practicum and student teaching situations, initial preparations are critical, because the cooperation of a supervising teacher must be secured. When school district personnel, such as special education supervisors, are to supervise the teaching, there are fewer preparations, although they are still important. When the supervisor is a peer, such as a student taking the same course, some mutual arrangements are crucial.

Practicum and Student Teaching

The first responsibility of a pre-service teacher-trainee is usually to be of assistance to the teacher. The trainee should also have the opportunity to pursue training objectives, however. To avoid misunderstanding between the teacher, the trainee, and the supervisor, these arrangements must be mutually agreed upon in writing within 2 weeks after the start of the experience. The agreement should specify the expectations of the cooperating teacher and the training objectives (Exhibit 11–1). It should be agreed that a sufficient amount of time will be allowed for the trainee to teach the prescribed child behaviors.

An important factor in the arrangement of a suitable direct teaching experience is the selection of the cooperating teacher and classroom. Ideal supervising teachers not only permit the trainee to pursue the required competencies, but also model these competencies in their daily routine. Practicum supervisors or teacher supervisors can often scan a classroom and determine whether a teacher employs appropriate planning and measurement competencies. For instance, one teacher's classroom may use displays purely to enhance visual appeal; children's work on display may reflect only the teacher's preferences for aesthetically attractive, novel, or humorous products. On the other hand, a teacher who displays student progress in charts, graphs, or other data forms is likely to value the daily measurement and progress monitoring procedures that are essential in promoting the acquisition of direct teaching skills.

Systematic planning (e.g., behavioral pinpoints, task analyses, or sequences) should also be readily evident in the teacher's classroom. If these records have been completed but filed away, it is unlikely that the teacher's day-to-day activities match what is written in individualized education programs.

A visit to the classroom to observe the teacher at work is recommended to help determine if the teacher would be an appropriate model for the trainee. Elements of teacher-child interaction to look for are (1) a high proportion of praise relative to neutral statements; (2) an absence of nagging (e.g., "Turn around and stop that." "Don't talk back."); (3) consistency in presenting instructional cues, prompting child responses, and providing subsequent teacher feedback; and (4) a focus on one task or type of response in each session, rather than several tasks or several responses at once. The importance of an appropriate role model for the teacher-trainee should not be underestimated. Although the college or university supervisor may issue the grades at the end of the semester, the supervising teacher is in daily contact with the trainee and is in a position to arrange training contingencies with immediate, powerful consequences.

In-Service Teacher Training

Typically, the competencies addressed in an in-service training program are applied in a teacher's own classroom. There are, however, some preparatory considerations. If a teacher's classroom approaches chaos, for example, it would be impossible to supervise the development of competent teaching there. In this case, the supervisor may suggest that

1. the supervisor working with the teacher establish instructional control before attempting the required competencies
2. the teacher select two or three students at a time and practice the competencies with them in isolation from the class until instructional control is established with the remainder of the class

Unlike pre-service teachers, in-service teachers have job priorities and daily routines that often interfere with their attempts to practice new tactics. Therefore, as part of the training preparations, teachers should schedule specific daily activities that will provide practice in the competencies to be supervised. For example, if modeling tactics are to be used in a one-to-one tutorial format to increase a child's math skills, a 10-minute session at the start or end of the math period should be written in the daily schedule. If questioning tactics are to be employed diagnostically during a roving tutorial activity (e.g., seat work), then the use of questioning tactics should be reflected in the teacher's written daily plans.

The supervisor should closely monitor the teacher's attempts to arrange opportunities to apply the direct teaching tactics, keeping in mind that beginning something new is often the most difficult step and that maintaining what has

Exhibit 11–1 Sample Practicum Agreement

Practicum Agreement

The purpose of this letter is to set forth the following items of agreement:

1. The practicum trainee will assist the cooperating teacher in the day to day operation of the classroom and will assist the following children to attain prescribed objectives:

    1. _John B._ (Child)   _Handwriting 17.0-17.1-17.5 Math 6.0-6.1_ (Objective) 6.11
    2. _Sara S._ (Child)   _Handwriting 17.0-17.1-17.5 Language 2.0 2.3_ (Objective)
    3. _Julie F._ (Child)   _Math 6.0-6.9 Reading 4.0-4.9_ (Objective)
    4. _Nancy R._ (Child)   _Handwriting 17.0-17.1-17.5 Reading 4.0-4.9_ (Objective)

2. The cooperating teacher will allow time in the daily schedule for the trainee to demonstrate targeting analysis, initial assessment, intervention, progress monitoring, and redirection competencies in the following programs:

    1. _Handwriting - group individualized format_
    2. _Language development - individual format_
    3. _Math - Small Group format_
    4. _Reading - Small Group format_
    5. _____

3. The supervisor will consult with the cooperating teacher and will make _5_ visits during the quarter to observe the trainee.

signed:

_____   _____   _____
Trainee   Cooperating Teacher Supervisor

been started is often in direct competition with a number of other school events. The supervisor of in-service training, in addition to providing feedback on the application of direct teaching tactics, must make it just as important for the trainee to practice new teaching tactics as it is to complete the myriad other school-related activities.

Planning Direct Teaching Programs

The level of specificity of the trainee's plans determines, to a large extent, the reliability of the supervisor in observing and redirecting the trainee. Supervision should be correlated directly to the tactics to be practiced. Hence, supervision begins with the planning forms: the Direct Teaching Program Checklist, the Preprogram Planner, and the Daily Planner.

Direct Teaching Program Checklist

The key to satisfactory supervision of people learning direct teaching competencies is to correlate supervision with the skills they are teaching to their students. The Direct Teaching Program Checklist (Exhibit 11–2) is the coordinating document for all other forms in this model. In essence, the checklist is a two-edged sword. For the trainee, it is a list of procedures for carrying out a direct teaching program. For the supervisor, those same procedures are teaching competencies that need to be demonstrated. When a supervisor approves a direct teaching program, inspects program planning procedures, observes direct teaching activities related to the program, and provides feedback to the trainees to improve their direct teaching, the results are ultimately reflected on the checklist.

Basically, the checklist is a contract. Each competency demonstrated by the trainee is verified by the supervisor by initialing the form in the righthand column of the checklist. The supervisor and trainee use the checklist as a contract for (1) initial approval of the skills to be demonstrated by the trainee and (2) final verification of the skills that the trainee has demonstrated. Before approving a program, the supervisor should evaluate written evidence of the following:

1. a targeted short-term objective that is both (a) specified in operational terms, and (b) agreed upon by the trainee, the supervising teacher, and the supervisor as a high-priority objective for the children to be taught
2. an analysis of the objective, preferably on the Preprogram Planner, that complies with the specifications
3. results of an initial criterion-referenced assessment of the child(ren)'s performance related to the targeted short-term objective showing the necessity of teaching that objective

4. appropriate instruction tactics described in scriptlike fashion on the Teacher Presentation Guide located on the back of the Daily Planner
5. appropriate progress measures

Preprogram Planner

For the supervisor, the Preprogram Planner is the connecting document between the Direct Teaching Program Checklist and the anticipated daily teaching sequence. All program decisions and activities should be included on this sheet.

Daily Planner

Whether a trainee selects a task or concept to teach, tries a one-to-one or group format, uses direct observation or a testing approach to measure progress, or selects a modeling or a questioning tactic, the Daily Planner standardizes the information for the supervisor. It provides a day-to-day reference for what the trainee is doing, not in relation to the individual vagaries of a practice site, but in relation to the competencies that are being demonstrated and, more importantly, to whether the child is making progress.

INSPECTING DIRECT INSTRUCTION PLANS

Although planning for direct instruction cannot be easily observed, the products of the planning can be examined. Examination of products is called an inspection because it implies a comparison to a "passing" or criterion performance. Inspection should begin before a program is started, to obtain initial approval, and should continue thereafter, to verify that the trainee is employing the planned teaching behaviors in direct teaching activities and to identify desirable program changes if children are not showing progress. The Direct Teaching Program Checklist has a column ("Verified") for recording the results of inspection.

There are any number of written products that demonstrate a trainee's planning. To help standardize the inspection process, these products can be grouped in a way that shows how they support the Preprogram Planner and the Daily Planner (Table 11–1).

Because the Preprogram Planner and Daily Planner are summaries of other documents, all documents should be examined to determine whether they correspond to the planning sheets. Likewise, the planned direct teaching activities should correspond to those observed. Criteria should be set for each planning activity inspected, because the use of predetermined inspection criteria can heighten the reliability of the process. A checkmark in the "Verified" column of the

Exhibit 11–2 Sample Checklist

DIRECT TEACHING PROGRAM CHECKLIST*

(For supervisors use only)

PROGRAM _____ *Jack* _____

	Approved Date	Verified (For supervisors use only) DATE Initial

TARGET *Written 2 and 3 place addition*
(What to teach) *computation with carrying* — 1/27 PB | 1/27 | PB

ANALYZE *Task Analysis*
(What to teach) — 1/27 PB | 1/27 | PB

ASSESS *Top rows of 7 daily worksheets*
(How measure) *(unprompted* — REVISE 2/19 PB

INTERVENE *Contingency attention, group,*
(What Teaching Tactic is used) — 1/27 PB

modeling, - individual

(SEE PRESENTATION GUIDE)
(ON BACK OF THIS PAGE)

Arranged Event *VI - 3 min. - each student* — 1/27 PB

Arrangement _____

CHECK PROGRESS/ *Top row of daily worksheet*
MASTERY (How measure) *(unprompted)* — REVISE 2/19 PB

REDIRECT _____
(What back-up teaching tactic may be used)

_____

(SEE PRESENTATION GUIDE)
(ON BACK OF THIS PAGE)

*Many of the procedures outlined on this checklist were adapted from the materials developed in the Field Based Special Teacher Education Program at George Peabody College for Teachers of Vanderbilt University.

Table 11–1 Materials That Support Preprogram Planner and Daily Planner

Form	Sections	Supporting Materials
Preprogram Planner (what is to be taught)	Short-term Objective	Individualized Education Program (IEP)
	Initial Assessment	Individualized Education Program (IEP)
	Task/Concept Sequence	The sequence as written on the Planner or on another written task analysis
Daily Planner (how to motivate, what tactics to use)	Subobjective	Written on the Preprogram Planner or written task analysis
	Materials	Materials that the teacher has collected or prepared for the planned program (See also the Teacher Presentation Guide on the back of the Daily Planner.)
	Presentation Mode	Teacher Presentation Guide or other written lesson description
	Child Response	Teacher Presentation Guide
	Consequent Event	Teacher Presentation Guide
	Arranged Event	Teacher Presentation Guide
	Monitoring Tactic	Selected or prepared test, probe, or observation recording materials; visual data display (graph or chart)
	Child Mastery/ Nonmastery	Results of tests, probes, or observations conducted by trainee

Direct Teaching Program Checklist indicates that inspection criteria have been met. To illustrate the inspection process, a hypothetical example follows:

Jack Turnbull, a special education student at Woahinks College, was completing one of his practicum requirements in a classroom for behavior-disordered children. His supervising teacher assigned him to instruct five of the students in the class during the independent math activity. Dr. Pauline Burz, Jack's practicum supervisor, had encouraged Jack to use this assignment to develop

and demonstrate group-individualized, as well as tutorial, competencies. Jack completed initial program planning using the supervising teacher's prepared IEPs and submitted the planning forms to Dr. Burz for review. After examining the planning forms; inspecting the supporting task analysis, initial assessment, and progress checking materials prepared by Jack; and checking with the supervising teacher, Dr. Burz approved the plan with some revisions, as indicated on Exhibit 11–2. Targeting and analysis were verified because competency in these areas had been demonstrated and did not require observation of the teacher's interaction with students.

Approximately 1 week after Jack had begun teaching, Dr. Burz visited the classroom. It was apparent from inspection of records and from informal observation that Jack was inconsistent in his teaching presentations. Also, inspection of results logged on Jack's Daily Planner revealed that the children had made no progress and that he had changed several aspects of the program (materials, consequent events, and arrangement) all at the same time. Dr. Burz instructed Jack to return to his original procedures and arranged a meeting to devise a means of systematically observing Jack's teaching presentations.

OBSERVING DIRECT INSTRUCTION

The results of casual or informal observation, even by experienced observers, have not been found to help teachers improve their direct instruction skills. Although casual observation is the predominant way in which supervisors obtain information and give feedback, it has been shown that the feedback provided by trainees who observe themselves through videotaped microteaching sessions is more constructive than that provided by supervisors who observe them informally (Borg, Kelley, Langer, & Gall, 1970). Direct observation is often the only way a supervisor can be certain that a teacher-trainee can perform a prescribed teaching tactic. Therefore, observations must be systematic, quantifiable, and comparable from one observation to the next in order to provide feedback that will consistently improve teaching performance.

A number of attempts have been made to develop a universal teacher observation system. These attempts have ranged from a 10-point teacher-child interaction system (Flanders, 1969) to simple measures of children's responsiveness to a teacher's actions, such as on-task behavior (Shores & Stowitschek, 1977). No single system for observing teachers appears to be acceptable in all instructional situations. Moreover, few situations can provide a supervisor with sufficient information at one time to assess the teacher's use of more than one or two instructional tactics.

To illustrate, the Field-Based Special Teacher Education Program, based at George Peabody College for Teachers of Vanderbilt University, was in need of a means of observing teacher-trainees. Because the emphasis of this program was supervision of practicum experiences, its success depended on the quality of the supervision provided. During the experimental phase, a period of nearly 1 year was devoted to the development of an observation system that supervisors could use to provide feedback to trainees. The participating supervisors were highly trained researchers, as well as teacher-educators who had previous experience with the observation procedures. Several teacher competence studies were conducted in which observation procedures were successfully used, but in spite of the considerable effort and attention to this task, no single observation procedure was found to be reliable and valid at all times.

An alternative approach to observing teacher-trainees resulted in both reliable and useful feedback to the trainees. Once a trainee had completed the planning steps, an observation procedure was devised that was tailored to the trainee's individual program. The Teacher Presentation Guide, Preprogram Planner, and Daily Planner actually specified the elements that the supervisor observed. For instance, a teacher observation system should answer three basic questions:

1. What does a teacher say or do in order to get a child to respond?
2. What is the child's response?
3. What does the teacher say or do immediately following a child's response?

Therefore, the supervisor uses observation primarily to determine whether a trainee is consistently using the teaching tactics specified in the written plans and to provide feedback if the trainee is using the tactic inconsistently or it is apparent that the teaching tactic is inappropriate to the student and target behavior being taught.

Uses of Observation Formats

Because observation of teaching often involves observing both the teacher and the child, it can be a complex, albeit crucial, supervision process (Rosenshine & Furst, 1973). General procedures for observing teacher-trainees include (1) identifying the teacher behaviors and child responses to be observed, (2) selecting or adapting an appropriate observation format, (3) completing observations and checking reliability, (4) summarizing the results of the observation.

Selecting Teacher and Child Behaviors to Be Observed

As an observer, the supervisor's purpose is to verify whether a teacher is correctly using a given teaching tactic and to provide feedback when that tactic is not being used. Therefore, only the teacher and child responses pertaining to the tactic in question need be recorded. This simplifies the observation task. In addition to teacher behaviors, child behaviors should be recorded because the use of the tactic must be judged by the child's responses to the teacher's behaviors and the subsequent responses of the teacher.

Preceding chapters have described the teacher and child behaviors for each tactic. These descriptions form the basis for observation and include operational specifications of what is to be observed (with the exception of inappropriate teacher behaviors).

Selecting an Observation Format

Observation formats vary according to the information needed. It is best to select the simplest format that will serve the purpose. The more complex the recording procedures, the greater the probability of unreliable observations. The less reliable the observations, the less effective the supervisor's evaluation and feedback.

Types of Observation Formats

There are several formats that can be used for teacher observation. Each varies in the simplicity and in the level of information obtained.

Anecdotal Format. The observer writes in a notebook, in quite terse statements, the sequence of actions and verbalizations of the teacher and the student(s) (Exhibit 11–3). In some cases, the observer may choose to exclude extraneous statements.

- *Advantages:* has flexibility, does not require coding, includes all information within the limitations of the observer, provides a more exact record of what transpired in the teaching session than do postsession recapitulations of what happened.
- *Disadvantages:* not readily quantifiable, observer may spend more time writing than looking, the action may be too fast at times to permit recording all of it, general impressions rather than specific observations may be inadvertently recorded, extraneous information that obscures pertinent information sometimes included, difficult to identify patterns of teacher behaviors to compare observation results to a criterion in verifying the occurrence of a tactic.

Exhibit 11–3 Sample of Anecdotal Record

Trainee *Harold W.*   Class *Ms. Jastings*

Date *9/30*   Subject *Study Hall*

Time Start *2:15*   Time Stop _____

Trainee began by asking children to remain seated throughout the session and use the time to complete the day's assignments – directed Johnny to get his books out – told Andrew to stop fidgeting – moved to back of room – two children in front of room began talking – trainee crowded beside one student who asked for help – three more students began talking – trainee said "I want it quiet in here", students quieted down – began talking within a minute – trainee walked up to desk – – – –

Behavior Checklist. The observer lists the teacher and child behaviors to be observed, observes the teaching session, and checks whether the behaviors occurred and were appropriately executed (Exhibit 11–4).

- *Advantages:* simple to use, provides quantifiable data (number checked yes or no), clearly determines whether something is or is not being done, requires little practice to use, focuses on behaviors of interest, observer can look at several behaviors during a session.
- *Disadvantages:* provides only nominal data, requires supervisor to decide what level of performance is to be checked "yes" or correct, has limited use for providing feedback to trainee and for pinpointing teaching problems, cannot describe a series of teacher activities.

Frequency Observation. The observer makes a list of teacher behaviors and child responses to be observed (similar to the checklist) and records the number of occurrences of each behavior within a specified time (Exhibit 11–5).

- *Advantages:* provides quantifiable data (number of times a teacher behavior or a child response is observed), allows comparisons between teacher behav-

iors (e.g., nags vs. praises), provides feedback and pinpoints problem areas.
- *Disadvantages:* requires practice to use reliably, does not show the sequential relationship between teacher behaviors or teacher behaviors and child responses, limits the number of behaviors that can be observed.

Event Recording. The observer selects and operationally specifies a limited number of behaviors to be observed, identifying how their occurrence is to be recorded (e.g., a code symbol). The observer also identifies how the occurrence of all other behaviors is to be recorded (e.g., a category and code for "other"). The recording sheet used permits the sequential recording of stimulus-response-consequence sequences (Exhibit 11–6).

- *Advantages:* provides a sequential picture of teacher-child interaction, permits the observer to pinpoint teacher behaviors that lead to appropriate or inappropriate student responses, permits accurate pinpoint feedback, provides quantifiable data, provides a standard format for observation across sessions.
- *Disadvantages:* requires considerable practice for reliable use, narrows the selection of teacher behaviors that

Exhibit 11–4 Sample Behavior Checklist Recording Form

Teacher_____	Date _____

	Yes	No
Materials	✓	—
Task Direction	—	✓
Model	✓	—
Praise	✓	—
Correction	—	✓
Data recording	—	✓
Behavior management	✓	—
TOTAL	4	3

Exhibit 11–5 Sample Frequency Recording Form

Teacher *Jack Turnbull*   Date *9/28*

Length of Sessions *10 minutes*

Task Direction	//	2
Question	THL THL THL THL /	21
Model	THL THL /	11
Physical Prompt	////	4
Student Correct Response	THL THL //	12
Praise	THL /	6
Correction	////	4
Data Recording	THL THL THL THL /	21

Exhibit 11–6 Sample Event Recording Form

	Trial 1			Trial 2			Trial 3			Trial 4			Trial 5			Trial 6			Trial 7		
	Teacher	Child Correct	Child Error	Teacher	Child Correct	Child Error	Teacher	Child Correct	Child Error	Teacher	Child Correct	Child Error	Teacher	Child Correct	Child Error	Teacher	Child Correct	Child Error	Teacher	Child Correct	Child Error
Question										1		1							12 7		
model							2	3		2 4	5	3	1			3			3 9		8
Praise																					
Nag										4			6						10		
Other																2 4			5 4 6		

Key:

A. Draw a line down the trial column if the entire sequence is correct

B. Draw a line down the child column to indicate child correct or error responses

C. Use numbers to indicate the sequence of events (e.g., 1 for first event, 2 for second event, etc.)

can be observed at one time, usually requires the use of a code for behavioral categories, is restricted by the task being taught, often provides more information than is needed, probably more a research tool than a clinical tool.

Interval, Point-in-Time, and Duration Formats. Although they have some utility for observing teaching activity, interval, point-in-time, and duration formats may not be useful for verifying teacher use of a given tactic other than behavior management. They are useful when a supervisor is interested in (1) the amount of time spent teaching, (2) teaching activity with a large number of students, and (3) trends in the teaching activities of a group of teachers. These formats often require timing devices, and their use is often not feasible in the typical pattern of supervision visits.

When a teacher first learns a new tactic, teaching errors are likely. At this point, observation formats that provide more information should be used to ensure adequate feedback. As teaching improves, the major purpose of observation shifts toward verification that the teaching tactic is used appropriately, and the checklist approach should be selected. A blank standard form is provided in Appendix A that can be adapted to differing observation purposes. Along the side of the form, the behavior(s) of interest are listed. These may be single teaching responses (e.g., praise, question), or they may be series of teacher-child interactions (e.g., open question-child error-constructed response question-child correct-praise). Units of observation, which are written in the boxes on the form, can vary considerably. For example, they may be teaching trials, units of time, or names of children being instructed. Regardless of content, a unit must be restricted to the smallest or shortest possible event, or series of events, that is consistent and distinguishable across the entire teaching session, because the units form the basis for quantifying the results of the observation. It is advisable to direct a teacher to keep teaching behaviors as succinct as possible for a given stimulus that is presented and to avoid excessive repetition. If a teacher asks the same series of questions and obtains several different responses to one reading word, the reliability of the observation will suffer.

The sample event recording form (Exhibit 11–6) shows how modeling sequences are written. On this form, teacher correction of errors can be recorded. In trials 1 and 2, a line was drawn through each teacher column, indicating that the entire sequence was correctly used. Trial 3 indicates that the teacher began the sequence appropriately, but responded inappropriately to the child's correct response. When teacher errors, like those exhibited in trial 3, occur on three consecutive or more trials, the supervisor should consider shifting to sequential recording in order to provide more accurate feedback. Trial 4 shows a sequential record of a teacher who used the correct modeling sequence and obtained a correct child response. Trial 5 shows a modeling sequence in which the child responded incorrectly at first. Trial 6 shows how a teacher erred in the use of feedback and modeling. Trial 7 shows a more common type of error, i.e., "kitchen sink" teaching, in which there is a great deal of teacher behavior and not much opportunity for child responding.

The checklist or sequential recording procedure can also be used when observing teachers' use of questioning tactics (Exhibit 11–7). Trial 1 shows how simple lines or hash marks are used when the child requires only minimal prompting (e.g., constructed response questions). Trial 2 depicts the correct use of the questioning sequence when the child requires more directed prompting. The sequential recording of teacher's correct and error responses is shown in trials 3 and 4. Correct use of questioning produces the sequence shown in trial 3. When teachers insert extraneous statements, such as directions or side comments, a sequence such as that shown in trial 4 may occur.

Other observation formats may be more useful for some child behaviors being taught. For instance, when chains of motor behaviors are being taught, physical prompting tactics are likely to be used. These present different observation problems.

Completing Observations and Checking Reliability

When observing the performance of a teacher-trainee, the supervisor should

1. be sure that the trainee is informed of the observation and understands its purpose (i.e., to verify or provide constructive feedback).
2. plan to conduct practice runs with the observation procedure before using it with a trainee in order to account for unanticipated events.
3. take a position close to the teaching activity in order to see and hear all the events as they unfold in the teaching session.
4. avoid interrupting or responding to children, because it may bias the observation. Planned ignoring is the most useful tactic while observing.
5. continue the observation, once it has begun, and adhere to the planned observation procedures as well as to the specified response definitions.

As mentioned earlier, direct observation of teacher-trainees is not helpful unless those observations are reliable. The most useful index of reliability is the extent to which two people agree on the teaching behavior they have observed. Therefore, it is strongly suggested that, in practice observations and during a sample of visits to practicum sites, the observer asks a colleague to participate in the observation—concurrently, but separately, observing a trainee or trainees by means of the same observation procedures. These observations must be independent; the recordings of neither observer can be visible to the other, and no discussion of the events observed can take place during the observation, and no changes should be made in what has been recorded.

There are several indexes of reliability. Typically, observers determine whether there was an agreement or disagreement between them on each recording unit, such as whether modeling was or was not employed on a regular trial. Then, the total number of agreements is divided by the sum of agreements and disagreements, and multiplied by 100 to arrive at a percentage agreement score. There are no set criteria of acceptability, but the percentages of agreement should average at least 80% and range no lower than 70%. If there is considerable disagreement, there are at least three possibilities: (1) the observation procedure is too complex for the information needed, (2) the observation procedures are inappropriate, or (3) the period of practice observations is too short. Reliability may be improved if the two observers

- rehearse before actually observing by calling out observed events as they occur in order to obtain an event-by-event indication of how close the agreement is

Exhibit 11–7 Sequential Record of Teacher-Child Interaction during Use of Questioning Tactics

Key:

A. Draw a line down the trial column if the entire sequence is correct.

B. Draw a line down the child column to indicate child correct or error responses.

B. Use numbers to indicate the sequence of events (e.g., 1 for first event, 2 for second event, etc.)

- discuss the operational definitions and refine their specifications
- consider eliminating behaviors that are not as crucial as others from those to be observed
- compare the two data sheets at a given point and more clearly define the units or trials observed if the data sheets do not correspond
- look for patterns of disagreement to help determine the source of problems
- simplify the recording procedure so that less time is spent writing and more time is spent observing (e.g., check marks or plus-minus recording instead of numbered codes)
- agree in advance on recording conventions for a particular problem event

In the earlier example of Dr. Pauline Burz' observation of Jack Turnbull's direct teaching tactics, Dr. Burz' first visit suggested that Jack was inconsistent in his teaching presentations. Because the exact nature of these inconsistencies was not readily apparent from informal observation, it was decided that a more complete and reliable observation was needed.

After Dr. Burz' first informal visit to Jack's practicum classroom, Jack and Dr. Burz met to work out a procedure for observing his teaching

Exhibit 11-8 Teacher Presentation Guide

TEACHER PRESENTATION GUIDE

INTERVENE:

Setting/Materials	Teacher Says/Does	Child Says/Does
Group Math, addition with 3 place addends and carrying, worksheets Individual Math, same worksheets	1. Pointed Praise ("I like the way you're staying in seat") 2. Examine problems —request response — Praise Model — request response — Praise	Sits in seat, looks at worksheet, completes problems errs/fails to complete problems (a) Answers correctly (b) errs Answers correctly

REDIRECT:

Setting/Materials	Teacher Says/Does	Child Says/Does

Exhibit 11-9 Dr. Burz' General Observation Form

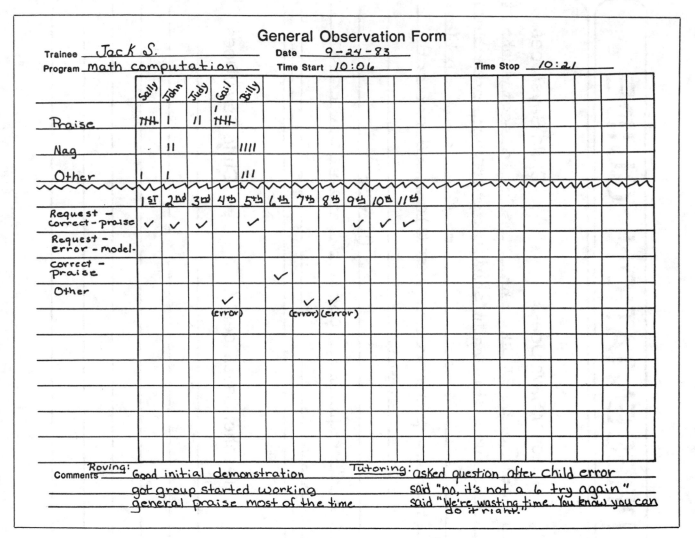

systematically. They began by examining the Teacher Presentation Guide that Jack had completed (Exhibit 11–8). In this program, Jack was practicing group-individualized instruction tactics and using modeling tactics in on-the-spot tutoring. They both decided that the object of the group-individualized practice was to increase Jack's use of pointed praise statements and reduce his negative or neutral comments. They agreed not only that it was important to check whether Jack was providing a disproportionate amount of attention to some children but also that his on-the-spot tutoring behaviors should be observed fairly closely.

Dr. Burz used the standard observation form (Appendix A), which had been filled in with the pertinent teacher behaviors, during her next visit to Jack's classroom. The top half of the observation sheet was used to tally the occurrences of these

three behaviors (numbers 1, 2, and 3) across the five children he was teaching (Exhibit 11–9). The lower half of the observation form was used to record Jack's use of a response-dependent modeling procedure during individual tutoring. Because the intent was to determine whether the sequence of teacher behaviors was correct, Dr. Burz simply checked Jack's correct use of the sequence request-correct-praise (number 1) or request-error-model-correct-praise (number 2), and the incorrect teacher behaviors (number 3). Each time Jack attempted the procedure it was considered a trial (e.g., first, second, third). Dr. Burz also wrote comments, particularly when teaching errors occurred, as a reminder of what happened. The results of this and subsequent observations, as well as the feedback Dr. Burz provided to Jack, are described in the next chapter.

Chapter 12

Redirection and Verification of Direct Teaching

S ome teachers, from the start, exhibit such appropriate teaching behaviors that they are said to be "natural teachers" who have made teaching an "art." Only a small percentage of the teaching force can be considered "naturally talented," however; the remainder of us (possibly 95%) must build the needed teaching skills through a concerted effort. This process can be such an arduous task that few teachers become skillful without assistance from teacher supervisors or colleagues. Supervision and guidance during field experience can potentially provide the most help, especially if it involves feedback and redirection regarding planning, measurement, and instructional presentation behaviors that are intended to change child behaviors. It is during early teaching experience that both good and poor teachers are made. The most succinct statement regarding this point was made by Hofmeister (1971), who observed that a pattern of teaching is established in the first year. Twenty years of experience, good or bad, may be 20 replications of that first year.

ADEQUACY OF FEEDBACK AND REDIRECTION

The effectiveness of many supervision procedures currently used in efforts to improve the teaching skills of teacher-trainees is at best unclear. The limited evidence suggests that the less systematic the supervision provided, the less the impact on the trainee. For instance, a study described by Borg (1970) demonstrated that teacher-trainees who used a videotape self-critique procedure in microteaching sessions became more skilled in employing prescribed teaching behaviors than did those who practiced under the supervision of college instructors. This is not to imply that direct supervision of teacher-trainees should be abolished, but rather that conventional supervision approaches may be falling short of their intended purpose.

The supervisor of a conventional student teaching or practicum experience typically makes one or two visits to the practice teaching site during the semester or quarter, either to get the trainee started or to determine whether the requirements of the experience have been met. Additional visits may be made if a problem arises. Because so many factors affect the success of the experience, supervisors frequently use a quite general checklist that notes personality, grooming, reliability, punctuality, general preparation, and management factors, as well as items directly related to instruction. For many of these factors, the completion of a checklist once or twice during the experience is sufficient. If direct teaching behaviors (planning, measurement, teaching presentations) were assessed in the same manner, however, the supervisor could be misinformed, and trainees who lack minimum competencies could be accepted into the teaching field. Supervisors should augment the more global checklist procedure in areas relating to direct teaching competencies. The time and effort required are often cited as the reasons that infrequent supervisory contact and general assessment of teaching practice are retained. In addition, the high student loads and diversity of situations in which teaching practice occurs are often believed to militate against a change in supervisory approach. Considering the importance of intensive supervision in conjunction with early teaching practice, however, these should be considered obstacles to be surmounted, rather than excuses for the continuation of potentially inadequate supervision.

Supervisors of in-service teachers are not always in any better position to provide systematic supervision than is the college or university professor. The special education supervisor in the schools must set up program operations, process diagnostic and individualized educational program (IEP) paper work, participate in hearings, testify in court, and put out a variety of "brush fires." Generally, observation of classroom teachers is restricted to occasional visits (once or twice per year) and, again, is generally unsystematic in content.

Typically, school district supervisors are based in the district office and must rely on indirect sources of information (e.g., school principals, parents, other teachers) to arrive at judgments regarding a teacher's adequacy. Granted, this information is useful and helps to identify glaring problems, but the precise identification of teaching deficiencies can seldom be arrived at through indirect information sources.

The consequences of infrequent and unsystematic teacher supervision can be seen in the manner in which in-service training targets are selected. Rarely is the selection of these training targets based on programmatic needs (West & Stowitschek, 1981). Because a "needs assessment survey" may go no further than asking the prospective participants what they would like, training is often focused on what is in vogue at the time. A programmatic approach to in-service training should be based on assessments of the educational performance of children taught by in-service teachers and the classroom performance of those teachers. Then, teacher opinions can be compared with these two assessments to identify needs.

When the Field-based Special Teacher Education Program shifted from low- to high-frequency direct supervision in 1975, a great deal of effort was devoted to the development and evaluation of the supervision model and to activities other than supervision. In later stages of operation (1980), the burden of support had been increasingly subsumed by the regular training program. The essential factor in this process was a shift in priorities.

An in-service version of the Field-based Special Teacher Education Program was used in a rural school district (Cavallaro et al., 1981). During the initial meetings, the special education supervisor identified the activity as a priority and planned with participants to resolve individual logistics problems. The district had no additional resources, but was able to arrange for direct and indirect supervision alternatives among existing personnel. Again, once established as a priority, the practical problems of carrying out systematic supervision were found to be manageable.

As discussed earlier, the first two components of the supervision process are (1) organizing direct teaching practice and (2) inspecting and observing direct teaching practice. The third component of the process, feedback and

Figure 12–1 Final Two Components of the Supervision Model

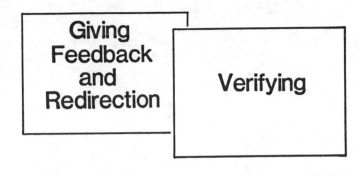

redirection, fosters skillful teaching; the fourth, verification, makes teaching competence a functional concept (Figure 12–1).

GIVING FEEDBACK AND REDIRECTION

Obviously, the components of the supervision process overlap; for example, giving feedback alternates with observing trainee performance. The important distinction to maintain is that feedback and redirection must flow systematically from appropriate sources of information (e.g., observation of trainee performance, reports from supervising teachers, trainee verbal reports). Because the interpretation of verbal reports can lead to erroneous assumptions, they should be corroborated by more direct inputs. Several problems actually encountered by supervisors in the field-based program were documented and subsequently used as benchmarks for other supervisors. These benchmarks for interpreting inputs on trainee performance are

- specific focus. The supervisor should avoid the temptation to look for general attributes of "good" or "poor" teaching and concentrate on prespecified teaching procedures, and deal with one at a time. Using a sequential model will help the supervisor to concentrate feedback on one type of teacher behavior.

- judicial selection. When the intent is to provide feedback regarding teaching procedures, the supervisor should place the greatest reliance on direct sources of information (e.g., inspection/observation). When teaching deficits or other problems are of serious concern to the supervisory teacher, the supervisor should rely more on that person's reports, but attempt to corroborate those reports with other information.

- preconditions for determining progress. At the time that the supervisor and trainee agree on the teaching tactic(s) to be practiced, the level of proficiency to be aimed for should be specified. Also, the rate of child progress considered minimally acceptable should be specified. These expectations for teacher and child behavior should assist the supervisor in judging the utility of the information being provided.

- consistency of information. If the current information is not consistent with information previously used to make decisions and give feedback, conflicts with previous suggestions made to the trainee may arise. The supervisor should not forget about the suggestions made to a trainee from one visit to the next.

Trainees may anticipate the process of receiving feedback and redirection as a negative experience. The supervisor can employ several techniques to ensure that the experience is both positive and constructive, however. First, if this type of supervision activity is a frequent and routine part of the supervisor's responsibilities, the trainee will not view it as inordinate. Second, if the feedback and redirective suggestions flow directly from what the supervisor and the trainee planned together (e.g., Direct Teaching Program Checklist, Preprogram Planner, Daily Planner), the sense of the unknown about the process will be reduced. Third, the manner in which the supervisor conducts the meeting can greatly affect its impact. The following are general guidelines for giving ongoing feedback and redirection:

1. Begin by summarizing the practicum experience. List the basic elements of the instruction program (e.g., what was targeted, what interpretation was specified) and the teaching tactics that were to be practiced and demonstrated.
2. Commend the trainee. Identify particular teaching activities or behaviors that were done well and describe how they were particularly useful. Do not attach a *but, however,* or *on the other hand* to the commendation. Do not commend the trainee for an utter disaster of an experience, however. When that is the case, it is probably best to get right to the point (corrective feedback) so as to avoid any misunderstanding about the acceptability of the trainee's teaching.
3. Encourage the trainee to identify his or her own perceptions of the experience. Ask the trainee to summarize the experience, including strong points as well as areas thought to need improvement. Acknowledge those points that are consistent with supervisory findings and seek clarification from the trainee on others. It may be necessary to prompt the trainee's responses with an initial suggestion (e.g., "Do you think any negative comments popped up in your teaching?").
4. Describe the teaching pattern. Verbally walk through a teaching sequence with the trainee, indicating what teaching errors occurred.

5. Describe, model, or prompt the desired teaching tactic(s). Redirect the efforts of the trainee to the extent permitted by the situation. Depending on the level of the trainee's understanding, this redirection may take the form of (a) orally describing the tactic; (b) providing a written diagram to follow, assuming the original description on the Teacher Presentation Guide was inadequate; (c) modeling the tactic in a role play situation; (d) modeling the tactic with the trainee's students; or (e) providing coaching (immediate prompting and feedback while the trainee is teaching). These alternatives are typically combined (e.g., verbal instruction, written diagram, modeling through role play). Direct prompting and feedback during teaching is probably the most effective redirection procedure, but it is also time-consuming and is not necessary with all trainees. The supervisor must be prepared to provide these redirection alternatives, if necessary, however.
6. Conclude in a positive vein. Sum up the meeting with a review of the positive aspects of the observed teaching session. If the entire experience is to be summarized, begin with areas that need improvement so as to end with the areas that were commendable.

Specific applications of the feedback guidelines are highly dependent on the unique events that surround each practicum, trainee, pupil, and program. In order to maintain a systematic approach, feedback should be focused on the documents and observations related to the planned instructional program. The following collection of problems were typical of the practicum experiences in Peabody's field-based program (Shores et al., 1979).

1. Problem area: practicum records

    - Discrepancies between recorded and observed events, indicated by comparisons of Checklist, Preprogram Planner, trainee's recorded data, and supervisor observation

      The trainee's plan indicated a daily probe with each session, but the daily schedule showed that the probe followed each session. Thus, the probe may have shown inflated results, owing to the priming effect of the session that preceded it.

    - Delay in updating of records, indicated by inspection of Daily Planner

      A trainee may wait until the end of the week to transfer raw data from the teaching session to the Daily Planner. Thus, a comparison of these results to previous results (on the same metric) would be delayed, putting off an important decision on needed program changes.

- Improperly coded records, indicated by Presentation Guide, Daily Planner, and perhaps other forms

A trainee using a modified Graduated Guidance strategy recorded prompt code 43 on every Daily Planner entry when physical assistance was used. Because full physical assistance (42), partial assistance (42), and shadowing (43) are included, it seems most appropriate to list the predominant tactic occurring in a session first and then list other tactics used. Physical assistance would then be listed first in the earlier sessions and, as progress occurs, the partial physical (42) or shadowing sequence, with full physical assistance eventually dropping out.

2. Problem area: targeting

- Selection of low-priority targets, indicated by comparison of trainee records with IEPs or teacher's records

A trainee may elect to teach color discrimination because it is a commonly selected target, even though the supervising teacher does not consider it functional. Another trainee may select to teach "eye contact" when it is not a prerequisite for an identified skill to be taught or even part of a social conversation program.

3. Problem area: analysis

- Instruction in a program's subtasks that does not contribute to the acquisition of the short-term (terminal) objectives, indicated by initial inspection of Preprogram Planner and results of daily instruction

A child referred to a resource teacher for illegible handwriting in daily work is assigned handwriting practice worksheets. His daily assignments continue to be illegible.

- Planned task sequence that may be logically sound but not effective for a particular child, indicated by comparison of Preprogram Planner with results recorded on the Daily Planner or on raw data

A trainee prepared a shoe tying program that employed the "double bow" (rabbit ears) method in the task analysis. For many children, this is the most efficient method. For others, the single loop-wrap around sequence best matches their motor skills.

- Selection of criteria inappropriate for the skill to be taught, indicated by initial inspection of Preprogram Planner and results of daily instruction

A trainee planned a toilet training program in which the step criterion for a portion of the program was stated as "will wipe with 90% accuracy."

- Criteria were increased too rapidly, indicated by comparison of Preprogram Planner with results of daily teaching when the student is working on task proficiency

When the number of 3-place multiplication problems a student was required to complete correctly was increased by 3 per day, accuracy diminished, and the child became frustrated.

4. Problem area: initial assessment

- Child placed at a level that is too advanced in the program sequence, indicated by comparison of initial assessment with results of daily teaching (as indicated on the Daily Planner)

A child was able to count a quarter and a dime and write 35 cents on the pretest. As instruction progressed, it was found that the child was not able to count any other combination. Further, it was found that the child could not count by any units other than ones. Fortunately, the trainee did not attempt to "press on," but dropped back to teach some more basic counting operations.

- Generalized responding taught but not assessed, indicated by comparison of teaching conditions specified on the Checklist. Presentation guidelines with the specified assessment condition.

In a program for teaching the concept *animal* the teaching presentation items are horse, mouse, house, dog, tree, person, coat; the probe items are house, mouse, coat, horse, tree, person, dog.

5. Problem area: intervention

- Intervention procedure continued when a student is not making progress, indicated by comparison of Daily Planner with raw data summaries (e.g., graph, tally sheet)

A child making little or no progress in his fourth-grade math computation practice exercise book was assigned to a student teacher. She planned a program based on the high amount of off-task behavior observed in this child. After 11 days of intervention (praise contingent on on-task behavior), no appreciable difference in the child's math computation skills was evident, even though he worked on task for most of the daily exercise period.

- Several changes in intervention made at the same time, indicated by comparison of Daily Planner with the redirect portion of the Teacher Presentation Guide or trainee notes describing the intervention

In the situation described previously, the trainee finally changed the intervention procedures. However, she changed the contingency (on-task behavior plus more problems covered per day), the arranged event (praise plus tokens exchanged for privileges), and the presentation mode (permanent models added to the exercise sheets). Even if the child's performance improved, the trainee would have no way of judging which change had the effect. Thus, a direct relationship, between teacher behavior and child outcome cannot be established to verify the successful acquisition of a teaching tactic.

- Teacher attending to child behaviors other than those targeted in the program, indicated by direct observation as compared with the Teacher Presentation Guide

Trainee presents a math flashcard with the fact 4 + 6 = and asks, "What is four plus six?" The child answers, "Four plus six equals ten," while looking down and turning in his chair. The teacher responds, "Now, sit up straight. Don't be a slouch."

- Supplying more teacher antecedents than necessary, indicated by direct observation and, perhaps, the Teacher Presentation Guide

Wanting to be of help during the math individual seat work activity, a teacher trainee spent several minutes with each child, asking questions, giving directions, supplying models and general encouragement. During this activity, the child spent most of the time looking and listening. The teacher, thinking he was helping, actually was reducing the child's opportunity to respond (writing answers to math problems on paper). In addition, the trainee subsequently reduced his opportunity to consequate correct child responses.

- Intermingling tactics prematurely, indicated by direct observation and, perhaps, the Teacher Presentation Guide

A teacher who has used antecedent modeling procedures for two sessions in a group-individualized reading exercise begins to add some diagnostic questions. The first tactic was not yet firmly established in her repertoire and, with the addition of questions, her use of modeling in sequence deteriorated.

6. Problem area: progress monitoring

- Changing the type of progress measure used during the program, indicated by Daily Planner or inspection of trainee's raw data

Little progress was occurring in teaching a young child to recognize pictures of common objects. The trainee decided to use actual objects and pair them with the pictures. At the same time, the progress measure shifted from pointing to pictures of objects to pointing to actual objects. It would have been acceptable to add this to the measurement procedure, but not to delete the picture recognition task. If it were deleted, data from neither the original assessment nor from the earlier intervention would be comparable.

- Violation of data graphing conventions, indicated by program graph or chart, raw data sheets

A trainee specified four subtasks in an expressive language program: saying nouns, verbs, pronouns and complete sentences (e.g., I want a cookie.). Each subtask was taught separately. However, each was assigned a portion on the ordinate (nouns 0% to 25%, verbs 25% to 50%, pronouns 50% to 75%, complete sentences 75% to 100%) with the ordinate labeled %correct. Although a child could respond correctly to all of the stimuli presented for a subtask ("say cookie"), the child would receive a mark no higher than 25% correct on the graph.

7. Problem area: redirection

- Basic changes in the program purpose when a change in intervention is all that is needed, indicated by Daily Planner, trainer's notes, Teacher Presentation Guide (redirection section)

A teacher-trainee, attempting to teach a child diagnosed as autistic to sign, was becoming frustrated with the lack of progress. The task was to give an acceptable approximation of the sign for common objects on request. About half the time, the child would give an acceptable sign, and the trainee would give him a raisin; about half the time, he would either give the wrong sign or an unacceptable approximation of the correct sign. The trainee planned the following changes: (1) switch the task to pointing out correct signs in a book, (2) add physical prompts to the presentation repertoire, (3) bring in a second trainee to serve as a correct model, and (4) add a token economy, with points exchangeable for toys. The supervisor's suggestion was to continue the program as before, but to require consecutive correct responses before delivering the raisin, beginning with three responses and systematically increasing the requirement to 10 responses. Within 4 days, all signs in the first set were used acceptably 100% of the time, and new signs were being added.

A REDIRECTION STRATEGY

Many suggestions for revisions to an instruction program are situation-specific. Although some simple program modifications consistently improve teacher and child performance, others consume time and effort, yet produce minimal results. A materials adaptation strategy suggested by Stowitschek, Gable, and Hendrickson (1980), termed the Consequence-Stimulus-Response (C-S-R) strategy, appears to have general applications for guiding the modification of many instruction programs. A sequential approach is used to consider modifications.

The vast majority of the instructional problems of trainees in Peabody's field-based program related to the manner in which they consequated targeted behaviors of their students. Problems often arose because they (1) selected consequent events that were not reinforcing to their students, (2) were inconsistent in their delivery of consequent events, or (3) did not schedule delivery of consequent events so as to make it clear to the learner that correct responses were necessary. Redirective suggestions to compensate for these problems are straightforward and relatively simple to implement. Thus, they should be considered as a first resort.

If it has been determined that the problem does not originate in this area, or additional problems are evident in other areas, the manner in which the task is presented (stimulus) could be the source of problems. A trainee may (1) be inconsistent in the manner of presentation, (2) fail to present the stimulus conditions in the teaching session that led the student to respond correctly to the stimulus condition in the test situation, (3) fail to provide sufficient prompts to ensure correct responding and keep errors to a minimum, or (4) have created a condition in which it is more reinforcing for the learner to respond under conditions of heavy prompting than to respond under unprompted conditions (e.g., full physical guidance may inadvertently provide physical attention for waiting). Redirection ranges from simply adding a prompt to extra coaching and supervised practice in order to increase the consistency of the trainee's use of a tactic.

Program changes relating to the learner's response may involve reanalyzing the task. In this case, it may be necessary to make many other program modifications. On the other hand, if a gap or misordering in the sequence of learning tasks is the problem, only minor changes may be needed. The redirective activities of Dr. Pauline Burz are described in the following as a continuation of the example in Chapter 11.[1]

Dr. Burz: "Well, Jack, I think you've come along quite well on the things we talked about last time. You used the demonstration and permanent model very effectively, and the entire group got right to the task on your signal. What are the things you noticed about this teaching session?"

Jack: "Well, I think I used more general than pointed praise and the on-the-spot tutoring didn't seem to go well. The kids weren't really tuned in to what they were doing, but I still think they are enjoying the new exercises."

[1] We recognize that it is not advisable to have a trainee practice two teaching tactics simultaneously. We are including them in the same example for purposes of brevity. In order to follow this example, it may be necessary to refer to Exhibit 11-9.

Dr. Burz: "You're right on the general praise thing. I'd suggest you drop the all right and think of the behaviors you're looking for—things like staying in their seats, looking at their own work, keeping that pencil moving, and including them in your verbal praise comments."

Jack: "Yes, maybe I should list them out first."

Dr. Burz: "Fine, if you think you need to. Two other things that are showing up on the observation form are the ratio of praise to negative and other comments and to whom you are directing them."

Jack: "Yes, I noticed I was getting on Billy's case quite a bit."

Dr. Burz: "Well, it seems easy to slip into with good old Billy pulling his tricks. Changing that ratio may help you start giving less attention to Billy's off-task behaviors. Right now, you are operating close to one negative comment for every four praise statements. Although it would be desirable to drop out all negative comments, it is probably more realistic to shoot for at least a high level of praises at first."

Jack: "Should I try and keep a count as I move around the room?"

Dr. Burz: "Well, that may interfere with your interactions with the students. You may try taping a tally sheet to your desk and dropping by it every 2 or 3 minutes to jot down an estimate of praises and nags. That way you don't have to count, but you only have to recall what occurred in the previous couple of minutes. Now, if you combine this change with more equal distribution of your positive attention across the students, I think you will find there are fewer occasions to nag. Even Billy is on task some of the time."

Jack: "Yes, I seem to recall one or two rare occurrences, but what about when I'm trying out the on-the-spot tutoring procedures?"

Dr. Burz: "Well, it's not easy, but if you can get yourself to glance around the room occasionally, you could do what we called 'shooting some praise.' I'll tell you what. If, by the next visit, we don't see more on-task work from Billy and the other students, we may focus entirely on the group-individualized attention procedures and bring the on-the-spot tutoring procedure back in later."

Jack: "All right, but I'd like to keep on with both for now if you think the tutoring is going all right."

Dr. Burz: "You are using the modeling procedure quite consistently when the child's responses are correct. It's when errors occur that

you are resorting to other things, such as questions or coaching. I think one thing you can do is to go back to using the modeling sequence chart when you tutor. Use the chart until you notice that these other comments have dropped out for 3 days in a row."

Jack: "I suppose I did move away from it a little too fast."

Dr. Burz: "Well, when you're moving from desk to desk, you don't want to have to carry things around forever."

AN INSERVICE SUPERVISION EXAMPLE

Systematic supervision has been combined with exportable training for paraprofessionals and their supervisors working with retarded persons. The systematic skill training workshops (Lent, Riall, & Stowitschek, 1981) included a system for supervising the acquisition and use of a modified graduated guidance teaching procedure applied to self-help skills of handicapped learners. The system included four phases: (1) observing with the trainer observation and feedback (TOF) sheet; (2) giving feedback using side two of the TOF sheet, (3) monitoring implementation of the training using the Progress Monitoring Chart, and (4) reprogramming when learner progress does not occur:

1. observing (Exhibit 12–1). A training trial conducted by a paraprofessional is observed by his or her immediate supervisor. The trainer responses preceding and following each task step of the training trial are circled if correctly performed or slashed if incorrectly performed or omitted. Criteria for trainer errors allowed (bottom left of sheet) are used to determine the adequacy of the training trial.
2. giving feedback (Exhibit 12–2). The feedback form is a checklist of questions regarding how the session was organized and taught and how results were recorded. Feedback procedures are applied as the supervisor progresses through the checklist.
3. monitoring progress (Exhibit 12–3). The Progress Monitoring Chart permits an ongoing comparison of observation training schedules and learner progress recorded by the trainer on a weekly basis. It allows the supervisor to track

* one trainer teaching several tasks to one learner (up to 20 observations)
* one trainer teaching several learners
* several trainers, each teaching one learner (5 observations per chart)

Exhibit 12–1 Example of an Observation Form Used in Training Paraprofessionals

Trainer Observation and Feedback Sheet (TOF)
Side One

Trainer: _____   Date: _____ Time: _____

Learner: _____   Supervisor: _____

Task Instruction:	Teaching Strategy:	Comments:
1.	S 0 1 2 3 4 + - C	
2.	S 0 1 2 3 4 + - C	
3.	S 0 1 2 3 4 + - C	
4.	S 0 1 2 3 4 + - C	
5.	S 0 1 2 3 4 + - C	
6.	S 0 1 2 3 4 + - C	
7.	S 0 1 2 3 4 + - C	
8.	S 0 1 2 3 4 + - C	
9.	S 0 1 2 3 4 + - C	
10.	S 0 1 2 3 4 + - C	
11.	S 0 1 2 3 4 + - C	
12.	S 0 1 2 3 4 + - C	
13.	S 0 1 2 3 4 + - C	
14.	S 0 1 2 3 4 + - C	
15.	S 0 1 2 3 4 + - C	
16.	S 0 1 2 3 4 + - C	
17.	S 0 1 2 3 4 + - C	

Total Steps   Goal to Be Met

____ 1-4   Can miss 0
____ 5-9   Can miss up to One
____ 10-14   Can miss up to Two
____ 15-19   Can miss up to Three
____ 20-24   Can miss up to Four
____ 25-31   Can miss up to Five

_____ correct step directions
_____ correct hand positions
_____ praise
Comments:

Key

(S) Task Instruction
(0) Step Direction
(1) Full Physical
(2) Partial Physical
(3) Shadowing
(4) No Help
(+) Praise
(-) Negative
(C) Correction

Source: Adapted from a preliminary version of the Systematic Training Program. George Peabody College for Teachers of Vanderbilt University. Nashville. Tennessee.

Exhibit 12–2 Checklist Used in Providing Feedback to a Paraprofessional Trainee

Trainer Observation and Feedback Sheet
Side Two

Set Up
1. Data Sheet close by during training . . . . YES   NO
2. Materials close at hand during training . . . . YES   NO
Comments: _____

_____

Teaching Strategy
3. All steps in the program completed? . . . . YES   NO
4. Trainer spoke the exact program words? . . . . YES   NO
5. Trainer gave correct hand positions? . . . . YES   NO
6. Final Reinforcement: Praise or Other? . . . . YES   NO
7. All steps in order? . . . . YES   NO
8. Praise/Correcton: Goal Met? . . . . YES   NO
9. Agreement on hand positions: Goal Met? . . . . YES   NO
Comments: _____

_____

Data Collection
10. Trainer recorded data immediately after trial? . . . . YES   NO
11. Trainer added data immediately after session? . . . . YES   NO
12. Data sheet up to date. . . . . YES   NO
13. Graph sheet up to date. . . . . YES   NO
14. Total # of trials for the week?_____At least_____? . . . . YES   NO
15. Highest total score for the week?_____Higher than
    last observation? . . . . YES   NO
Comments: _____

_____

Reminder
Begin with a statement of praise on a strength area.
Systematically review this sheet with the trainer.
Give appropriate suggestions and/or demonstrations where needed.
Answer any questions and encourage comments and/or suggestions.
End with a statement of praise on a strength area.

Source: Adapted from a preliminary version of the Systematic Training Program. George Peabody College for Teachers of Vanderbilt University. Nashville. Tennessee.

Exhibit 12-3 Monitoring Form Relating Trainer's Behavior to Client Performance

Progress Monitoring Chart

Supervisor _____

	Trainer, Learner			Trainer, Learner			Trainer, Learner			Trainer, Learner		
	Task			Task			Task			Task		
OBSERVATION OF TRAINING												
Date												
Time												
Set Up												
1-2 Questions all yes? (If not-which questions)												
Teaching Strategy												
3-7 Questions all yes? (if not-which questions)												
3 Praise/Correction Goal met?												
9 Agreement with trainer Goal met?												
Data Collection												
10-13 Questions all yes? (If not-which questions)												
Trainer Proficient Yet?												
TRAINING SCHEDULE												
Days												
Time(s)												
14 Target number of trials for that week												
Actual number of trials for that week												
Difference												
LEARNER PROGRESS												
Long term goal score												
15 Highest and lowest score for that week												
Higher than last week?												
DATE TRANSFERRED TO IHP OR IEP												

Source: Adapted from a preliminary version of the Systematic Training Program, George Peabody College for Teachers of Vanderbilt University, Nashville, Tennessee.

and decide

- the point at which observation of trainers can be faded out
- the point at which observation of trainers must be resumed
- whether the teaching procedure is in error
- whether the learner is receiving a sufficient number of teaching trials
- whether learner progress is occurring as a result of the teaching procedure and the scheduling of a specified number of teaching trials

4. reprogramming. When the learner is not making progress, it may be necessary to modify either the consequent events that the trainer is providing or the task steps being taught. As a last resort, the presentation procedure may also be modified.

VERIFICATION

The culminating act of verifying direct teaching competencies is simple, but the planning, inspection, observation, feedback, and redirection activities that verification represents are quite involved. In the more limited sense, competency verification can be an exact way of determining when a trainee has successfully completed a practicum experience. In an expanded sense, it can serve as a means of determining the utility of instructional offerings in a program. The greatest significance of competency verification lies in teacher certification and maintenance of quality in teaching, however. Competence should not be a construct that pertains only to pre-service preparation or to didactic instruction. It should be a common reference point for professional standards and for critical decisions spanning an individual teacher's career.

The initial preparation of special education teachers has been programmatic to the point of graduation. The renewal or updating of in-service teachers has been decidedly unprogrammatic. Attempts to use teacher certification or recertification as a means of bringing continuity to teacher preparation have met with varied success. The more successful attempts have been those that established some classroom-related reference points and did not rely on the number of course credits accrued. Other certification programs that purport to be based on competency or performance have added a list of competency statements, but have continued to certify teachers based on the accrual of course credits. Many have lacked a means of verifying (1) that competencies have been attained and (2) that their application has at least a concurrent relationship with changes in the educational per-

formance of handicapped children. Of course, this effort required to verify competence is greater than that required to count credits, but the real and potential benefits far outweigh the disadvantages. Potential benefits include the following:

- Reciprocity of teacher certification across state lines could become standardized because the unit of evaluation (competency statement) could be clarified. Now, it is often unclear whether one course is equivalent to another with a similar title or catalogue description.
- The reputation of a teacher education program would not vary with the number of acceptable or unacceptable teachers hired in school systems, but on the quality its graduates demonstrate beyond the minimum level.
- The problem of locating acceptable model teachers to supervise trainees would be reduced because they would probably "speak the same language."
- Needs assessments for in-service teacher training need not rest on opinions alone, but on demonstrations of classroom teaching and on child outcomes.
- In-service training activities could be sequenced programmatically, and training could begin to move away from the "one-shot" workshop approach.
- Follow-up evaluation of the effects of training could be directly referenced to the assessed teacher needs.

Competency verification has been used to upgrade teaching standards in some cases. For example, although initially focused on core teaching competencies, the verification procedures used in Peabody's Field-based Training Program evolved into a complete special education certification program. Using prespecified guidelines, a departmental committee reviewed documents submitted by students as evidence that they had attained necessary teaching competencies. The certification review also listed courses taken by the trainee so that the procedure would be compatible with certification programs that were dependent on course credits as the certifying unit.

A performance-based teacher certification program was instituted in Georgia (Bryan & Roederer, 1979). This program is based partially on the premise that "teacher development should continue into the early years of employment so that new teachers could actually demonstrate their professional competence" (p. 1). Beginning teachers receive a nonrenewable certificate after successfully completing an approved degree course in education and passing an examination in their subject matter area. This certificate is valid for a period of up to 3 years. In order to obtain a renewable certificate, teachers must demonstrate on-the-job mastery of teaching skills. Master teachers from each participating school district are trained as data collectors; they gather information on teaching plans and materials, classroom procedures, interpersonal skills, professional standards, and student perceptions. A profile of teacher ratings relative to 52 generic competency statements is compiled and used for personnel preparation as well as certification decisions. Although the Georgia certification procedure does not reference its performance-based component to child outcomes, it is a significant step in that direction.

In addition to surveying teachers and administrators regarding appropriate targets for in-service training, the state of Utah has launched a pilot program to select topics by combining direct observation and assessment of child performance with these surveys. It is hoped that, in this way, the selection of topics and objectives for teacher renewal activities will more accurately reflect not only the perceived needs of special education teachers, but also the measured needs of handicapped children.

Just as other professions have recognized the need to ensure the competence of all their members through examination and reexamination, so are the education professions acknowledging the need to verify teaching competence, demonstrated as teacher performance that positively affects child performance.

References

Abt Associates (1976). *Education as experimentation: A planned variation model* (Vol. 3). Cambridge, Mass.: Abt Associates.

Abt Associates (1977). *Education as experimentation: A planned variation model* (Vol. 4). Cambridge, Mass.: Abt Associates.

Adams, T. (1964). The development of a method for analysis of questions asked by teachers in classroom discussion (Doctoral dissertation, Rutgers University). *Dissertation Abstracts International*, A-2809 (University Microfilms No. 64-11, 745).

Adamson, G., Shrango, M., & Van Etten, G. (1972). *Basic educational skills inventory*. Rolling Hills Estates, Calif.: B.L. Winch & Associates.

Allen, K.E. (1980). The language impaired child in the preschool: The role of the teacher. *The Directive Teacher, 2*, 6–10.

Anderhalter, O., & Shands, F. (1976). *Analysis of skills: Reading*. Bensenville, Ill.: Scholastic Testing Service.

Armstrong, J. (1977). The use of a diagnostic questioning strategy to teach educationally handicapped children to solve verbal reasoning problems. Unpublished education specialist thesis, George Peabody College for Teachers.

Aschner, M. (1961). Asking questions to trigger thinking. *National Education Association Journal, 50*, 44–46.

Azrin, N., & Besalel, V. (1980). *How to use overcorrection*. Lawrence, Kans.: H & H Enterprises.

Baer, D.M., Peterson, R.F., & Sherman, J.A. (1967). The development of imitation by reinforcing behavioral similarity to a model. *Journal of the Experimental Analysis of Behavior, 10*, 405–416.

Bandura, A. (1965). Influence of models' reinforcement contingencies on the acquisition of imitative responses. *Journal of Personality and Social Psychology, 1*(6), 589–595.

Bandura, A. (1968). Social-learning theory of identificatory process. In D.A. Goslin (Eds.), *Handbook of socialization theory and research*. Chicago: Rand-McNally.

Bandura, A. (1969). *Principles of behavior modification*. New York: Holt, Rinehart & Winston.

Beatty, L., Madden, R., Gardner, E., & Karlsen, B. (1976). *Stanford diagnostic mathematics test*. New York: Psychological Corporation.

Becker, J., & Jackson, D.A. (1974). *The behavior analysis phonics primer*. Lawrence, Kans.: Jill Becker and Student Behavior Laboratories.

Becker, W.C. (1977). Teaching reading and language to the disadvantaged—What we have learned. *Harvard Education Review, 47*(4), 518–544.

Becker, W.C., Engelmann, S., & Thomas, D.R. (1975). *Teaching I: Classroom management*. Chicago: Science Research Associates.

Becker, W.C., & Gersten, R. (1982). A follow-up of Follow Through: The later effects of the Direct Instruction Model on children in the fifth and sixth grades. *American Educational Research Journal, 19*(1), 75–92.

Becker, W.C., Madsen, G.H., Jr., Arnold, C.R., & Thomas, D.R. (1967). The contingent use of teacher attention and praise in reducing classroom behavior problems. *Journal of Special Education, 1*, 287–307.

Belch, P. (1975). The question of teacher's questions. *Teaching Exceptional Children, 7*, 46–50.

Belch, P. (1978). Improving the reading comprehension scores of secondary level educable mentally handicapped students through selective teacher questioning. *Education and Training of the Mentally Retarded, 13*, 385–389.

Bellamy, T., & Brown, L. (1972). A sequential procedure for teaching addition skills to trainable retarded students. *Training School Bulletin, 69*, 31–44.

Biberdorf, J.R., & Pear, J.J. (1977). Two-to-one versus one-to-one student-teacher ratios in the operant verbal training of retarded children. *Journal of Applied Behavior Analysis, 10*(3), 506.

Birnbrauer, J.S., Wolf, M.M., Kidder, J.P., & Tague, C. (1965). Classroom behavior of retarded pupils with token reinforcement. *Journal of Experimental Child Psychology, 2*, 219–235.

Boning, R. (1974). *Understanding questions: Supportive reading skills*. New York: Dexter & Westbrook.

Borg, W.R., Kelley, M.L., Langer, P., & Gall, M. (1970). *The minicourse: A microteaching approach to teacher education*. Toronto: Macmillan.

Brigance, A. (1976). *Brigance diagnostic inventory of basic skills*. Woburn, Mass.: Curriculum Associates.

Brophy, J., & Good, T. (1974). *Teacher-student relationships: Causes and consequences*. New York: Holt, Rinehart & Winston.

Brown, L., Bellamy, T., & Gadberry, E. (1971). A procedure for the development and measurement of rudimentary quantitative concepts in low functioning trainable students. *Training School Bulletin, 68,* 178–185.

Brown, L., Hermanson, J., Klemme, H., Haubrich, P., & Ora, J. (1970). Using behavior modification principles to teach sight vocabulary. *Teaching Exceptional Children, 2*(3), 120–128.

Bryan, B., & Roederer, S. (1979). Personal communication.

Buchanan, C.D. (1963). *Programmed reading.* St. Louis: McGraw-Hill.

Buchanan & Sullivan Associates. (1964). *Programmed reading.* St. Louis: Webster Division, McGraw-Hill.

Burney, J.D. (1976). Effects of teacher use of a precision lesson-planning technique on instructional interaction and pupil achievement. Unpublished doctoral dissertation, George Peabody College for Teachers.

Buros, O. (Ed.) (1978). *The mental measurements yearbook* (Vols. 1 & 2). Highland Park, N.J.: Gryphon Press.

Bushell, D., Jr. (1973). *Classroom behavior: A little book for teachers.* Englewood Cliffs, N.J.: Prentice-Hall.

Bushell, D., Jr. (1978). An engineering approach to the elementary classroom: The behavior analysis Follow Through project. In A.C. Catania & T.A. Brigham (Eds.), *Handbook of applied behavior analysis.* New York: Irvington.

Carnine, D. (1976). Effects of two teacher presentation rates on off-task behavior, answering correctly and participation. *Journal of Applied Behavior Analysis, 9*(2), 199–206.

Cavallaro, C., Stowitschek, C., George, M., & Stowitschek, J. (1980). Intensive inservice teacher education and concomitant changes in handicapped learners. *Teacher Education and Special Education, 3*(3), 49–57.

Cawley, J., Fitzmaurice, A., Goodstein, H., Lepore, A., Sedlak, R., & Althaus, V. (1977). *Project MATH.* Storrs, Conn.: Educational Development Corporation.

Chall, J. (1967). *Learning to read: The great debate.* New York: McGraw-Hill.

Clark, H., & Sherman, J. (1975). Teaching generative use of sentence answers to three forms of questions. *Journal of Applied Behavior Analysis, 8,* 321–330.

Connolly, A., Nachtman, W., & Prichett, E. (1971). *Key diagnostic arithmetic test.* Circle Pines, Minn.: American Guidance Service.

Cook, T.P., & Appoloni, T. (1976). Developing positive social emotional behaviors: A study of training. *Journal of Applied Behavior Analysis, 9,* 65–78.

Day, R. (August 1979). Personal communication.

Dixon, R., & Engelmann, S. (1980). *Corrective spelling through morphographics.* Chicago: Science Research Associates.

Dixon, R., Engelmann, S., Meier, M., Steely, D., & Wells, T. (1980). *Spelling mastery.* Chicago: Science Research Associates.

Eaton, M., & Hansen, C. (1978). *The fourth R: Research in the classroom.* Columbus, Ohio: Charles E. Merrill.

Educational Development Corporation. (1976). *Individualized criterion referenced testing: Reading.* Tulsa, Okla.: Educational Development Corporation.

Eichols, R.E., O'Daffer, P.G., & Fleenor, C.R. (1976). *Investigating school mathematics (primer).* Menlo Park, Calif.: Addison-Wesley.

Engelmann, S. (1970). *Preventing failure in the primary grades.* Chicago: Science Research Associates.

Engelmann, S., & Bruner, E.C. (1969, 1974). *DISTAR Reading I: Teacher's guide.* Chicago: Science Research Associates.

Engelmann, S., & Carnine, D. (1970). *DISTAR Arithmetic: An Instructional System.* Chicago: Science Research Associates.

Engelmann, S., & Carnine, D. (1975). *DISTAR Arithmetic I: Teacher's guide.* Chicago: Science Research Associates.

Engelmann, S., & Carnine, D. (1982). *Corrective mathematics.* Chicago: Science Research Associates.

Engelmann, S., & Osborne, J. (1976). *DISTAR Language I: Teacher's guide.* Chicago: Science Research Associates.

Engelmann, S., & Osborne, J. (1973). *DISTAR Language III: An Instructional System. Teacher Presentation Book.* Chicago: Science Research Associates.

Engelmann, S., & Steely, D. (1980). *Mathematics modules.* Chicago: Science Research Associates.

Engelmann, S., Becker, W., Carnine, D., Meyers, L., Becker, J., & Johnson, G. (1973). *Corrective reading program: Teacher's management and skills manual.* Chicago: Science Research Associates.

Fine, M., Allen, C., & Medvene, A. (1968). Verbal interaction patterns in regular and special classrooms. *Psychology in the Schools, 5,* 265–271.

Flanders, N.A. (1960). *Teacher influence, pupil attitudes, and achievement.* Minneapolis, Minn.: University of Minnesota Press.

Floyd, W. (1960). An analysis of the oral questioning activity in selected Colorado primary classrooms (Doctoral dissertation, Colorado State College). *Dissertation Abstracts International,* CSC-XXI, p. 46. (University Microfilms, No. 60-6253).

Freitas, L., Nelsen, K., & Whalen, C. (1967). The establishment of imitation and its use for the development of complex behavior in schizophrenic children. *Behavior Research and Therapy, 5*(3), 171–181.

Gall, M. (1970). The use of questions in teaching. *Review of Educational Research, 40,* 707–721.

Gallagher, J., Aschner, M., & Jenne, W. (1967). Productive thinking of gifted children in classroom interaction. Research Monograph No. B-5. Washington, D.C.: Council for Exceptional Children.

Gessel, J. (1971). *Diagnostic mathematics inventory.* Monterey, Calif.: CTB/McGraw-Hill.

Goodman, I., Bellamy, T., & Pierce, L. (1972). Teaching trainable level students basic spelling skills. In L. Brown & E. Sontag (Eds.), *Toward the development and implementation of an empirically based public school program for trainable mentally retarded and severely emotionally disturbed students: Part II.* Madison, Wis.: Madison Public Schools.

Greenwood, C.R., Sloane, H.N., Jr., & Baskin, A. (1974). Training elementary aged peer-behavior managers to control small group programmed mathematics. *Journal of Applied Behavioral Analysis, 7,* 103–114.

Guess, D., Sailor, W., & Baer, D.M. (1978). *Functional speech and language training for the severely handicapped.* Lawrence, Kans.: H & H Enterprises.

Guess, D., Sailor, W., Rutherford, G., & Baer, D.M. (1968). An experimental analysis of linguistic development: The productive use of the plural morpheme. *Journal of Applied Behavior Analysis, 1,* 297–306.

Hackett, M. (1971). *Criterion reading: Individualized learning management system.* New York: Random House.

Hall, R.V. (1971). *Managing behavior: Part I.* Lawrence, Kans.: H & H Enterprises.

Hall, R.V., & Hall, M.C. (1980). *How to use systematic praise and approval.* Lawrence Kans.: H & H Enterprises.

Hall, R.V., Panyan, M., Rabon, D., & Broden, M. (1968). Instructing teachers in reinforcement procedures which improve control. *Journal of Applied Behavior Analysis, 1,* 315–322.

Hansen, C., & Eaton, M. (1978). Reading. In N. Haring, T. Lovitt, M. Eaton, & C. Hansen (Eds.), *The fourth R: Research in the classroom,* Columbus, Ohio: Charles E. Merrill.

Haring, N., & Gentry, N. (1976). Direct and individualized instructional procedures. In N. Haring & R. Schiefelbusch (Eds.), *Teaching special children.* New York: McGraw-Hill.

Haring, N., Lovitt, T., Eaton, M., & Hansen, C. (1978). *The fourth R: Research in the classroom.* Columbus, Ohio: Charles E. Merrill.

Hasazi, J.E., & Hasazi, S.E. (1972). Effects of teacher attention on digit-reversal behavior in an elementary school child. *Journal of Applied Behavior Analysis, 5,* 157–162.

Hendrickson, J., & Stowitschek, C. (1980). Teacher use of diagnostic questioning and modeling in language development, *Journal of Special Education Technology, 4,* 17–27.

Hillman, S. (1972). The effect of question type and position on four types of learning among mentally handicapped children (Doctoral dissertation, Indiana University). *Dissertation Abstracts International, 33,* 4174-A (University Microfilms, No. 73-2714).

Hofmeister, A. (1970). *Diagnostic arithmetic combinations test.* Logan, Utah: Outreach and Development Division, Exceptional Child Center, Utah State University.

Hofmeister, A. (May 1971). Personal communication.

Hofmeister, A., Gallery, M., & Hofmeister, J. (1977). *Training for independence.* Niles, Ill.: Developmental Learning Materials.

Hopkins, B.L., Schutte, R.C., & Garton, K.L. (1971). The effects of access to a playroom on the rate and quality of printing and writing of first- and second-grade students. *Journal of Applied Behavior Analysis, 4,* 77–87.

Howell, K., Kaplan, J., & O'Connell, C. (1979). *Evaluating exceptional children: A task analysis approach.* Columbus, Ohio: Charles E. Merrill.

Jobes, N.K. (1975). The acquisition and retention of spelling through imitation training and observational learning with and without feedback. Unpublished doctoral dissertation, George Peabody College for Teachers.

Kamm, K., Miles, P., Stewart, V., & Harris, M. (1972). *Wisconsin tests of reading skill development: Word attack.* Minneapolis, Minn.: NCS Interpretive Scoring Systems.

Knapczyk, D.R., & Livingston, G. (1974). The effects of prompting question-asking upon on-task behavior and reading comprehension. *Journal of Applied Behavior Analysis, 7,* 115–121.

Lahey, B.B., & Drabman, R.S. (1974). Facilitation of the acquisition and retention of sight-word vocabulary through token reinforcement. *Journal of Applied Behavior Analysis, 7,* 307–312.

Lent, J., Riall, A., & Stowitschek, J. (1981). The development of a replicable model inservice training package for paraprofessionals working with severely handicapped children and youth: Final report. U.S. Office of Education, Grant Number G007801468.

Loughlin, R. (1961). On questioning. *The Educational Forum, 25,* 481–482.

Lovaas, O.I. (1981). *The ME book.* Baltimore: University Park Press.

Lovaas, O.I., Berberich, J.P., Perloff, B.F., & Scheffer, B. (1966). Acquisition of imitative speech in schizophrenic children. *151,* 705–707.

Lovitt, T. (1977). *In spite of my resistance . . . I've learned from children.* Columbus, Ohio: Charles E. Merrill.

Lovitt, T. (1978). Arithmetic. In N. Haring, T. Lovitt, M. Eaton, & C. Hansen, *The fourth R: Research in the classroom.* Columbus, Ohio: Charles E. Merrill.

Lovitt, T.C., Guppy, T.E., & Blattner, J.E. (1969). The use of a free-time contingency with fourth graders to increase spelling accuracy. *Behavior Research and Therapy, 7,* 151–156.

Lynch, W., & Ames, C. (1972). A comparison of teachers' cognitive demands in special EMR and regular elementary classes. Center for Innovation in Teaching the Handicapped, Indiana University, Bloomington, Indiana. Final Report 28.3.

Mager, R.F., & McCann, J. (1961). *Learner-controlled instruction.* Palo Alto, Calif.: Varian Associates.

Maggs, A., & Maggs, R.K. (1979). Direct instruction research in Australia. *Journal of Special Education Technology, 2(3),* 26–34.

Markle, S., & Tiemann, P. (1970). *Really understand concepts.* Champaign, Ill.: Tiemann Associates.

McNeil, J.D. (1959). Concomitants of using behavioral objectives in the assessment of teacher effectiveness. *Journal of Educational Psychology, 50,* 239–246.

McNeil, J.D. (1967). Concomitants of using behavioral objectives in the assessment of teacher effectiveness. *Journal of Experimental Education, 36(1),* 69–74.

Meyerson, L., Kerr, N., & Michael, J.L. (1967). Behavior modification in rehabilitation. In S.W. Bijou & D.M. Baer (Eds.), *Child development readings in experimental analysis.* New York: Appleton.

Moyer, J. (1966). An exploratory study of questioning in the instructional process in selected elementary schools (Doctoral dissertation, Columbia University). *Dissertation Abstracts, 147,* 27-A.

Okey, J., & Humphreys, D. (1974, April). Evaluating outcomes of competency-based teacher education. Paper presented at the annual meeting of the American Educational Research Association, Chicago.

O'Leary, K.D., Becker, W.C., Evans, M.B., & Saundergas, R.A. (1969). A token reinforcement program in a public school: A replication and systematic analysis. *Journal of Applied Behavior Analysis, 2,* 3–13.

O'Leary, K.D., & Drabman, R. (1971). Token reinforcement programs in the classroom: A review. *Psychological Bulletin, 75,* 397–398.

O'Leary, K.D., & O'Leary, S.G. (Eds.) (1972). *Classroom management.* New York: Pergamon Press, 1972.

Osborne, J.G. (1969). Free-time as a reinforcer in the management of classroom behaviors. *Journal of Applied Behavior Analysis, 2,* 113–118.

Panyan, M.C. (1980). *How to use shaping.* Lawrence, Kans.: H & H Enterprises.

Peniston, E. (1975). An evaluation of the Portage project: A comparison of a home-visit program for multiply-handicapped preschoolers and head start program. Paper presented at the annual meeting of the American Educational Research Association, Washington, D.C.

Porterfield, J.K., Herbert-Jackson, E., & Risely, T.R. (1976). Contingent observation: An effective and acceptable procedure for reducing disruptive behavior of young children in a group setting. *Journal of Applied Behavior Analysis, 9,* 55–64.

Premack, D. (1959). Toward empirical behavior laws: 1. Positive reinforcement. *Psychological Review, 66,* 219–213.

Reese, E.O. (1973). A general procedure for applied behavior analysis. Unpublished paper, Mt. Holyoke College.

Rogers-Warren, A., & Warren, S. (1980). Mands for verbalization: Facilitating the display of newly trained language in children. *Behavior Modification, 4,* 361–382.

Royal Canadian Air Force Exercise: Plans for Physical Fitness. (1962). New York: Pocket Books.

Rosen, T. (1976). *Management system for Sullivan reading.* Logan, Utah: Exceptional Child Center.

Rosenshine, B. (1977, April). Academic engaged time, content covered and direct instruction. Paper presented at the annual meeting of the American Educational Research Association, New York.

Rosenshine, B., & Furst, M. (1971). Research on teacher performance criteria. In B.O. Smith (Ed.), *Research in teacher education—A symposium*. Englewood Cliffs, N.J.: Prentice-Hall.

Rosenshine, B., & Furst, N. (1973). The use of direct observation to study teaching. In R. Travers (Ed.), *The second handbook of research on teaching*. Chicago: Rand McNally.

Rowbury, T.G., Baer, A.M., & Baer, D.M. (1976). Interactions between teacher guidance and contingent access to play in developing preacademic skills in deviant preschool children. *Journal of Applied Behavior Analysis, 9*, 85–104.

Salzberg, C.L. (1972). Freedom and responsibility in an elementary school. In G. Semb (Ed.), *Behavior analysis and education, 1972*. Lawrence, Kansas: University of Kansas Support and Development Center for Follow Through.

Salzberg, C.L., & Rule, S. (1973). *El Paso County Association for Children with Learning Disabilities' Summer Learning Project: A Progress Report.* Unpublished paper.

Sasser, R. (1978). Adapting packaged measurement systems to monitor the classroom performance of handicapped persons. *Journal of Special Education Technology, 1*(1), 51–57.

Schreiber, J. (1967). Teachers' question asking techniques in social studies (Doctoral dissertation, University of Iowa). *Dissertation Abstracts, 28*, 523-A.

Scott, J.W., & Bushell, D., Jr. (1974). The length of teacher contacts and students' off-task behavior. *Journal of Applied Behavior Analysis, 7*, 39–44.

Shores, R.E., Roberts, M., & Nelson, C.M. (1976). An empirical model for the development of competencies for teachers of children with behavior disorders. *Behavior Disorders, 1*(2), 123–131.

Shores, R., & Stowitschek, J. (1977). Final report: Prototype model for developing empirically-based special education teacher competencies. U.S. Office of Education, Grant Number G007503450.

Shores, R.E., & Stowitschek, J.J. (1975). Final report on In-STEP. U.S. Office of Education, Bureau of Education for the Handicapped. Grant Number OEG-0742177.

Shores, R.E., & Stowitschek, J.J. (1976). Year-end report: Prototype model for developing empirically based special education teacher competencies. U.S. Office of Education, #G007503450.

Shores, R.E., Stowitschek, J., Salzberg, C., & Kerr M.M. (1979). Evaluation and research. *Teacher Education and Special Education, 2*(3), 68–71.

Shumaker, J., & Sherman, J.A. (1970). Training generative verb usage by imitation and reinforcement procedures. *Journal of Applied Behavior Analysis, 3*, 273–287.

Smith, B.O. (1971). *Research in teacher education: A symposium*. Englewood Cliffs, N.J.: Prentice-Hall.

Smith, D.D. (1981). *Teaching the learning disabled*. Englewood Cliffs, N.J.: Prentice-Hall.

Smith, D.D. (1973). The influence of instructions, feedback and reinforcement contingencies on children's abilities to acquire and become proficient at computational arithmetic skills. Unpublished doctoral dissertation, University of Washington.

Smith, D.D., & Lovitt, T.C. (1973). The use of modeling techniques to influence the acquisition of computational arithmetic skills in learning disabled children. Unpublished manuscript, University of Washington.

Smith, D.D., & Snell, M.E. (1978). Classroom management and instructional planning. In M.E. Snell (Ed.), *Systematic development of moderately and severely handicapped*. Columbus, Ohio: Charles E. Merrill.

Steinberg, L., Sedlar, R., Cherkes, M., & Minich, B. (1978). *Essential math and language skills*. Chicago: Hubbard Scientific.

Stevens, R. (1912). The question as a measure of efficiency in instruction: A critical study of classroom practice. *Teachers College Contribution to Education*, No. 48. New York: Teachers College, Columbia University.

Stevens, R., & Rosenshine, B. (1981). Advances in research on teaching. *Exceptional Education Quarterly, 2*(1), 1–10.

Stowitschek, J., & Armstrong-Iacino, J. (1978). Teacher questioning as a programming strategy. *Improving Human Performance, 6*, 143–155.

Stowitschek, J., & Gable, R. (1978). Effects of a mediated training package on teachers' modeling behavior and subsequent student performance. Unpublished paper.

Stowitschek, J., Gable, R., & Hendrickson, J. (1980). *Instructional materials for exceptional children: Selection, management, and adaptation*. Germantown, Md.: Aspen Systems Corporation.

Stowitschek, J., & Hofmeister, A. (1974). Effects of minicourse instruction on teachers and pupils. *Exceptional Children, 40*, 490–495.

Striefel, S. (1974). *Teaching a child to imitate*. Lawrence, Kans.: H & H Enterprises.

Sulzer-Azaroff, B., & Mayer, G.R. (1977). *Applying behavior analysis procedures with children and youth*. New York: Holt, Rinehart & Winston.

Suppes, P. (1962). *Sets and numbers*. New York: Random House.

Thiagarajan, S., Semmel, D., & Semmel, M. (1974). *Instructional development for training teachers of exceptional children: A source book*. Reston, Va.: Council for Exceptional Children.

Thomas, D.R., Becker, W.C., & Armstrong, M. (1968). Reduction and elimination of disruptive classroom behavior by systematically varying teachers' behavior. *Journal of Applied Behavior Analysis, 1*, 35–45.

Tiegs, E., & Clark, W. (1970). *The California achievement tests*. Monterey, Calif.: CTB/McGraw Hill.

Wessel, J. (1976). *I can*. Chicago: Hubbard Scientific.

West, R., & Stowitschek, J. (1981). The development, demonstration, and replication of programmatic inservice training for special education. Proposal submitted to the U.S. Department of Education, Special Education Programs.

Wheeler, A.J., & Sulzer, F. (1970). Operant training and generalization of a verbal response form in a speech deficient child. *Journal of Applied Behavior Analysis, 3*, 139–147.

White, O., & Liberty, K. (1976). Behavioral assessment and precise educational measurement. In N. Haring & R. Schiefelbusch (Eds.), *Teaching special children*. New York: McGraw-Hill.

Whitney, R., & Striefel, S. (1981). Functionality and generalization in training the severely and profoundly handicapped. *Journal of Special Education Technology, 4*(3), 33–39.

Wolfe, M.M., Risley, T.R., & Mees, H. (1964). Application of operant conditioning procedures to the behavior problems of an autistic child. *Behavior Research and Therapy, 1*, 305–332.

Woodcock, R. (1972). *Woodcock reading mastery tests*. Circle Pines, Minn.: American Guidance Service.

Young, J. (1972). *Precision teaching*. Provo, Utah: Brigham Young University Press.

Zahorick, J. (1974). Questioning in the classroom. *Education, 4*, 358–363.

Zetlin, A., & Gallimore, R. (1980). A cognitive skills training program for moderately retarded learners. *Education and Training of the Mentally Retarded, 15*, 121–131.

Appendix A
Blank Forms

DIRECT TEACHING PROGRAM CHECKLIST*

(For supervisors use only)

PROGRAM _____

	Approved Date	Verified (For supervisors use only) DATE Initial
TARGET _____ (What to teach)		
ANALYZE _____ (What to teach)		
ASSESS _____ (How measure)		
INTERVENE _____ (What Teaching Tactic is used)		
_____		
_____		
_____		
(SEE PRESENTATION GUIDE ON BACK OF THIS PAGE)		
Arranged Event _____		
Arrangement _____		
CHECK PROGRESS/ _____ MASTERY (How measure)		
_____		
REDIRECT _____ (What back-up teaching tactic may be used)		
_____		
(SEE PRESENTATION GUIDE ON BACK OF THIS PAGE)		

*Many of the procedures outlined on this checklist were adapted from the materials developed in the Field Based Special Teacher Education Program at George Peabody College for Teachers of Vanderbilt University.

PREPROGRAM PLANNER*

Name _____   Service Program _____

Long Term Goal # _____   Instruction Schedule _____

Short Term Objective _____

_____

_____

Initial Assessment: _____

Sub-Skill Objectives: (Please number each one)

S.T.O. No.	Conditions:	Behavior:	Criterion:

*Many of the procedures outlined on this checklist were adapted from the materials developed in the Field Based Special Teacher Education Program at George Peabody College for Teachers of Vanderbilt University.

TEACHER PRESENTATION GUIDE

INTERVENE:

Setting/Materials	Teacher Says/Does	Child Says/Does

REDIRECT:

Setting/Materials	Teacher Says/Does	Child Says/Does

DAILY PLANNER*

Planning		Instructional Tactics					Measurement	
Ⓐ	Ⓑ	Ⓒ	Ⓓ	Ⓔ	Ⓕ	Ⓖ	Ⓗ	Ⓘ
	Sub-Objective	Materials	Presentation Mode	Child Response	Arranged Event	Arrangement	Progress Checking Tactic	Child Mastery/ Non Mastery

KEY

Ⓐ **Date:** date for which planned

Ⓑ **Sub-Objective:** (number from Program Plan Sheet - up to 30)

Ⓒ **Materials:**
- 30 = no materials
- 31 = published materials
- 32 = teacher made
- 33 = other

Ⓓ **Presentation Mode:**
- 40 = modeling
- 41 = questioning
- 42 = physical assistance
- 43 = prompt
- 44 = other

Ⓔ **Child Response:**
- 50 = oral
- 51 = motor/gestural
- 52 = written
- 53 = other

Ⓕ **Arranged Event:**
- 60 = social
- 61 = token
- 62 = consumable (edible)
- 63 = activity (e.g., free play)
- 64 = other

Ⓖ **Arrangement:**
- 70 = variable interval
- 71 = fixed interval
- 72 = continuous
- 73 = variable ratio
- 74 = fixed ratio
- 75 = other

Ⓗ **Progress Checking Tactic**
- 80 = criterion-referenced test
- 81 = daily record
- 82 = normative test
- 83 = other

Ⓘ **Child Data:**
- 90 = non-Mastery
- 91 = Mastery

*Many of the procedures outlined on this checklist were adapted from the materials developed in the Field Based Special Teacher Education Program at George Peabody College for Teachers of Vanderbilt University.

General Observation Form

Trainee _____

Program _____

Date _____

Time Start _____ **Time Stop** _____

Comments _____

Index

Note: Italicized page numbers indicate an entry in an exhibit, table, or figure.

About the Authors

Joseph J. Stowitschek

Joseph J. Stowitschek completed doctoral studies in special education and instructional technology in 1972. He currently directs the Outreach and Development Division of the Exceptional Child Center and is associate professor of Special Education at Utah State University. Previously, he had been associate professor of special education and Kennedy Center scientist at George Peabody College for Teachers of Vanderbilt University.

Dr. Stowitschek is senior author of *Instructional Materials for Exceptional Children: Selection, Management and Adaptation.* He has published numerous research and theoretical articles in the field of special education and is editor of the *Journal of Special Education Technology.*

Carole Stowitschek

Carole Stowitschek completed her Ph.D. in special education at George Peabody College for Teachers of Vanderbilt University in 1981. She is currently affiliated with the Intermountain Plains Regional Resource Center and the Department of Special Education at Utah State University. Other professional pursuits include the direction of the SAM project, a federally funded project to develop microcomputer software to supplement secondary mathematics curricula.

Dr. Stowitschek's teaching experience includes work with both nonhandicapped and handicapped children, including the mildly handicapped, specific learning disabled, and emotionally disturbed. She has conducted research on teacher planning as it relates to child performance, the use of behavior-disordered adolescents as instructional agents, and teacher questioning tactics.

Jo Mary Hendrickson

Jo Mary Hendrickson received her Ph.D. in the Program for Human Development Specialists from George Peabody College for Teachers of Vanderbilt University and her M.A. in behavioral disabilities from the University of Wisconsin (Madison). Currently, she is vice-president of professional services and product development at Continental Learning Systems, Inc., Nashville, Tennessee.

Dr. Hendrickson has experience as a classroom teacher, diagnostician, and teacher trainer. She has conducted and published research in the areas of language intervention, social development, and special teacher-student interaction. Dr. Hendrickson has also authored several instructional programs, including materials for disadvantaged and handicapped learners.

Robert Day

Robert Day received his M.E. from the University of Washington and his Ph.D. from George Peabody College for Teachers of Vanderbilt University. He is currently the coordinator of staff development and research at the Special Purpose School at Parsons State Hospital and Training Center in Parsons, Kansas. He also holds an adjunct appointment to the Bureau of Child Research at the University of Kansas.

Dr. Day has worked with handicapped children for 15 years as both a teacher and researcher. Furthermore, while pursuing his doctorate at Peabody College, he had an opportunity to work on a nationally recognized teacher training project.

About the Contributors

Sarah Rule

Sarah Rule is currently involved in the application of teacher training procedures and direct teaching tactics to mainstream preschool settings as a researcher at the Exceptional Child Center, Utah State University. She has served as director of teacher training at the Eastern Regional Teacher Training Center for the Behavior Analysis Follow-Through program. She has been teacher and principal of a mainstream elementary school. Dr. Rule has authored several articles on teacher training.

Charles L. Salzberg

Charles L. Salzberg, Ph.D., is a Professor of Special Education at Utah State University, where he is engaged in preparation of teachers for handicapped students and is conducting research on vocational training and placement. Previously, Dr. Salzberg was the director of the Eastern Regional Teacher Training Center for the Behavior Analysis Follow-Through Program serving economically disadvantaged children throughout the United States. Subsequently, he helped to initiate the competency-based teacher training program developed at George Peabody College for Teachers in Nashville, Tennessee. Currently, he coordinates the vocational special educator program in the Department of Special Education and conducts a variety of research and development projects serving handicapped people.

K. Richard Young

K. Richard Young, Ph.D., is an Associate Professor in the Department of Special Education at Utah State University and coordinator of the personnel preparation program for teachers of severely handicapped persons. Previously, he has been a teacher and program director for children and youth with behavioral disorders, autism, and other severe handicaps. He is also a licensed, practicing psychologist and has published in the fields of psychology and special education.